The EVERYTHING
Dating Book, 2nd Edition

Dear Reader:

Through my work as a life and career expert, online advisor, and personal image consultant, one truth I have learned is that while dating can be fun, romantic, and exciting, few people put themselves out into the "meet market" to date because they really love it. Most people embark upon a dating journey because they ultimately want to *meet someone*, stop dating, and enjoy a personal relationship with a special person.

I've met and advised single people of all ages, cultures, lifestyles, and relationship goals. They tell me on a daily basis that dating is challenging, and sometimes frustrating. Above all, they want to know exactly when they will meet someone and end the dating journey successfully. I tell them that dating is a *process*—a means to an end—not a goal in itself, and like anything worthwhile in life, this goal often takes time to accomplish. The good news is that each person can affect the outcome of his relationship goal; it's not only up to luck or fate. Regardless of what your relationship goal is, you will get there *faster* aided by good information and ideas, an organized, viable plan, and a healthy perspective.

It has been my pleasure to create a dating book that delivers exactly what its title suggests—information on virtually everything that makes up a modern, adult dating experience. Let this book be your guide as you learn to be a smart, savvy, effective, and satisfied single, and to date well and happily, until you find your match. Love, success, and happiness truly can be yours!

Best of luck,

Alison Blackman Dunham

The EVERYTHING Series

Editorial

Publishing Director	Gary M. Krebs
Associate Managing Editor	Laura M. Daly
Associate Copy Chief	Brett Palana-Shanahan
Acquisitions Editor	Gina Chaimanis
Development Editor	Katie McDonough
Associate Production Editor	Casey Ebert

Production

Director of Manufacturing	Susan Beale
Associate Director of Production	Michelle Roy Kelly
Cover Design	Paul Beatrice
	Matt LeBlanc
Design and Layout	Colleen Cunningham
	Holly Curtis
	Erin Dawson
	Sorae Lee
Series Cover Artist	Barry Littmann

Visit the entire Everything® Series at *www.everything.com*

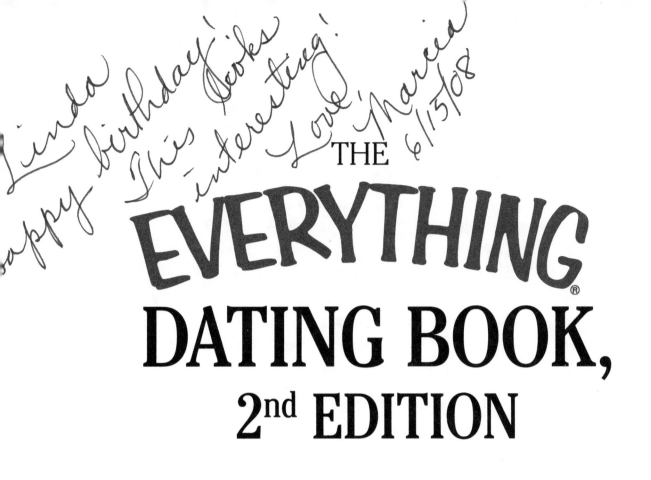

Linda
Happy birthday! This books
"interesting"! Love, Marcia 6/15/08

THE EVERYTHING®
DATING BOOK,
2nd EDITION

Meet new people and find
your perfect match!

Alison Blackman Dunham

Adams Media
Avon, Massachusetts

To my twin sister Jessica Blackman Freedman, AKA "Advice Sister Jessica," and my wonderful husband, John R. Dunham.

An Everything® Series Book.
Everything® and everything.com® are registered trademarks of F+W Publications, Inc.

Published by Adams Media, an F+W Publications Company
57 Littlefield Street, Avon, MA 02322 U.S.A.
www.adamsmedia.com

ISBN: 1-59337-372-4
Printed in the United States of America.

J   I   H   G   F   E   D   C   B

Library of Congress Cataloging-in-Publication Data
Dunham, Alison Blackman.
The everything dating book : meet new people and find your perfect match! /
Alison Blackman Dunham.-- 2nd ed.
p.   cm.
ISBN 1-59337-372-4
1. Dating (Social customs) 2. Man-woman relationships.
3. Single people--Psychology. 4. Courtship. I. Title. II. Series.
HQ801.D78 2005
646.7'7--dc22
2005026440

This publication is designed to provide accurate and authoritative information with regard to the subject matter covered. It is sold with the understanding that the publisher is not engaged in rendering legal, accounting, or other professional advice. If legal advice or other expert assistance is required, the services of a competent professional person should be sought.

—From a *Declaration of Principles* jointly adopted by a Committee of the American Bar Association and a Committee of Publishers and Associations

Many of the designations used by manufacturers and sellers to distinguish their products are claimed as trademarks. Where those designations appear in this book and Adams Media was aware of a trademark claim, the designations have been printed with initial capital letters.

This book is available at quantity discounts for bulk purchases.
For information, call 1-800-872-5627.

Contents

Acknowledgments

First, my thanks, love, and gratitude go to my amazing husband, John R. Dunham. He brightens my life every day with his intelligence, feedback, patience, and love. He is also a great editor!

A very special thanks to my agent, Jacky Sach. You found me, encouraged me, and helped me throughout the creation of this book. Jacky, I couldn't have done it without you. Special thanks also go to Jessica Blackman Freedman, my twin sister and former coauthor. Her influence as the "other half" of The Advice Sisters® is still present in everything I write.

Other people who have contributed not only to this book but also as a major influence on my life and views include my parents Norman and Sylvia Blackman, who will never stop loving each other. My cousin, Hillary Bader, who was a wonderful and talented woman, inspired me to follow my dreams and make them come true. Tillie Bader, my grandmother, was a quietly wise woman with timeless advice that appears throughout these pages. I hope what she told me will help present and future readers to live happier, more successful lives.

Finally, thanks to my dear friends (in no particular order): Icer, Stu, Kelly, Josh, Brandon, Bruce, Jeff, Amy, Bill, Sharon, Vicky, Chris, Jean, Jules, Evelyn, Tony, Janet, Howard, Clare, Stephanie, and the countless other men and women around the world who have sought my advice and shared their true-life stories, situations, and tips in this book.

Top Ten Things for a Safe, Successful, Satisfying Relationship Journey:

1. You can't get to your destination if you don't know what that is. Set a goal. Be clear about what you want to accomplish on your dating journey.

2. Use your head (and your past) to guide your heart.

3. Be clear about who you are seeking. Know your assets and liabilities. Define what you will accept in a partner and what is unacceptable.

4. Remember that dating isn't *always* fun or romantic. Dating is the process you follow to reach your relationship goal.

5. Keep a dating journal during your relationship quest. What you write will give you invaluable insight into yourself. It will guide you today, tomorrow, and always.

6. Be prepared. The more information you have and the more you think about how to manage your dating journey, the better it will be.

7. Setbacks are all part of the dating process. Validate your goals and stick with them. Make a commitment to succeed—and you will.

8. Let go of anger and beat the broken-heart blues. If you haven't met the right person yet it just means that he is still out there, waiting to connect with you.

9. Don't make your relationship journey the only focus in your life. A happy person is one who is well balanced.

10. Good relationships take work. Don't take your partner for granted. Work at your relationships every day.

Introduction

▶ The urge to connect with others, and to love and be loved, is ageless and universal. No matter what your age, lifestyle, or personality, whether you're seeking a one-night fling, a whirlwind weekend, a summer romance, or a lifetime love, dating is the way to find it! Perhaps you're reading this book with the intention of getting married, or you just want to increase your social circle and find a loving companion. Maybe you've been too busy to date and have little experience with it, or it's your first time back in the meet market for decades. Perhaps you have been dating for a while but haven't yet found what you are seeking. Whatever your relationship experience and whatever your heart's desire, this book is meant for you.

The experience of searching and finding someone special, and then making a genuine connection, is magical, but just about every dating journey is filled with bumps, surprises, and detours. The more you know about the challenges you may face on your dating journey, the better prepared you will be to avoid the obstacles, adjust your route, and enjoy your experience as a whole.

If you are embarking upon a dating journey now, you're in luck. Tremendous evolutions in technology have significantly changed the way we connect and relate to one another. On the other hand, some of these technological improvements actually cause us to be even busier than ever before. As time passes and responsibilities increase, you may find that you have a lot less time (and less energy) to be social. Adults also bring more "baggage" (experiences good and bad) into new partnerships. The more birthdays you have celebrated, the more likely you are to be selective about who you are willing to date. But don't worry—you'll soon know how to quickly identify a good prospect, from an iffy one.

Younger singles are busy and looking for love, too, and they will also benefit from the wisdom in this book. The process of making connections, regardless of age, is the same, and this dating book is geared to appeal to the tastes, needs, and challenges of adults of every generation, living varied lifestyles and savoring varied dreams. You can read, enjoy, and use this book as a young person, and then pass along what you've learned to your single-and-dating-again parents and friends.

If you wanted to learn a new skill, or brush up on an existing one, chances are you'd do some reading on the subject. Dating is no different. This book will give you a fresh perspective and supply new and appropriate ways to handle adult dating situations. The topics in the chapters are presented in the same order they would occur in the dating process, so it's best if you don't skip around. You might miss something that could potentially save you lots of time and help you avoid disappointment and frustration.

As with any goal, the key to being successful is to know what you want, know what you have to offer, make a plan, maintain a positive attitude, find satisfaction in the journey, and believe that if you chart your course, you will get to where you want to be. You will face challenges and may find yourself questioning your choices. You may even wonder whether this is a goal worth pursuing. It is! Every goal, no matter how large or small, begins with a first step. Reading this book is just the beginning of an exciting dating journey.

Chapter 1

Getting Started

When you embark on any journey, it helps to know what the final destination will be, especially if you'd like to get there with as little stress as possible. The same is true of your dating experience. This chapter will help you get off to a great start by giving you a holistic view of what dating actually is, and jump-start your thinking about what you are seeking and why. You'll not only define your goals but you'll also learn to stay focused and remain motivated until you reach them.

What Is Dating?

For the purposes of this book, dating begins the moment you decide that you want to find a romantic relationship with someone, followed by the process of identifying that person. However, it is the specific *activities* that you undertake to find new people and the process of getting to know them (with the goal of making a romantic connection with one of more of them), that make up most people's definition of "dating."

For many, dating is a mixed blessing. There's anticipation and suspense, as you prepare to go out and wonder who you might meet. There's excitement, when you meet someone and find a genuine mutual attraction to be explored. There's fun and perhaps romance, as you meet new people and experience new activities (new ideas, new cuisine, new films, new music, etc.).

FACT

Up until nearly the middle of the twentieth century, it was assumed that every young man or woman would marry in his or her teens or early twenties. Many matches were often still arranged by parents, and respected elders still had a major role to play in suggesting and approving suitable mates, and then making the appropriate introductions. Even if you did meet someone on your own, limited mobility forced you to choose from people in your local community.

However exciting and fun dating can be, it is also a process of personal selection. You are judging others, and they are judging you. You can't select everyone you meet as your special partner, so dating is also an activity of elimination (moving on from those you aren't interested in and who aren't interested in you) as well as selection (finding mutual interest). It's a given that not every person you meet will pan out as a potential partner. Even when you do click with someone, somewhere in the dating process you may discover that you aren't right for each other. Uncertainty, disappointment, frustration, and sometimes sadness can also be part of the dating process. But then there's that heart-stopping moment when you realize you've met the person you want—the one you've been dreaming of—and she feels the same about you! Dating gives you the opportunity to experience your options until you find that special person.

Dating was done differently in past years. In the early 1900s, for example, a man would typically ask for a father's permission to "call on" his daughter. If permission to "come calling" or "court" was given, the couple didn't actually go out together very much. Popular choices for their dating activities were daylight walks, cultural events such as lectures or concerts, or rides in a carriage or, later, a car, always accompanied by a responsible married person or couple.

ALERT!

Perhaps you are familiar with this scenario: Your mother is nagging you for grandchildren (before she gets too old), and your friends have all paired up and are pushing you to do the same (before *you* get too old). Watch out! It's very important that you don't try to please the people you love at the expense of your own happiness. This is your life, and no one knows what you want from a relationship better than you do.

Although the formality of a parent's choice still exists in certain cultures, today's singles are mostly expected (and required) to find their own partners. The good news is that there is much better access to singles around the world, as well as next door. For instance, we have the Internet, which allows singles twenty-four-hour access to possible partners they ordinarily might never meet in their daily lives.

When you're single and looking to date, you should start with a clear vision of what you want, who you want, and why. Armed with this information, you can then consider the various ways and places that appeal to you in seeking out potential partners. After you've gone through these thought-provoking exercises, you will want to take action—actually go out, meet new people, make connections with one or more, and get to know them through dating activities. If a romantic relationship with just one special person is your goal, the two of you will continue through the getting-to-know-you phase of dating and venture into a relationship as a couple. Assuming that the bond you've created is a good one, the relationship will eventually go beyond dating entirely, and turn into a long-lasting or permanent relationship.

Modern dating takes time and effort. For some, dating is best described as an experience to endure until you meet someone to take you out of the meet market. However, if you are excited about meeting people, are able to keep an open mind, and are also prepared to manage your dating journey, your confidence level will soar, your expectations will be met, and your dating days will be remembered as some of the best of your life.

Evaluate Your Motives

The first step in successful dating is to figure out what you want out of the experience. Ask yourself why you want to meet someone. It sounds like a simple question, but there are often many factors influencing your decision. Perhaps you're only looking for companionship—someone to grow old with. Maybe you want to get married or have children. Or perhaps you just want to fill a void in your life.

Everyone has a different reason for dating and a different end goal. Whatever your reasons are, being clear about what you want (and why) is the key to feeling satisfied with the result of your journey. You may be surprised to find that your idea of what you want changes as you go through the dating process. Men and women are no longer expected to pair up at a very young age, and it isn't considered unacceptable, or even undesirable, to remain single or unmarried for a long time, or perhaps for a lifetime. When couples do marry today, it's often much later in life. Women are entering the work force in much greater numbers. They are delaying marriage and family to pursue higher education, further their careers, and get a better sense of the world and themselves before making a commitment to someone else. Men are delaying marriage longer, too. Medical breakthroughs in fertility research have made starting a family later in life more viable for couples.

Divorce is also significantly changing the singles scene. It is sending new people into the dating pool on a daily basis. Many of these are older and (presumably) wiser than they were when they first married. Most already have established households, and perhaps children from their former marriages. Most will pair up again. When they begin to think about finding a new partner and start going out again, they are dealing with new issues such as the emotional well-being of their children, who makes more income (and therefore who pays), the blending of families and friends, and safeguarding financial and material assets. Many are living longer, losing long-term partners, and finding new love into their eighties and nineties!

Dating no longer requires marriage as the only acceptable end goal. Today's couples do not necessarily expect to marry until they are more established in their lives and careers. Dating can be solely for self-exploration and companionship at any age. There is no need to rush!

Your Commitment Level

How serious do you want your relationship to be? Are you really ready for a new love, or do you just want to dip your toe into the singles pool and see if you want to dive in? Relationships can be made at any age and for as many reasons as there are stars in the universe. It's not always an easy task to decide what you really want, but it's the key to your happiness and success. Are you seeking marriage, or just romance—or perhaps just a supportive friendship? The time to figure this out is preferably before you start actively going out dating. If you really aren't sure what you want or why, it helps to consult people you admire who can help you sort out your true feelings and goals.

You may be surprised to find that your goals and vision change as you go out and meet new people. This is just fine. You may decide that you'd rather not meet anyone for a serious relationship at the moment, or that you would like to have a romantic relationship but want to remain single. You may start dating just to find a supportive friend or no-strings romance, and realize through the dating process that what you really want is a long-term, committed relationship or marriage. The final choice of commitment level is up to you, but it takes honesty, information, courage, and confidence, to know what you've chosen is best for you.

FACT

If you're not sure what type of relationship you want, it helps to talk to friends, family, and trusted mentors. You might consider attending relationships-oriented self-discovery seminars, or perhaps consulting an online advisor or in-person therapist or professional counselor.

Even if you're never kept a journal and don't think you are a talented writer, you'll want to document your feelings, thoughts, and desires on your dating journey. You can go low-tech (a spiral, lined notebook and a pen are all you need) or put all your thoughts into a word processing program or even a complicated database on your computer. No matter how you document it, writing down your thoughts, goals, and feelings and then keeping notes on the people you meet is a great way to remember all sorts of reactions and details about someone your brain might not retain. As you read through your notes, you will begin to see significant patterns in the types of people you select and in how you date. For example, are many of the people you've been choosing legally separated but not divorced? Are you finding that many of your dates end up with an invitation to "get cozy at my place"? Have you spent the past four weekends at the same singles bar? Do you have a history of getting past a few dates, then having a blow-out fight that ends the relationship? Documenting your dating journey can also be a great way to relieve stress and frustration. Writing about a particularly funny or gruesome dating experience is a bit like coming home from a bad date and calling your best friend to debrief.

Even if you think you're ready to date, there is one more test you should try. Consider the following lists of "A" and "B" statements. After reading the two lists, decide which list you identify with more, or acknowledge that you identify with half of each list.

"A" Statements
- I can't wait to share my life with someone.
- I enjoy my life as it is, but being in a couple would make it even better.
- I am willing to do whatever it takes for as long as it takes to find true love.
- I am flexible and open-minded about relationships.

- I am looking forward to the challenges of being part of a couple.
- I am willing to risk rejection and negative feelings to find love.
- If I don't find someone right now, that's fine—I will just keep looking.

"B" Statements

- I can't wait to be a mom/dad.
- I do not want to die alone.
- I doubt I will find someone, and I'm afraid of rejection.
- I can't wait to get someone so my parents will stop bugging me!
- I am unsure about my sexual preference.
- I am set in my ways and in my requirements.
- I couldn't choose a good match if it stood up and waved in my face.

If you identify more with the "A" statements, you're probably ready for that new relationship and willing to do what it takes to make it work. If the "B" statements are more in tune with your feelings, you may want to reconsider whether a love search is the best thing for you right now. If you have a mix of both A and B, chances are you have some mixed feelings. In this case, you'll definitely want to take a very close look at your past relationships to help sort out these feelings.

ESSENTIAL

Keeping notes about your dating journey and the people you meet is essential to your success—and it makes for fascinating reading later on. Just remember that if you want your notes to be private, keep them that way. You might consider keeping your notes hidden or even using initials instead of the full names of those you write about.

If you've decided to go ahead and start the dating journey, you will need a few tricks to keep yourself motivated when times get tough. Complete the following sentences and keep them for future reference. In times of doubt, you can reread your reasons for dating and reaffirm your goals.

- The things I'm most excited about in starting a new relationship are:
- The things I'm most apprehensive about in starting a new relationship are:
- The aspects of dating that are easiest for me are:
- The aspects of dating I find the most challenging are:
- The things I like most about being single are:
- The things I like least about being single are:
- The things I like most about being part of a couple are:
- The things I like least about being part of a couple are:

How do you get the information, courage, and confidence to make great decisions? Reflecting upon your past and identifying patterns from past relationships is a great way to start. Not only will you determine what you want for today—what you learn about yourself will be invaluable for your dating journey.

Your Past: Your Key to a Great Future

Imagine what a timesaver it would be if you could spend just a little time with someone and quickly know if she has what it takes to make a great relationship with you. This might sound impossible, but it's not. You can figure out what makes you desirable to others, and, just as importantly, what will make one of them a good match for you. The keys lie in your past relationships. It's pretty likely that you've had a least one romantic experience, even if your relationship experience is very limited.

Take a trip down memory lane, starting with your first date. Write down the name of the person who first asked you out. How did you meet? What was this special person like? What initially attracted you to each other? What did you do on your first date? Was it a good experience? Did you see each other again? Why or why not? What things did you particularly like or dislike about this person? How did your relationship end? Why?

If you have never been on a date in your life, were there any people you might have dated? Who were they and why didn't you ever make a connection with them?

ALERT!

If you don't consider your past dating history seriously, you may be condemned to repeat it. Be honest about your experiences and learn from them. No one ever needs to know your results, and the only person who can judge you is you.

Now, go through all your past significant romantic relationships, and for each of them write down the answers to the same questions. If you haven't had any significant relationships, write down the names and particulars of people you have dated a few times, or had a crush on or were attracted to, and what happened to your relationship with these people.

Your Relationship History

Your tastes may have changed over time, but your basic personality and the types of people who attract you (and whom you attract) are probably the same. Perhaps all of your partners were emotionally needy. Perhaps many were adventurous. Did most of your past partners have a good sense of humor or a positive, upbeat outlook? Do you see a history of physical violence, verbal abuse, and constant fighting? Were many of them unable to commit or unavailable?

ESSENTIAL

If you do an assessment of your past relationships, you'll get a snapshot of not only the physical types you're most attracted to, but also positives and negatives (both yours and your potential partner's) that you should look for when you meet new people. These will most likely indicate success or failure in a relationship with them.

Go back through your notes and select the top six assets (those you absolutely require from a partner) and the top six liabilities (things that you will never accept in a partner) and note those. Try to determine what assets and liabilities you bring to a relationship that seem to be most valued or rejected by others. Armed with this information, you will be able to zone in more quickly on "your type" of potential partner; once dating them, you can quickly spot red flags in their past, personality, or values signaling that this person isn't a great candidate for a relationship with you.

Their Histories Matter, Too

Most of the people you meet will have had experience with past relationships and loves. Learning about their past relationships can help you figure out whether someone will be a good match for you. You may find some people who can't wait to blurt out their entire life's history the moment you meet them. Others may be very secretive through at least the first few dates.

ALERT!

Not everyone is forthcoming with personal information. You don't have to give your date an interrogation worthy of the FBI. Gently directed questions and chatting will keep the conversation (and the information) flowing, and will help you both identify red flags that could make or break a relationship.

When you go on your first official date, it's acceptable to ask a few questions about your date's past. Things to work into the conversation might include: Have you had many serious relationships? How long did these relationships generally last? Have you been married? Divorced? How long has it been since you were separated from your last ex? What do you want from a relationship now? A good general question to ask is, What's most important to you? Is it career? Family? Religion? Politics? Money?

Be an astute listener and read between the lines for clues to your date's assets and liabilities. Does it appear that your date only blames other partners and personally takes none of the blame for things not working out in the past? Is there any aspect of the person's past or present life that might suggest trouble for you in a relationship—e.g., substance abuse, physical abuse, criminal record, bankruptcy, mental or physical health problems, inability to keep a job, rocky family relationships, or sexual perversions? Does this person have good manners? A healthy level of personal hygiene and fitness? Is your date forthright in discussing opinions, interests, and ambitions, or uncommunicative and withdrawn? All of these points are important in determining whether or not you'll make a good match.

You don't have to delve too deeply on date one, but both you and your date should exchange information about significant aspects of your lives. For instance, don't try to keep it hidden that you have children or that you're not yet legally separated from your ex. Anyone who isn't interested in a relationship based on this information isn't the right person for you.

When you're dishonest with a date, the only person you deceive is yourself. If you realize that your date has qualities that you absolutely do not want and cannot accept in a potential partner, there's no point in continuing to date him. Obviously, if you love babies and animals and can't imagine a life without a houseful of both, and your date says that he hates kids and loathes animals, chances of a happy, long-term relationship with this person are pretty low. You can't change these things about a person, and ignoring real aspects of a person's values, history, and personality can sabotage your dating success. The warnings you ignore will come back to haunt you later on—guaranteed!

On the plus side, there is a nearly infinite selection of great people out there, in a huge range of styles and characteristics. Once you know what you are looking for, what assets are desired and what liabilities acceptable, you will more easily pinpoint the potential partners who will be attracted back to you. Being flexible is the key to dating success. No one can meet all of your requirements, but you'll know when you've found someone who fits enough of them.

Chapter 2

What Are You Looking For?

Did you ever reject someone who could have been the love of your life, just because you were pining away for a fictionalized version? Fantasy and dreams are fun, and real people are definitely more complex and not nearly as perfect as their fictional counterparts. However, a fictional lover can't hold your hand, make you laugh, console you through life's tragedies, or share your joys. If you want to meet someone real, not just dream about storybook romances, you've got to have a detailed idea of what you want.

Setting Your Sights Too High or Too Low

One thing's for sure: If you cut off every potential partner at the pass, you'll never succeed in reaching the end goal of your dating journey. Having too many criteria for dates can be just as bad as having too few. Take Petra's situation, for example:

> *My perfect partner isn't out there but it's not my fault. I'm not picky, really. I just don't like guys under six feet, and definitely no paunches or thinning hair. If he wears baseball caps or T-shirts with logos, I won't date him again. A six-pack of rippling muscles is good, and so is someone who is extremely successful in his own business, so he can lavish expensive gifts on me. I can't tolerate it if he puts me second. He should be willing to drop everything and be with me when I'm feeling lonely. Brian was close to my ideal, but he insisted on reading the newspaper every morning, and that really bugged me. Steve was romantic and had lots of good qualities, but I didn't like his hair, and I hated his taste. He kept buying me expensive jewelry I didn't like. It's obvious why I ditched him. (Petra, 39, City Planner)*

Does Petra's sentiment sound familiar? Have you ever let someone special get away because you felt that there might be someone better? Even a fictional romance hero might want to read the newspaper in the morning or wear a baseball cap! Amazingly, Petra has still found potential partners that come close to meeting her requirements, but her standards are so exacting and contradictory that she is bound to continually be disappointed. This woman is unlikely to find anyone, even in fiction, who will satisfy her. Petra thinks the reason she can't meet anyone is that all the men are not worthy of her, not that her vision might be unrealistic. And although Petra has plenty of potential liabilities of her own, she ignores them.

QUESTION?

Could *you* live up to the requirements you've set?
Being choosy about who you date is fine, but being picky to a fault is unreasonable. Also, don't forget to think of how the other person might view your assets and liabilities. Consider who you are and what you have to offer.

Perhaps you've never expected too much from your dates, but have you ever expected too little? Have you ever continued dating someone you really weren't interested in, just because you didn't feel confident that your special someone was still out there waiting? If so, don't feel bad. Many people have blind spots when it comes to what they want, what they should have, and who can meet their expectations. And singles aren't guilty only of creating sky-high, unrealistic requirements for their potential partners; they often do the opposite as well.

Many people stay in unsatisfying or even unhealthy relationships because breaking up is too messy, or because they don't want to be the bad guy. Every time you do this, you do yourself a disservice. Wasting your time on someone who doesn't treat you well, doesn't appreciate you, or doesn't care about you will only set you back in your dating adventure. Just as setting your sights too high can leave you dateless, setting them too low can leave you stuck in a dating nightmare.

Narrowing Down Your Options

You now know not to set your sights too high or too low, but you may be wondering exactly what your date criteria should be. Here's one easy way to figure it out: Imagine you are a business executive who needs a new assistant. You would probably contact the human resources office and tell them you have a job to fill. In order to find a good candidate for the position, they will need a description of the job, a detailed account of the type of person you are seeking, and a list of skills and experience this person should have. To give them this information, you would need to compile a list. When you are single and seeking a relationship partner, you can make a similar list. You are searching for someone with particular attributes to fill a certain "position" in your life.

Chances are you can already think of a few assets that you'd like in a partner and maybe a few things you don't want. However, the more descriptive and honest you are, the better your chances are of finding a good match. To save yourself a lot of time and grief, you will also want to note the things you really can't accept in a partner.

FACT

Most singles don't know what they are looking for beyond the basics—blond hair, sense of humor, and a good job, for example. But when they take the time to sit down and actually figure out a more holistic view of their desires, they make better, faster, happier matches.

Following are a list of assets and a list of liabilities you might find in a potential partner. These lists are by no means complete, but they contain a few of the basic attributes you might be looking for (or avoiding). Check all the points that are significant to you. Then go back and circle the top six assets (the things your perfect partner must have) and top six liabilities (the things that you cannot accept in a partner). Circle the assets and liabilities that you think best describe you as well. If you don't see your preferences, add them to the list. Keep these notes for future reference.

Assets:

- Has sense of humor
- Generous
- Communicative
- Confident
- Attractive
- Healthy (mentally and physically)
- Financially secure
- Wants/does not want children
- Geographically desirable
- Hard-working
- Sexually compatible
- Sociable
- Honest
- Ready for commitment
- Loyal
- Compassionate
- Romantic
- Intelligent
- Open-minded

- Similar/dissimilar background, interests, and values
- Other

LIABILITIES:

- Greedy/cheap
- Lacks confidence
- Unattractive
- Unhealthy (mentally or physically)
- Financially unstable
- Wants/does not want children
- Geographically undesirable
- Sexually incompatible
- Antisocial
- Dishonest
- Fearful of commitment
- Unromantic
- Unintelligent
- Depressive
- Violent
- Jealous
- Disloyal
- Substance-abuser
- Prejudiced
- Similar/dissimilar background, interests, or values
- Other

If you were given a stack of resumes and asked to select the best ones for the open assistant position, you would first go through the bunch and eliminate any that blatantly didn't display your "must haves" or that displayed any obvious negatives or "can't stands." To find your best love applicants, you go through a similar process of elimination. Once you have a clear idea of what you want, you can go out into the world and find it!

Mother Doesn't Always Know Best

When you meet someone, do you automatically size this person up to your mother's standards? Many otherwise successful, intelligent singles do just that. It's also quite common to be pushed into a relationship by well-meaning others when you're not ready.

One piece of truth people often forget is that going through life without a committed partner is not a failure in any way. Some people are late bloomers, others are happier being by themselves, and still others might value friendships and family relationships above romantic partnerships. This choice is yours to make, so make it wisely! It is selfish and destructive to be in a serious relationship with someone else if that's not what you want. It's even less responsible to reluctantly or prematurely bring children into your life because your mom wants to be a grandmother or all of your friends are having babies, instead of from your own genuine desire to be a parent.

ALERT!

Some singles feel such pressure from outside sources to pair up that they marry the first acceptable person who will say "I do." These relationships rarely work out well. In most cases, these couples find that they are not at all compatible. Be honest with yourself and your partner before making a permanent commitment.

The best advice dating singles can get is to heed their inner voice. Dating can actually help you figure out what you want. Most people who are in the meet market are seeking long-term committed relationships, but if you're not sure that this is what *you* want, it's kindest to tell potential partners up front how you feel. If someone wants instant marriage and family and you don't want that, be honest and don't waste their time, or yours. Consider Barbara's story:

> I really wanted to get married, but Peter told me right away that he intended to remain single. I should have found someone with more similar goals, but Peter was cute, clever, and rich, and I was in love with him. He was devoted to his mother, who always told us that her greatest joy would

be to hold her first grandchild. After dating for two years, I got tired of waiting for Peter to change his mind about marriage. I accepted a job in another town. Peter begged me to stay, but I told him I wouldn't, unless we got married. The next weekend, Peter got down on one knee and proposed to me in front of his mother. Then he became very sullen and withdrawn. By our wedding day, I realized that I was a bride with a very reluctant groom. It never occurred to me that Peter hadn't actually changed his mind about marriage, he had just caved in from the pressure his mother and I put on him. Our marriage wasn't happy, and lasted less than a year. I later learned that when Peter told his mother that I was leaving, she went out and bought my engagement ring and gave it to Peter, saying she would never forgive him if he let me go! Today I'm remarried, but Peter is still single and seeing a man he met at a bar. I guess he always knew where his heart was. Only the need to please the people he loved, the pressure to conform, and the pressure we put on him forced him into a marriage he knew he couldn't handle. In the end, we all suffered. (Barbara, 54, Psychologist)

Be true to yourself. Take the time to be sure of what you want, don't let anyone else tell you what that should be, and never change your heart's desire just to please someone else! If people care about you and want you to be happy, they will let you live your life and make your own relationships, at your own pace. Then they will be supportive of your choices.

Avoid Carbon Copies of Your Exes

If you've dated a number of people but still haven't found your match, you may be making a common mistake: dating carbon copies of your former partners. Even if a past relationship was damaging, many people often end up in new relationships with similar people. This can happen for a myriad of reasons—it's comforting, you miss your ex, or you haven't learned from your bad experience. However, repeatedly dating the same kind of person and having it not work out is a huge waste of time.

Take Joey's situation, for example. Joey is an easygoing, soft-spoken man. His ex-wife Melinda is a loud, controlling woman. When Joey and Melinda married, she immediately set about alienating all of Joey's friends and family so they couldn't influence him. She pushed him around, and when he tried to fight back, she always blamed and attacked him.

After ten years, Joey had finally had enough and divorced Melinda. Soon, he was in love again! Joey told everyone that his new love, Melany, was "not at all like that witch, Melinda." However, when Joey introduced Melany to friends at his fiftieth birthday party, everyone was dumbstruck—Melany was a nearly perfect copy of Melinda. She not only looked, sounded, and dressed like Joey's ex, but she pushed him around all evening, loudly demanding that Joey do this, get that, and go there.

Even if you don't blindly pick a clone of your ex over and over, be aware that you might be sabotaging your efforts in other ways. For example, if you want to meet a college professor, you're far more likely to find one at an academic conference than at the local bar. If you have a specific type of partner in mind, head to the spots where she might hang out to double your luck.

At one point, Melany even yanked a drink out of Joey's hands, screaming, "You don't need another beer!" When one of Joey's best friends tried to defend Joey, Melany snarled that Joey was "my man and my business." In private, Joey's friends voiced their concerns and pointed to the similarities between Melinda and Melany, but Joey didn't seem to see any. Joey agreed with Melany that their lives would be just perfect if he would change and see things her way.

If Joey's experience sounds familiar to you, perhaps it's time you broke with tradition and tried someone new! If you usually date uptight perfectionists who don't make you happy, for instance, maybe it's time to look for a more laid-back partner.

Identifying Your "Type"

How many times have you or a friend said something like the following: "She's attractive and very nice, but I'm not interested her romantically. She's just not my type." Probably plenty. It's not necessarily a bad thing, as long as you know what your type is and keep your expectations reasonable.

In your dating journey you're likely to meet a few people who seem to have nearly everything you want, at least at first. But in reality, there's just no way around it: You can't imagine yourself in a romantic relationship with them. There's no chemistry—they're just not your type.

On a visual level, your type is a physical image that you find appealing. But chemistry is also based on things you cannot even see. When you size people up, you generally consider their assets and liabilities. At first glance, these are often grouped together to form generalized opinions or stereotypes (e.g., tough guy, momma's boy, gold digger, etc.). But there's even more to it. Animals, including humans—and even insects—respond to something so elusive that you can't even categorize it: pheromones. Without going into all the details, these are chemicals that bypass conscious systems to trigger specific, often sexual, responses. The key things to know about pheromones are that every person has his or her own unique pheromone molecule that carries a one-of-a-kind chemical signature. Although you might not be aware of it, your personal pheromone messenger molecules are continuously whirling off your body and into the air around you. They rise up from the recesses of your sweat glands, and they linger in strands of your hair.

Obviously, an attractive scent is not the only way to choose a mate. You also have to use all the information receptors you have, including your five senses and the assets and liabilities that you already know you must have or won't accept in a mate. Even if you think you can appreciate the good in everyone, you can't possibly be equally attracted to everyone on earth. Likewise, you can't force chemistry where there isn't any.

FACT

Most scientists agree that humans process pheromones as strong sexual stimulants. If you want to take advantage of the personal power of your pheromones, you should know that the most potent pheromone-generating regions of the body are located in the groin, the armpits, and the narrow strip of skin between the base of the nostrils and the upper lip.

Is Your Type Really Important?

Physical attraction is a nearly instantaneous reaction—an initial response to another person. It's one of the reasons some people can tell immediately whether they could be friends with someone else. It's also the same reaction that some people call "love at first sight." Of course, love at first sight isn't genuine love at all, because you can't love someone you know nothing about. But this sensation is a powerful attraction to a particular type of person. Your type should consist of a mixture of physical and intangible factors that draw you to someone else. Jacky's story is a great example of the importance of types:

> *Some people mistakenly think I'm a ballerina, because I'm thin and very graceful, but I am not a dancer. I have two left feet! In college, however, I went to a fraternity party and a tall, intellectual-looking blonde man immediately caught my eye. He had the bluest eyes I've ever seen and I also like tall, sensitive-looking intellectual men. From his thin, sensitive face, topped with horn-rimmed glasses, to his tweed jacket with patches, this guy was "it." Our eyes locked. I could tell that he was also attracted to me. As he made his way to me, a friend of mine whispered that he was a catch, a third-year medical student. My heartthrob was not only good looking, but he was almost a doctor! He was absolutely my type. As my heart thumped wildly, he asked if I was a ballerina, because he was a sucker for that type of woman. I knew right then and there that we would connect as a couple, and maybe get married. (Jacky, 33, Homemaker)*

Jacky and her heartthrob actually did connect, marry, and live happily ever after, but not until they spent nearly six years getting to know one another. Their "types" did lead them to each other across a crowded room filled with plenty of other possibilities, but it took much more than being the right types for each other to make their relationship last.

So, what's *your* type? Close your eyes, and think about what kind of person you'd most like to be with in a romantic setting. Imagine getting physically close to this person, perhaps holding hands or getting ready to lock lips. Free association is the best way to make this exercise work, so don't think too much about your answers to the following questions:

- What vision immediately springs to mind?
- What kind of person are you with?
- What does this person look like?
- What images do you see?
- What setting are you in?
- What are you doing in that setting?
- What is the person doing?

Write down your answers for future reference. Now, close your eyes again and do the same exercise, but "age" each of you about twenty years.

- What picture immediately springs to mind?
- What kind of person are you with?
- What does this person look like?
- What images do you see?
- What setting are you in?
- What are you doing in that setting?
- What is the person doing?

Write down your answers for future reference. But how do you figure out what your answers to this exercise might mean? Consider Marianne's experience with this exercise:

> *I had already determined that my ideal partner would be a hard-working, devout, family man—who wouldn't mind if I stayed home once the babies started coming along (I'd like a baseball team of boys!). So I was surprised that I didn't envision the mild-mannered man in a business suit that I thought I'd see during this exercise. Instead, he was a man on a very large motorcycle, wearing a metallic purple helmet with orange flames on it. I have never even been on a motorcycle! He handed me a matching purple helmet, and whisked me away down a tree-lined country road. In my fantasy, I felt natural, and free. Then, when I did the twenty-years-ahead exercise, the business suit still didn't appear, but the biker was back, with gray hair, a few more pounds, and a big smile. When we started riding away, I realized that there was a line of other riders behind us. But we were the leaders of the pack! At first, the visions didn't make any sense to me, but as I*

thought about it, I realized that besides the intrinsic qualities that I wanted in a mate that might be considered "staid," my type was someone who was adventurous, who would retain a youthful outlook, and who was a natural leader. There are plenty of men I could meet that fit my needs and my "type." (Marianne, 25, Court Reporter)

Now check out Abe's experience:

I never really thought I had a "type," so I was really surprised when I envisioned myself rock-climbing with a very physically sculpted woman wearing very bright, very tight bike shorts. I always liked women with confidence and intelligence, but not body-builders or athletes. In fact, I always picked women in helper professions, like teachers or nurses. When I did the twenty-years-forward exercise I envisioned myself (sporting my beer belly) running a track race, but the woman I was with was in much better physical shape, and she was beating me although I tried to win. The vision was unsettling, but the more I thought about it, the more I realized that I am most attracted to women who care about their bodies and their health, and who challenge me to be my personal best. Not long after this, I met a woman who turned out to be a yoga instructor. I wasn't sure whether we were going to click or not, but she had the confidence to ask me out, and then she challenged me to a game of chess for our first date. I was hooked! (Abe, 49, Community Leader)

Like Abe and Marianne, you may be surprised to see what your visions hold. And keep one thing in mind: Just because you envision a biker doesn't mean you are mostly attracted to bikers, but it does give you a hint of what your subconscious desires. You don't have to be a trained counselor to pick out patterns. In most cases, they will be fairly obvious to you.

Armed with this information about your type, you can now venture out into the meet market to find your special someone in the places where those types of people are likely to be. Just keep an open mind—and have fun with your adventure.

Chapter 3

Self-Evaluation

You've already defined what you want in a partner, but your potential partners have requirements, too. Essentially, you are a unique product, and it's your job to market yourself to a receptive audience who appreciates that you have something the other products don't. Additionally, you have to understand yourself well enough to know when a person is right for you and when you've been mismatched. So, before you head out into the meet market, consider what makes up your identity and all the things you bring to a relationship.

What You Have to Offer

The more you know about your own assets and liabilities, both inside and out, the easier your quest for a partner will be. The trick is in finding a way to be honest with yourself. Most people have a somewhat skewed self-image, and it takes a lot of time and experience to gain the confidence needed to find a good match. A little self-knowledge can go a long way, so taking a good hard look at who you are and what you have to offer is a great idea.

The following exercises may be challenging for you, so keep in mind that you don't have to share your results with anyone else. They are for your consideration only. The more honest and open-minded you are about yourself, the better you will be able to focus your dating efforts when you go out.

ESSENTIAL

Here's a good way to change your attitude when it comes to looking for dates: Stop and think about what you have to offer instead of what someone else has to offer you. Once you can see yourself from this angle you can more accurately assess the likelihood of a successful relationship with a particular partner.

Wouldn't it be convenient if you could just go to the "dating store" to find your perfect match? You would simply key in a list of your own attributes and the attributes you want in a potential partner, and out would pop a perfect mate who automatically also wants you! This fantasy has gotten a bit closer to reality in recent years with the advent of online dating. This method involves searching a database for specific attributes such as age, religion, education, eye color, height, and weight. However, even if you can select people you are attracted to, you still can't control the level of attraction someone else feels for you in return.

Should you ever change yourself to suit someone else? No—it's a horrible idea. You can change a hairstyle to resemble a popular movie star, but you can never change what makes you *you*. If you try to make significant changes to please someone else, the real you will still remain, and you won't be able to keep up the facade forever. Besides, you want to be with someone who appreciates your true identity! Complete the following sentences to reaffirm your self-image and locate trouble areas:

- Some things I might like to change about myself are:
- Some patterns my life tends to follow are:
- Others think my best qualities are:
- Others think my potential liabilities are:
- Some ways I might adjust my dating style are:
- I would like my next partner to be someone who:

Reality Check

Taking a realistic look at what you have to offer, as well as what the other person is offering you, is essential. You can't know what people want just by looking at them, but it's a sure bet that some people will love what you have to offer and some people will not. Consider Unissa's experience:

> *I am fifty pounds overweight. I exercise regularly, but I have always been big, and I'm satisfied with that. I meet lots of men in my sales job that I might like to date, but all too often, they aren't interested in me. I have great inner qualities and I wish that more people would take the time to know me better. When I began dating more actively, I realized that my weight might be considered an obvious liability, but I really want a man who can accept me as I am and who wants to date all of me! I didn't get a lot of dates, but when I met Gerry, the first thing he told me was that he was attracted to me because I was a confident, big, beautiful woman! He never saw my size as an issue. In fact, he told me that he wasn't attracted to skinny women. He always says that I'm the sexiest woman on the planet because there's more of me to love. In the year that we've been going out, we've learned that we're very compatible in other ways, too. I know this relationship is going to go far. (Unissa, 34, Sales Manager)*

Appearance isn't everything, but it very often affects people's self-confidence as well as how they are perceived by others. Before you jump into dating, it's a good idea to make an honest assessment of your appearance and decide how you feel about it. Choose the answers that best complete the following statements:

I consider my overall appearance to be:
- Attractive
- Average
- Unattractive

I would describe the way I feel about my appearance as:
- Satisfied
- Indifferent
- Dissatisfied

I consider myself to be:
- Underweight
- Average
- Overweight

I consider my overall health and physical condition to be:
- Excellent
- Average
- Poor

You can't control someone else's perceptions and feelings, but you can change your own personal self-image. If there are things you'd like to change about yourself, think seriously about how to make those changes and then get started! As you dive into dating, continue to improve upon your self-confidence and stay open to new ideas.

FACT

Be aware: What you consider one of your greatest assets might be a major liability for someone else. For example, if you are a true animal lover with three dogs, a person with severe pet allergies and intense fear of dogs probably won't be your perfect match.

Makeover Magic

As you make changes on the inside, you might also want to consider how you appear on the outside. Later on in this book you will learn specific ways to boost your physical selfimage. You'll learn that even something as simple as new makeup or a great-fitting suit can do wonders for your appearance and your ego and help you enhance romance. However, don't forget that it's the internal qualities that are most lasting and important. Consider the assets and liabilities that you use to describe yourself, along with those your critics (friends) mentioned before deciding what parts of yourself to make over.

While you're working on your image, keep in mind that others might be doing the same. Don't let an outdated hairstyle or a bad tie cloud your vision. These minor details should never turn you away from an otherwise wonderful potential partner. A woman named August almost made this mistake:

> When my friend Paulette set me up with Carl, I immediately loved his voice over the phone. He sounded like Barry White, and imagined he looked very sexy. Meeting him in person was another matter entirely. Carl was tall as he had described, but he wasn't well built and had badly yellowed teeth, my personal turnoff. I told him I couldn't stay for more than one drink. Carl just smiled (with his yellowed teeth) and handed me a personally inscribed copy of his recently published book of photographs. I was really touched.
>
> As we talked, I realized that he was not only talented, but he was romantic and caring, and had nearly all the attributes I was seeking. One drink turned into two, and two drinks turned into dinner. By the time we said goodbye I realized that I really liked Carl, but I wasn't sure I could get past his looks. Six months went by and I ran into Carl at a fundraiser. He had slimmed down and had obviously been to a dentist. Now he was attractive both inside and out. We have been dating for six months and I'm so much in love, I can't believe I almost totally rejected him! (August, 34, Nonprofit Manager)

Constructive Criticism from Friends

Think you know what others think of you and what kind of first impression you are likely to make? Some people have a fairly accurate image of themselves, but most people are too partial to be brutally honest. One way to find out how you appear to others is to enlist the help of several trusted friends whose opinions you respect. A man named Martin tried this method to learn why he was having unsuccessful relationships with women:

> *At age forty, Martin felt he knew everything there was to know about himself. He thought he was a pretty good catch, although he admitted that he liked to boast about his job where he met high-profile celebrities, and he tended to drop names in conversation. When Martin's last relationship fizzled, he asked his friends why they thought he wasn't scoring well with women, and what they considered his assets and liabilities. He was shocked by their responses. They all agreed that Martin's most pronounced liability was his insecurity and his need to be the center of attention. They also pointed out that this need to show off became even more pronounced when he was around a woman he wanted to impress.*
>
> *Martin's friends also suggested that Martin needed to pick women who challenged him more, as his usual choice of partner was predictably submissive and quiet (someone who wouldn't hog his spotlight) and he would quickly get bored with these women. Martin took his friends' critiques seriously. The next woman he met was named Linda. She was a talented musician who had gathered a crowd at a party by playing folk songs on her guitar. Martin resisted the urge to gather his own crowd, and joined her group. After she finished playing he complimented her, and suggested they meet for coffee. He quickly discovered that they were soul mates, and he is grateful to his friends for pointing out things that he would never have noticed on his own.*

After you have asked your friends for their basic assessments, you may be shocked to see aspects of yourself you never considered, much like Martin was. If your friends have made a clear and honest critique, you should see areas where you could make a few adjustments to your image, outlook, dating style, and attitude.

What if you get defensive during a personal critique by your friends?
It's extremely important not to get defensive and upset with your friends if they tell you something you don't want to hear. They are doing you a huge favor by critiquing you. Treat them with kindness and gratitude, and be sure that you write down what they say for future reference.

Consider your friends' responses. Do you agree? Disagree? Is there a pattern? Have they mentioned anything that you might want to change? Make a note of these things. Here are a few specific questions you might choose to ask your friends:

- How would you describe my personality?
- How would you describe my dating style?
- What do you consider my greatest asset?
- What do you consider my greatest fault?
- How do you think I could improve my chances of finding a great partner?
- If you were choosing a partner for me, what type of person would you select?

Go for It!

One thing you want to avoid when it comes to dating is regretting a missed opportunity. Too many people let great opportunities pass them by for fear of being rejected or being hurt like they have in the past. The only way to get over this fear is to face it, head-on. If you see an attractive, well-dressed, and obviously single person smiling at you from across your favorite art gallery, go over and make conversation! You've got nothing to lose—except a possibly great opportunity if you don't.

Just because you've had negative experiences in the past doesn't mean that history is doomed to repeat itself. Don't let fear or insecurity hold you back when it comes to love. A woman named Harriet almost made this very mistake:

I met my David at our local park. My live-in lover had left me for someone twenty years his junior, leaving me with two young boys to support. I was so bitter and so busy just trying to be a single mom that I was completely out of the dating scene. David always seemed to be in the park with his little boy every time my boys and I were there. He would say hello and I'd quickly nod and walk away. I told myself I wasn't interested in getting to know anyone, and I didn't like the fact that he had a kid when I already had two. But David seemed like such a nice man, and he was so good with his little boy, that one day I let him strike up a conversation. Slowly, our feelings for each other grew. Even better, our kids got along so well that they became good friends. A friendship grew between us, as well as between our kids. Two years after we met we married, and yes—we got married in that park. (Harriet, 39, Cosmetician)

Making a connection with someone can happen at any time, in any place, and at any age. Love often happens when you least expect it. As long as you're open to new experiences and different types of people, you will be ready to meet your perfect match—whenever that person comes along.

Try Something New

It makes perfect sense that the best place to find your type of person is at the places that correspond with the traits you're looking for in a potential partner. For example, if you are hoping to meet a musician, it seems obvious that you're more likely to meet such a person at a jazz club than at a racetrack.

ALERT!

Making snap judgments about people can end your dating journey before it's even begun. If you decide that there's only one type of person you want to meet and only one place where you can possibly meet him, you're narrowing your options down to almost none. This mistake will put you back at square one every time.

However, one mistake people often make is never leaving their comfort zone. For instance, if you like music and enjoy the company of musicians but have never had a successful relationship with one, perhaps you're looking in the wrong place. Maybe you don't need a musician to be happy—you just need someone who will appreciate music as you do. That opens up your options quite a bit. You're likely to find music fans at any number of places, from shopping malls to cafes. The important thing is that you get out there and make yourself available. Be open to new ideas, and you just may find what you seek. This sentiment helped Frank dig himself out of the depths of a bad breakup:

> *After my fiancé, Arlene, broke our engagement, I didn't have the heart to date again for nearly a year, but I finally got tired of sitting home alone. When my friends pushed me into a cooking class, I figured that at least I'd know how to cook for one. I never expected to meet anyone and I wasn't really up to looking, but Cynthia was my potato-peeling budding, and we really got along well. She actually asked me out, but I'm glad I said yes because I had a great time. Since then, I've met a few other women and I am beginning to feel that perhaps I could make a romantic connection with someone again. I'm still wary of getting hurt, but just because one woman broke my heart doesn't mean that every woman will. It takes courage to get back in the saddle after you've fallen, but I'm ready, and this time I'm going to stay the course. (Frank, 30, Accountant)*

Chapter 4
Meeting People

Now that you have a better idea of what you want in a romantic partner, it's time to start your search. Your active dating experience begins with an attraction formed by a first impression, but you first have to put yourself out there. The best way to do this is to use your tried and true methods in new and exciting ways. If you've never answered a personal ad, taken a dance class, or experienced speed dating, why not try? New activities will enhance your life, as well as boost your chances of finding love.

Personal Introductions and Blind Dates

Personal introductions don't always result in great matches, but they are one of the most common and time-honored ways to get two people together. An in-person introduction gives you something in common (you both know the person matching you) and you can quickly size up whether there is any chemistry. Even if the match doesn't work out well, at least someone you know (not always your mom or your single aunt) thinks enough of you to help you find true love. And it's a win-win situation when it does work out. Here's Michelle's story:

> *When I first saw Dick, I thought: "Oh no! What was my friend Susan thinking? This is going to be a disaster." Dick was so nervous that he shredded all the napkins on our table without even realizing it. I don't think he expected someone like me, either. But as we chatted, Dick and I both realized that we had a lot in common and Dick had nearly all of the qualities I had hoped for, with no significant liabilities. Thanks, Susan! (Michelle, 55, Artist)*

Blind dates, though similar to personal introductions, are a particularly frightening prospect for some people. Nearly everyone with any dating experience at all has a blind-date story, and there are even television shows that capitalize on how wild this experience can be. These are the most risky setups because you are meeting someone you've never seen and haven't chosen, and you probably have just a few basic details about him or her. Blind dates have a bad rap, but they have successfully joined countless grateful couples.

Even if your gut tightens when someone suggests this kind of setup, don't automatically turn down the offer. Get as much information as you can, and if you think the person has been represented fairly and might actually have potential, *go for it!* If you can't stand the thought of idly picking at your pizza with someone whose company you don't enjoy and to whom you're not attracted (or vice-versa, as it works both ways), ask your "matchmaker" to double-date, or to invite you both to dinner or to another type of social activity (e.g., a football game, fundraiser, dance, or party). That way, you both have your mutual contact to turn to if things don't work out—and your mutual contact to *thank* if they do.

Bars and Clubs

Bars and clubs are popular places to meet people, especially if you enjoy drinking, dancing, dressing up, and being in a high-energy atmosphere with lots of noise. People do meet in bars and clubs, especially those geared specifically toward singles. Bars are best left for socializing with friends or to the lounge lizard/barfly types who are there solely so they don't have to drink alone. These types of places don't encourage the kind of interpersonal interaction you need to make good connections. They are often overcrowded, poorly lit, smoky, and so loud that you can't hold a conversation. Connections are superficial and made on quick first impressions, so an eye-catching appearance and outgoing personality really help. You might give or get a fistful of phone numbers, but never connect with any of them again.

ALERT!

If you're not into one-night stands, limit your drinking so you can use good judgment and avoid anyone who is obviously only looking for a "good time." Also, if you go searching for a date at a bar or club, you might consider bringing a friend along with you. This way, you can keep an eye on each other and fight off any undesirable attention.

Singles bars (or bars with singles nights) and singles dances are a better bet, but still a poor choice if you are serious about meeting and dating. You will meet a lot of single people, but not necessarily any with whom you can connect on a real level.

Meeting and Eating Activities

Food and love go together, and a great way to meet quality people are "meeting and eating" activities. Getting together over a meal always stimulates conversation, and provides an easy, enjoyable, natural setting in which to exchange ideas and information. You need to eat anyway, so why do it alone?

Progressive Dinners

If you liked musical chairs as a child, you'll love this adult version, where no one is eliminated and everyone wins! Here's how it works: A group of singles meets at a restaurant and each person gets a number. After each course or time period (e.g., twenty minutes) those with odd numbers move one space around the table clockwise, and those with even numbers move one space counterclockwise. This gives everyone a chance to sit and chat with everyone else. If you don't make a match, you still have enjoyed good food and conversation.

It takes great organizational skills to plan a progressive dinner, but you can usually find advertisements for them in singles-oriented publications, on the Internet, and as featured events promoted by the restaurant. These dinners usually have a set fee, which includes the tip (drinks may be extra), and you must reserve your place in advance.

Bring-a-friend dinners are the social version of a swap meet. You and some friends each invite some unattached people of the opposite sex (people you like but aren't romantically interested in), to a party, brunch, dinner, dessert, or cocktails. This is a great way to meet new people in a relaxed social setting where no one is a total stranger, since everyone personally knows at least one host. Your friend's neighbor (nice man, no sparks for her) may just set off sparks with you. Your coworker's cousin who hasn't scored a second date for some time might just hit it off with your neighbor.

Another version of this is to collaborate with some friends who live within walking distance (or a quick commute) of one another. Each host or hostess invites a few singles to join them for a party—with a twist: The group moves to a new location every half hour. You and the other hosts provide directions and maps, share the cost, and enjoy a fun experience.

If you are adventurous, another version is the blind-date dinner. You and your single friends (male, female, or even both) place a group personal ad that offers a short description of each of you and what you are looking for, just like you'd do in a solo personal ad. The ad goes on to say that you are all selecting a group of special guests to attend a blind-date dinner. The guest will not only meet you, but all the other guests, too. When the responses arrive, pick the best ones and invite them to a dinner or brunch at a modestly priced restaurant at which you've reserved a table. A prix fixe brunch is best, because it's affordable (and many include a drink) and everyone's cost will be the same. As in a progressive dinner, every other person moves after each course (or after fifteen to twenty minutes).

FACT

Whether you choose a cooking class, wine or liquor-tasting event, or any variation of singles dining, meeting and eating activities are enjoyable ways to pair good food, good beverages, and good people. Also, a table full of food and drinks will always give you something to talk about when conversation comes to a halt.

If you like these meeting and eating ideas but are more traditional, consider joining or starting a dining club. Some dating services organize lunch and dinner groups (e.g., gourmet singles, solo suppers). The "regulars" meet every week or month for breakfast, lunch, or dinner in the same or different restaurants (you pay your own way or your share of the bill) or in each others' homes, and they are encouraged to bring guests. If you start your own, you can advertise for participants and mix them with people you know. The camaraderie of a regular dinner with newfound friends is wonderful, and if someone arrives who is intriguing, the personal introductions are easy!

Speed Dating

This is a relatively new concept that lets you meet a lot of people in very quick (under four minutes) one-on-one encounters. Speed dating seems to work best for people who have schedules so demanding that they don't have much time to date, and who are outgoing, communicative, visually attractive, and aren't afraid of rejection. Typically, the women are seated on one side of a table (or tables) and the men line up in front of them. Each couple gets three or four minutes to chat, and keeps notes on the conversation. A timekeeper asks the men to move down the table one person at regular intervals. The conversations continue until all the men and women in the room have met. Then everyone gets a list with the names of all the participants, and are asked to indicate which ones they'd be open to have more contact with. Their choices are compared (usually by the organizers after the event) and if there is a match, the couple is given contact information and encouraged to get in touch.

ALERT!

Whether in-person or online, speed dating is fast-paced and not for everyone. You are making choices based on quick first impressions, limited information, and possibly flawed assumptions. On the plus side, if you like the idea of meeting lots of potential partners quickly, it's worth trying to see if it's fun for you.

If one person is interested but the other isn't, the contact information isn't given to either. Some of the online dating sites have started offering online speed dating events (you chat by phone as you view a photo and profile online). For some, this is a less intimidating way to try speed dating.

Continuing Education and Singles Travel

Remember how naturally and easily you met people when you were in school? You and your classmates went through school together and had common interests and something to talk about. Going to school for lifetime learning is still a fun and effective way to meet single people. You don't have to be working toward a degree. Even a one-night class brings opportunities to learn and to love. At worst, you will learn new skills or discover a new hobby. At best, you might meet your love match. These short seminars are inexpensive, and many places will let you participate at reduced rates if you help out at the class or in the office for a few hours. You might just meet your new love while answering phones or collecting feedback forms.

You can find a wide variety of adult education classes on practically every topic from winning in the stock market to winning the game of love. Even if you live in a very small town, local community groups often have short seminars on everything from composting to pottery. These places are often advertised with tip-off names such as Alternative University, Adult Learning Center, or Senior Seminars. One type of class that has always been popular is ballroom dancing. You will meet lots of people and learn a new social skill. Group classes require students to rotate partners after every dance, so you will always have a partner, even if you didn't come with one. You can even practice those new moves in a club or disco—the perfect first date.

Adult education classes aren't restricted to singles, so when you register, don't be shy about asking which of the classes is likely to attract the most singles. It makes sense to select topics that genuinely interest you, but "Solo for the Holidays" will attract more unattached people than "Planning Your Dream Wedding."

Travel is another great way to continue your education, but it also includes a bit more romance, intrigue, and excitement. It's a great way to see the world, share new experiences with new people, and even save on the cost of traveling solo by taking group trips. There are numerous agencies that cater just to singles, and even special-interest singles and specific age groups. The upside of going on a singles-oriented vacation is that you are bound to meet single people, many of whom are looking for the same type of relationship you are. It's also a way for singles who hate being alone in a strange place or who are worried about their safety to relax and see the world.

Choose your travel group carefully. Always check the Better Business Bureau to see if anyone has lodged a complaint, and get references if possible from others who have used their services. Be aware that in many groups, the type and age of the singles may be varied, and you may be one of just a few that suit your age and interests.

Depending upon the group and how it's run, the pressure to pair up may be a bit overwhelming. If you don't click with your travel group, you are stuck with them for the duration of the trip. Another version of this is a singles-club vacation where most, if not all, of the guests will be single. It's not for everyone, but singles travel is definitely a fun alternative to always traveling alone, or staying home. Even if you don't go on a solely singles trip, let people you meet know you are "looking." You never know who they know who could be perfect for you, once you are at home! That's how Sam met his wife, Inez:

> *My wife, Inez, met an elderly couple from Queens when she went on a bus tour of the West. She told them that she was single and had never been to New York. When they invited her to visit them, she took them up on their invitation. The elderly couple, who were my neighbors, asked me if I would do them a favor and show Inez the sights. I guess they figured that the nice single man next door might be a better tour guide for Inez than an elderly couple. We actually never even had a formal first date. We met, walked around town, and discovered that we had an instant attraction and nearly everything that each partner wanted in the other! We were married within the year. (Sam, 56, City Planner)*

Volunteering

Be giving, and possibly find love! What could be better? It's a powerful, enriching experience to do something positive for others, such as serving a meal at a shelter or soup kitchen. You'll be with other caring people and you'll be busy doing something that makes you feel good about yourself. You'll also be able to make easy conversation with other volunteers, so you'll naturally be able to make connections. The gratitude you'll receive from those less fortunate than you will lift your spirits. And it can't hurt to remind yourself that being dateless isn't the worst thing that can happen to someone.

If volunteering doesn't particularly interest you but you have a favorite pastime, that might be a great opportunity to lend a hand. For example, offer support to a political candidate, raise funds for a community chorus, or pitch in and join your company's softball league. You will meet lots of like-minded people, and even if you don't find a new love, you'll have a good time supporting a cause or activity you believe in. It worked for Freida:

" I volunteered to deliver meals to elderly shut-ins on Christmas Eve. They were so grateful for attention and the food. It made me feel good, and much less lonely. John was driving the delivery van. By the time we'd finished our rounds, my spirit had been lifted and I even had a date for New Year's Eve. (Freida, 28, Engineer)

Religious Institutions and Special-Interest Groups

Nearly every religious group offers events, worship services, study groups, retreat weekends, and social events just for singles. This is a time-tested way to meet others who share your religious beliefs, in a safe and familiar setting. An easy way to make connections is in after-service get-togethers (e.g., Jewish people share light refreshments called Oneg Shabbat after Sabbath services).

ALERT!

At a religious event, don't just make a beeline for the singles. Be friendly to everyone. Let it be known to others in your congregation that you are single and looking. It's a sure bet that some of them will know someone they think is perfect for you, and will be more than eager to arrange an introduction.

If you don't practice religion, you can still seek a partner in a special-interest group. Everyone knows that if you enjoy what you are doing, your feelings will radiate to others. In a special-interest singles group, you are bound to meet like-minded people. There are groups and societies to meet every special interest, from the association for unmarried naturists (nudists) who wish to meet other singles in a social setting to postcard collectors, Star Trek fans, competitive chess players—just about anything you can name.

Research your special interests online, in the phone book, or through special-interest publications. The chances are great that there are local groups, or active Internet communities, of like-minded singles who have the same passions, hobbies, and interests that you do.

Weddings and Funerals

Weddings provide a very romantic setting. There is a beautiful bride and a beaming groom, pledging their love to one another. Weddings are fertile ground for romantic pairings (other than the bride and groom). If you are single and invited to a wedding without a date, don't panic. The chances are great that you'll be seated next to (or introduced to) other single guests. At least you'll all have something in common—you'll know one or both members of the couple. Don't be shy and sit out the dancing and toasts to the bride and groom. These are good ways to honor the couple, get yourself noticed, and make connections.

Funerals are obviously not romantic events, but everyone there is bound to have something in common with you (they know the deceased or the bereaved). While funerals are not intended to be social events, they are places where you can reconnect with relatives, colleagues, and friends. Consider Harriet's experience:

> *I attended the funeral of my coworker's mother, but misjudged how long it would take me to get to the church and arrived nearly an hour early. When I walked inside, I didn't see my colleague or anyone I knew and I was too tired to walk around outside. I sat down in the back pew and quietly waited for the service to start, when a man sat down next to me. The service wasn't starting for another twenty minutes, and I was feeling a bit awkward about not knowing anyone, so I struck up a conversation. We discovered that we knew several people in common, even though he didn't work for the same company I did, and that he grew up in Brooklyn and I grew up in Manhattan. Imagine that! By the time the mass began, we realized that we had a lot in common. A few weeks later Gino asked me out and I figured, why not? We've now been married fifteen years. (Harriet, 50, Office Manager)*

Funerals are also becoming a popular meeting ground for some seniors, especially those who live in retirement communities. These days, mature singles are living longer, living life better, losing partners, and looking for love again.

Office Romance

The workplace is a natural breeding ground for romance. You are spending a lot of time with people who have at least one thing in common with you, and, of course, you are in close proximity. If you have a pulse (not to mention hormones), that attractive person at the next desk—or your cute, powerful boss—could look pretty tempting.

However, workplace romance is risky. You still have to function in the same work setting if the relationship fizzles—imagine trying to concentrate on work while your ex is e-mailing poetry to a new love at the next desk. Workplace romance is also harder to keep under wraps than a celebrity scandal, so be prepared to be the hot topic at the water cooler. People do meet and even marry someone from the workplace, but not every office coupling has a happy ending. Dating a coworker (or worse, the boss) could cost you your job, your reputation, and good references for future jobs.

ALERT!

Many companies have very definite policies about workplace fraternization. Not every employer thinks love at work is a beautiful thing. Always make sure you know what your official company policy is before you dip your toe into the love-at-work waters.

If Cupid strikes and it's a coworker you're attracted to (and this person is sending signals back to you), be careful. Even if the company gives a thumbs-up to your potential relationship, there's more at stake than just being the subject of office gossip. Both of you need to ask yourself the following questions:

- Are you looking for romance, or are you just interested in having a closer friendship because you are bored or lonely?
- Who else knows that the two of you are interested in each other? Would your romance make these people uncomfortable, or cause them to hurt your ability to be discreet?

- How will you agree (in advance) to handle things if the relationship sours?

If you decide that the risks are acceptable, or you just can't control your feelings, don't start screaming it from the rooftops. Office romances should be handled very carefully and quietly. Canoodling coworkers can make others uncomfortable.

However, if you are lonely, bored, or attracted to someone who might harm your career, consider getting out of the office more, not getting involved at work. The workplace is a place to do business. There are potential new loves outside of your nine-to-five life, just waiting to meet you.

Matchmakers and Dating Services

Matchmakers and personal dating services (including video dating services) have been helping to make successful love connections for singles for a long time. They are the matchmaking community elders for modern daters, and they might be the way to find your perfect partner. Keep in mind that your success depends a great deal upon the quality of the service, the type of search, and your requirements.

ESSENTIAL

> Know how a dating service works before you sign up. Some rely on quantity, not quality, and just match bodies to bodies with the thinnest of criteria. Others will search extensively for exactly what you are seeking. Still others may recruit help from outside of their service. Matchmakers and dating services might be a good option for you if you are super-busy, very selective, or not willing to try it on your own.

Matchmaking services are not charities, they are profit-making businesses. Additionally, they can only match you up with others who have also come to seek help. Before you sign up, check things out with the Better Business Bureau to see if there are any complaints against the agency on file. Then get references. Be sure to know how long you have to use them, how many contacts you will be allowed to make, and whether you can refuse contacts without being penalized. Will you be able to get a refund? Can you change your requirements without charge? Don't be pressured to sign up immediately if you're not ready, and don't let them force you to make your requirements so broad that you can't target your needs properly.

Video dating is similar to traditional matchmaking services. Instead of just having a print profile, you will provide a photo of yourself and make a short videotape for potential partners to watch, in which you talk about yourself and what you are seeking in a mate. Your profile will be kept in the office for others to view, and you will be able to view and choose from their profiles, too. As in speed dating, if one person is interested and the other isn't, the contact information won't be given out.

ALERT!

The high-quality dating services are not inexpensive, and your success with them depends largely on the skill of the "matchmaker" in picking out potential partners and how honest and specific you are in describing yourself and your needs. They're worth considering if you have the money and don't count on the matchmaker for all of your potential partners.

Video dating works best for people who look good on film, are articulate and personable, are willing to risk rejection, and are concerned about how someone looks, sounds, and acts. It doesn't as work well for people who are aren't photogenic, don't express themselves that well, are afraid of being judged, or get nervous in front of a camera. A print profile is usually available as well to let you know more about a person's intrinsic qualities, but it's tempting to select those who look the best on the tape, rather than those who might actually be best for you overall.

Personal Ads

One of the easiest, most exciting, and fun ways to meet potential dates is to "play" the personals. You don't even have to leave home to make connections! Online dating is similar to playing the personals, and many of the same rules apply.

Personal ads often have tip-off statements that will tell you volumes about an advertiser or respondent's life and expectations. Here are a few common ones, with a "translation" of what they actually indicate:

- "For marriage" (that's what they want)
- "For friendship" (that's what they want)
- "For a committed relationship" (not necessarily marriage)
- "With no strings" (no commitment)
- "Seeking anyone" (either gender)
- "Afternoon fun" (most likely, sex)
- "No smokers/drinkers/kids/pets, etc." (if they're specific, they mean it)
- "For whatever happens" (they're not sure what they want)
- "To meet my friend" (someone else placed the ad; the single might not even know about it yet)

Not every ad you place or respond to will generate dates, in-person chemistry, or a true love, but it's an exciting way to meet lots of people. You don't have to be a clever writer to write or respond to personal ads, but you do need to be upbeat and be able to handle rejection.

ESSENTIAL

The following are some abbreviations you should know when perusing the personal ads: S=single; M=married; D=divorced; F=female; M=male; BI=bisexual; G=gay; TV=transvestite; TS=transsexual; L=lesbian; HIV=HIV positive; W=white; B=black; H=Hispanic; A=Asian; J=Jewish; C=Christian/Catholic; PROF=professional; NS=non-smoking.

If you want to place an ad, you'll get to set the requirements and choose from all the responses. Singles respond directly to your ad, and you get to select those you'd like to meet. A less expensive alternative is to enjoy "shopping" the listings, select the ones that sound best to you, and respond to just those ads. Either way, once you've made contact, you will still have to go out and meet in person.

How to Write or Respond to an Ad

Start by researching the publications where you are likely to attract the kind of singles you most want to meet. You will get the widest range of readers from newspapers and general-topic magazines. One special-interest newspaper for intellectuals has been running personal ads in their publication for more than five decades!

Here are some tips to help you write or respond to an ad:

- Most publications charge by the word, so be succinct. Do mention anything very relevant to meeting you (e.g., personal/physical restrictions, religious, or geographic constraints).
- To help readers decide if they'd enjoy meeting you, put some character into your ad. It's better to say "Let's create a romantic dinner together" instead of "I like romantic dinners (doesn't everyone?)." If you have long hair, call it "Rapunzel-esque" instead of revealing its exact length.
- Words and style do matter in personal ads. Proofread your ad or ask someone else to do it, so that what's written really reflects your personality and preferences and doesn't have typos or poor grammar.
- Don't insist upon a photo with print personals. No one ever provides a bad one, but sometimes they supply seriously out-of date ones. It's different in online dating, where posting a photo is a must.
- Be safe and use just a first name—or a clever nickname (remember *Sleepless in Seattle*?). In most cases you will be assigned a mailbox, an e-mail address, or a voice mail, so there's no reason to reveal where you live, or give clues.

If you've written an ad, separate the responses into piles: those who meet your requirements, those who are weaker possibilities, and the obvious "wrongs." It may take a while for people to get around to responding to your ad, and the first ones to answer may not be the best matches. Consider that the personals are an activity of quantity, but not always quality.

You don't have to respond to everyone who contacts you. No response just means "I'm not interested."

QUESTION?

What about safety, when it comes to personal ads?
The good news is that most people will be pretty much as they represent themselves. However, you might come across someone who is truly bizarre, a pathological liar, or a heartless scammer. Adults already know that their safety is their responsibility. When you are meeting a stranger (even online contacts) for the first time, exercise reasonable caution.

If you are answering someone else's ad, choose carefully. If someone has set specific limits on age or mentions other specifics, take them seriously. For example, if an ad requests a specific age range and you're considerably older or younger, don't respond. The author won't make an exception for you. If an ad mentions that an ideal partner will want to spend every weekend sailing, and the very thought makes you queasy, choose someone else. If you aren't honest about who you are and don't stay focused on what you want, you're wasting everyone's time.

Six Steps for Making Careful, Considerate Contact

Here are six steps you can follow when making contact with someone whose personal ad has caught your attention:

- Call or agree to talk only when you really have the time. Don't call when you've got to catch a train in ten minutes, or pick up your children from school.
- Make contact when you're alone and unlikely to be interrupted. Keep the letter or notes about your contact in view. If you are responding by voice mail, not letter or e-mail, work out your opening lines in advance to keep your nerves calm.
- For safety's sake, never give your real name. Identify yourself only as "the Cat-Loving Glamour Gal, who placed an ad in last month's

Savvy Single magazine," and ask if it's a good time to talk (if it isn't, arrange a time to call back).

- Keep the first conversation short and let the other person know whether or not you'd like to have more contact. If you do, exchange phone numbers or e-mail, never addresses (leave this for when you've gotten to know each other better).

- Once you make a date to meet in person, keep the contact short, inexpensive, and public (a coffee bar is a good choice); never meet in a private place or in your home.

- At the end of your initial conversation, if you decide you don't want to have more contact, be clear about it, and don't be offended if someone doesn't want to meet you. The most tactful way to indicate lack of interest is: "We really don't have as much in common as I'd hoped. You deserve someone who is right for you and I clearly am not. I think it would be best if we don't take up any more of each other's time."

Chapter 5
Online Dating

Today just about everyone uses computers. Most workplaces have computers for various purposes, students rely heavily on them for research and word processing, and they're rapidly becoming the foremost venue for communication between family and friends. An increasing number of households have one or more computers these days. The availability of user-friendly, affordable computers and Internet services has been a boon to singles, too. This chapter is entirely devoted to the information you need to meet potential partners online.

What Is Online Dating?

Online dating is simply another way—not necessarily the best or only way—to connect with other people. This dating method is very similar to other dating avenues discussed previously, only it uses technology to make the romantic connections happen. People of every type and generation are logging on, in increasingly large numbers. The Internet offers twenty-four-hour access, immediacy, and anonymity along with interactive communication and the ability to screen prospective dates in the comfort and privacy of home. This concept is particularly attractive to younger people who view online activities as part of daily life, and older singles seeking to revitalize and expand their social circles.

ALERT!

Online Web sites and services change more frequently than outfits at a fashion show. For the best and most current choices, consult computer-savvy colleagues and friends. Also seek out sites being reviewed and recommended in current magazines, newspapers, and e-zines.

It's easy to think of the Internet as magical, but in reality, the computer is just a machine and the Internet is just a networking program. The Internet attracts a representative sampling of everyone in the real world. The Internet doesn't change who you really are. Most of the people you meet will be decent, normal, honest, and safe to meet. You may also run into a few who are unkind, unbalanced, or perhaps even dangerous. Cloaked in the relative anonymity of the Internet, you can have an active, online fantasy life. That means you also can't ever be completely sure that people are who you think they really are (until you investigate them and get to know them in person).

The Internet was started by academics who wanted to gather and exchange information. Its primary use is still to search for information and advice. You can find information in seconds about nearly any topic. For singles, this means access to thousands of relationship-oriented Web sites that range from general to very specific sites. There are sites specifically for redheads, pet lovers, and even tattooed daters!

F A C T

You can use search engines such as Yahoo (*www.yahoo.com*) or Google (*www.google.com*) to search for singles events, to find reviews of dating services and Web sites, to make online reservations for concerts, restaurants, and other social activities, and even to research singles-oriented travel (complete with online quotes for trips).

If you want to meet other singles online, the best way is to join an online dating service (or several). Most charge a fee, but they are more than just a place to view profiles of other singles. You will have access to instant messaging, e-mail, chat rooms, bulletin boards, speed dating, video profiles, and other high-tech services that can enhance your online dating experience. Some sites are virtual communities with shopping, singles trips, chat rooms, articles, Web cams, and even offline events and trips. Most also have double-blind e-mail and instant messaging systems that let you immediately correspond with possible partners without giving out your full name, address, or phone number.

Chat Rooms

A chat room is like a virtual party where everyone is in a group conversation. If you click with someone, you can even go into a "private chat" and get acquainted right then and there. Most fee-based online dating services offer chat rooms for various age groups and interests. If you aren't ready to sign up for an online dating service, you can still find plenty of free chat on the Internet (type "singles chat" plus the specific type of people you want to talk to). Participating in a chat can be an interesting experience. Many chat rooms attract a dedicated core of "regulars" and you may find that a lot of the conversation doesn't interest you. However, you might also find some fascinating people with very similar interests to yours. That's what happened to Joan:

" *My boyfriend and I met in a chat room for snowboarding fans. We chatted for awhile, then exchanged e-mails and photos. At first I didn't think we could have a future because he lives six hours from me. Still, we have managed to get together fairly often. I am moving next year to be closer to my boyfriend. Then I won't have to rely on the computer anymore! (Joan, 32, Sales Manager)*

Chat rooms have developed a reputation as clubhouses for kids (partially true) and therefore of interest to predators (also partially true). If you really want to connect with a potential partner, you'll do better in the chat rooms provided by singles associations or dating services. The visitors are more likely to be adults genuinely hoping to make a relationship. Chat rooms are a great place to improve your social skills, alleviate loneliness, or just pass a bit of time. Don't expect any serious connections from them—but there is always the chance the person you want will be there, too.

Choosing the Right Dating Site

Choosing the right online dating site(s) is your key to successful online dating experiences. Some services may not have enough of the types of people or the demographics that you need to make a match. If you are a senior single, for example, you might be better off joining a smaller service that caters more closely to your age requirements, rather than a large site with more singles but fewer who would be potential matches for you. Make sure the service is reputable and has a privacy policy that is acceptable to you. A large number of members who are off the market but still posted as active are also useless to you.

Beware of sites featuring "brides," primarily from Eastern Europe, Asia, or South America. These sites are run by marriage brokers who connect men to women for a fee. While some are legitimate, many are scams or prostitution brokers, or actually engage in modern-day slavery.

Also, if most of the members are in Illinois and you live in Ohio, that won't help you get in-person dates! Consider Angel's experience:

> *I specifically requested only men within a twenty-mile radius of my home, but a man who lived four hours away contacted me anyway. I have a great job and two small children and I'm not about to move. Neither was he. There was no point in our continuing the contact. (Angel, 39, Sales Representative)*

Another aspect to think about is cost. On nearly all dating sites, you can post a profile for free, but you won't be able to contact or respond to anyone until you pay a monthly fee. There are other services you may want to add such as an enhanced listing, a video or audio message, and online speed dating. If you don't have a good photo, you will have to add the cost of getting one and digitizing it.

FACT

"Free" sites will still require something of you, even if it's not money. You might need to provide personal information and may be required to download special software to get the chat service working on your computer. Check the site's privacy policy and don't be surprised if you get spam (junk mail) from "adult" oriented advertisers.

You might also want to consider for-a-fee online advice, dating coaching, or even someone to create or edit your online profiles. If you join several different dating sites to maximize your chances, and you continue subscribing for more than six months (most people do), you can end up with quite a bill.

Online Etiquette

Once you have joined an online dating service, you will select a username (e.g., MarilyninManhattan) and a password that gives you access to the Web site. Many sites will reserve an anonymous e-mail account for you to access your messages and respond to them. In other cases, the service's e-mail server will remove your real e-mail address from messages you send. These systems are important features that help protect your privacy.

You will also be asked to create a member profile with photos and descriptive text about you and what you are seeking. Give serious thought to what you say, as this is the only way people can judge whether you could be a potential match. Certain criteria such as age, height, body type, religion, marital and parenthood status, and smoking and drinking habits will be used to help locate your best matches. Some sites have psychological and even physical attraction "tests" that you can take to help you find appropriate matches. These are usually very basic.

Commonly Used Acronyms and Emoticons

There are standard abbreviations used in Internet conversations. Even if you choose not to use them, others will. People may type these all in caps or all in lowercase:

- BTW: By the way
- BRB: Be right back
- IMHO: In my humble opinion
- IMNSHO: In my not so humble opinion
- IMOL: In my other life
- IOW: In other words
- IRL: In real life
- LOL: Laughing out loud
- ROTFL: Rolling on the floor laughing
- WRT: With regard to

Many people use icons called emoticons to further express themselves. You are likely to see (or want to use) some of these popular ones:

- :-) Smile; laugh; "I'm joking"
- :-(Frown; sadness; "Bummer"
- ;-) Wink; denotes a pun or sly joke
- :-O Yelling or screaming; or completely shocked
- :-D Big delighted grin
- :-P Sticking out your tongue
- %-(Confused and unhappy
- :'-(Crying
- :-| Can't decide how to feel; no feelings either way

- ANY COMBINATION OF CAPITAL LETTERS = screaming (considered rude)

Make Your Profile Stand Out

Your profile and photo are what potential partners will use to decide whether they want to connect with you. Most online dating sites have a set form with questions you answer, such as: Who has influenced you most? Describe your ideal first date. This makes it easy to complete a profile, but limits your creativity and how much you can say. Luckily, through the exercises you completed earlier in this book, you already know the main points you want people to know about you, what you are seeking, and what is unacceptable. If you aren't sure that what you've written expresses the real you, ask others to offer suggestions. You might also use a fee-based editing service specializing in creating personal ads.

How Specific Should You Be?

It's important to give people a sense of what makes you tick. Everyone likes "moonlit walks" and "home-cooked meals," so be more specific. Mention your love of terriers, your belly-dancing prowess, your pride in your Armenian heritage, etc. Mentioning liabilities will limit your responses, but if there is something very important about you that isn't going to change, mention it. You want to attract the *right* types for you, not just a lot of contacts.

Be honest, but upbeat. If you are extremely tall, for example, you could describe this as "You might need a stepladder to kiss me!" not just "I'm very tall." If there is something you absolutely must have or will not accept, say so. If you will only date Jewish men, or only women over 5'5", or only someone with children, it lets people know not to waste their time contacting you if they don't have these qualities.

Following the Rules

Read the Web site rules before you write your profile. The Internet is still self-policed to some degree, and laws governing it are often unclear. You will not be allowed to use objectionable language or make offensive comments. You will also be blocked from using personal identifiers (e.g., your Web site or e-mail address). Check how long posted information stays up, how to update your posting, and how to remove it when you are ready. Some sites will flag your listing as "new" every time you make a change to your profile, so you'll get more attention if you update often.

Once you've found the site you like, you will be tempted to get started right away, but don't! Take the time you need to create a great profile, then let it mellow. Go back to it—ideally a day later, or at least in a few hours—and you'll catch omissions and errors, and can then feel confident that you have put your best foot forward.

QUESTION?

Can you mention your past relationships in your online dating profile?
If you've been divorced several times and definitely do not want marriage again, this is something to consider mentioning. But never, ever specifically mention ex-partners or display that huge chip on your shoulder! If you find yourself being negative, it is a sign that you aren't ready to be seeking someone new just yet.

Photo Essentials

It is absolutely essential to post a recent photo of yourself in your dating profile. If you are going to post just one, choose a color head shot that clearly shows your smiling face. Secondary photos should ideally include a full length shot of just you, and others that give information about who you are. Pose with your sports car, your adored pet, your pottery, or show yourself on vacation, sailing, playing the piano, etc. Even a less than perfect photo is better than none. However, it is unproductive to post one that is really old, or shows you in an unflattering pose. It also makes no sense to post a photo that isn't of you, one with someone obviously cut out of the photo, or one that is blurry.

Making Contact

You've posted your profile. You are getting responses or you are ready to contact others. From here, the process is much the same as for print ads. To contact people, search for profiles that interest you by geographic location and age, by key word, or by personality or physical preferences. Some sites will even suggest matches for you. Keep in mind that these sites use very simple matching technology. Even those with long questionnaires just boil down to basic physical and personality types.

If you want others to contact you, be sure keep your profile public. You (or they) can send a "wink" to show interest without an e-mail letter, or you can opt for e-mail and describe yourself in more detail and ask questions of potential partners, too. Every e-mail note you write has to be personal. Would *you* respond to a form letter that implies that person has sent out a bulk mailing but hasn't specifically chosen you? It's the ultimate turn-off! Your note doesn't have to be long and complicated (it is actually better to keep the first one brief), but it does have to be accurate. Write as you normally express yourself, and don't try to impress with fancy words or false claims. Draft it first to check for typos and grammatical errors.

FACT

It can be very time-consuming to respond to everyone who contacts you. The best way to handle unwanted initial contacts is just not to respond. When they don't hear back from you, they will know you are not interested and will go on to contact someone else.

AIM (AOL Instant Messenger) allows you to type a text message to another person and she can respond instantly, if she wishes. An icon next to her profile or name will show that she is logged in and online. IM is an easy way to reach the next step in interacting with someone new. When you're ready to go offline, phone calls will reveal a host of things about communication style, social skills, and how you respond to one another in person.

Use a cell phone if possible, or get a device that blocks your number in Caller ID. Be wary if an increasingly familiar online contact refuses to speak to you by phone, fails to provide direct answers to direct questions, or offers inconsistent information about age, interests, appearance, marital status, profession, employment, etc.

Safety Net

You must consider your safety when venturing into the online dating world. It's very easy for people to conceal their true identities, and meeting an online friend in person for the first time is risky. For these reasons, you should take certain precautions when searching for dates on the Web.

Online Safety

For your safety, use the instant messenger and e-mail provided through your dating service. A trustworthy person who really wants to get to know you will appreciate your caution, and will also feel that trust needs to be earned. Stop communicating with anyone who pressures you for personal information or tries to trick you into revealing it. Be wary of anyone who offers too much information of their own, too quickly. Learn from Lorraine's experience:

> *Brian told me that he had graduated from Harvard, and that his grandfather had invented a popular household cleaner. As the tone of our e-mails started to get steamier, I went to check him out. My online search revealed that he hadn't ever been to Harvard. Lots of his other claims didn't check out, either. When I confronted Brian, he acted like it was no big deal—but it was, to me. I'm glad that I checked him out before we got more intimate, even though we were just doing it online. (Lorraine, 43, Realtor)*

In-Person Safety Tips

When you meet an online contact in person, be particularly aware of displays of anger or frustration, demeaning or disrespectful comments, any inappropriate behavior, or any attempt to control you. If something seems wrong, immediately excuse yourself to consider the situation privately. If you feel compromised in *any way*, don't worry about being embarrassed or not being "nice." Just make an excuse, even if it is a bit lame, and leave. Your life and safety are much more important than the opinion of someone you're not likely to ever see again! You don't want to find yourself in a situation like Kirsten's:

> *I met Dru in a chat room. We met in person at a local bistro and were waiting for our table when Dru suddenly asked: "Are you a virgin?" I was shocked that he would ask that right away, but I wasn't really thinking, so I said yes, I was. "Then you're useless!" Dru replied, and whirled around and walked out the door! I was initially upset, but then I realized that Dru didn't want a relationship with me. He only wanted me for sex (or worse). I went home, feeling disappointed, but very lucky that I didn't get any deeper into a situation I couldn't handle." (Kirsten, 23, Student)*

Taking Things OFFline

If your computer screens are both covered with kisses to each other, it's time to think about taking things offline and moving forward, in person. Meeting someone for the first time is exciting but can be scary. Even if you can't wait to meet your cyberlove, be sensible and smart in how you go about it. Make the first meeting short and in a public place. If you really click, there will be other meetings in the future. Arrive and leave on your own. Make sure to tell a good friend where you will be, when you will return, and your date's name and contact information. Here's Simone's experience:

> *After Gary and I e-mailed for a while, he couldn't wait to meet me. As the date approached, Gary changed the details several times, then asked if we could meet in another town. When I asked why, he got really defensive and said he was just protecting his kids because I could be a child molester! I think he was just hiding something—maybe a wife? (Simone, 59, Medical Administrator)*

You may have heard romantic stories about couples who meet online, fall in love, and travel great distances to be together in person. If this is the situation you face, plan carefully and wisely. Arrange and pay for your own transportation and lodging. Always make sure a friend or family member knows your plans and has your contact information. Never give your potential partner details, since if things don't go well, you will want to get out without any interference. If something seems "off" when you arrive at the date location, trust your gut. Make an excuse—or don't—and leave. That's what Nancy had to do when she realized that Larry wasn't all he boasted to be:

> *I met Larry online in a chat room and immediately liked him. He seemed very kind and chivalrous—two traits I value highly. A friendship developed between us and we decided to meet in person and go see a movie. I held our place on line while Larry went to the box office to get our tickets but he returned with only one ticket, saying: "Ok, you can go now to get yours." I was really surprised and annoyed, since I figured he would either buy both of us tickets or purchase them and ask me to reimburse him for mine. I decided to let it ride, and bought my own ticket. About twenty minutes into the movie Larry said he was going to get some popcorn. When he didn't return for a long while I looked around and noticed him, three rows in front of me, with popcorn and a drink! I was so disgusted that I left the movie without seeing the end. It was definitely the end for the two of us! (Nancy, 42, Programmer)*

Though something could go wrong, as it did for Nancy, chances are you will have a pleasant time. It might be *so* good that you might be tempted to throw caution to the winds. Staying with your date for the duration of your stay is risky and not recommended for a first visit away from home. If this is what you want to do, however, do it as a responsible adult who is prepared to deal with the consequences. After all, you could face consequences like these:

> *When Roxanne finally flew from London to New York to meet me, we were so intensely attracted to one another that we went directly to my place and didn't leave for three whole days! I thought I had found my true love, but when Roxanne returned home, she stopped returning my calls and e-mails, and even rejected a gift I sent her. To this day I still have no idea what happened. I was humiliated and brokenhearted." (Sam, 40, Web Designer)*

When the Online "Honeymoon" Is Over

Not all of your online connections will pan out to become the prince or princess of your dreams. And some relationships might even end badly. Luckily, most online dating sites have "blocking" options. You may feel that this is sufficient to let someone know that you are no longer interested, but even a new acquaintance deserves the consideration of closure. Behind every computer screen is a person with a real ego, and real emotions that cause real pain. It's better to send a brief note to say that you aren't a match and you are moving on.

Rarely (but it does happen) someone will react so badly to rejection that he takes revenge. Stalking, slander, and other threats online (and off) are criminal acts. The best thing to do is inform the administration of the dating Web site on which you met. If you've gone past the safety measures to your own e-mail and phone number, you may want to change this (you can always get new ones). In the rare case where a threat escalates to violence, contact your local police.

ALERT!

If you find yourself logging on for love for hours a day instead of balancing it with other activities, you may be addicted to your new online dating hobby. Just remember: an online date isn't the same as an in-person one, and cybersex is not equivalent to the physical act (although the emotional consequences can be very much the same).

Online, as with in-person contacts, most of the people you meet will not be your perfect match. If you have invested time and emotion in someone online, it will hurt just as if you had met in person. However, if you find the rejection so upsetting that it affects your daily life, get some support and take a break from dating. For suggestions for dealing with taking a dating break, see Chapter 17.

If you have been deceived by someone, consider him a single bad apple. The entire world isn't out to get you! Don't let one bad experience ruin your enthusiasm for making connections. Most people you will meet are decent and have honest intentions. They are genuinely looking for love just as you are. And even if you don't find that great love you seek, you can still have some terrific conversations with interesting people, as Reana has:

> *I'm a single mom with three toddlers and a demanding job. My free time is spent doing chores, and spending time with my kids. I don't have the luxury of going to parties or singles events and I wouldn't be meeting anyone if it wasn't for online dating! I can log on late at night when my children are sleeping. I meet new people, every time. I have met about a dozen eligible men for lunch or after-work coffee dates. Although I haven't found a match yet, I am glad I can date on my own time schedule. (Reana, 48, Hostess)*

Chapter 6

Focus Your Search

Everyone wants to believe that a story of fateful meeting with a happy ending is in their future. Perhaps you wake up hoping that today will be the day that you accidentally find love—at the library, on the ferry, at the bank, at the market, or while fixing a flat. The potential to meet someone special exists just about everywhere, as long as you are open to it. However, if you'd rather not leave romance to chance, then it's time to consider ways to focus your search.

Where to Find Your Type

Where is the best place to look for the type of person you want? Since you already know approximately what you are looking for, you can further adjust your search to focus on the places where you will find your type in the highest quality and quantity.

The results of the envisioning exercises you did in Chapter 2 will help you hone your search. Review the notes you took during the exercise and ask yourself some questions. What was the most dominant theme of your vision? Were there additional characteristics that your ideal partner should have? What general type does your primary vision fall under? Whatever types you are most attracted to, they are likely to display dominant characteristics (intellectual, artistic, adventurous, etc.) and other less significant ones (dress, hairstyle, etc.).

How can you define your type when it likely has many different, and possibly contradictory, aspects? Furthermore, where should you look for such complex personalities? Consider Sharon's experience: Sharon was drawn to politicians, but she also wanted someone who was very athletic and into cooking and fine wines. She finally met (and married) a local community organizer who ran marathons for fun, and had studied one summer at Le Cordon Bleu in France. Mark had a similar situation: He was highly attracted to family-oriented women, but he was also attracted to power and sought someone with a head for business and who shared his passion for collecting antique advertising signs. He found the perfect match at an auction—a vegan environmentalist who also owned her own antiques business. The moral of the stories: Don't limit your search to one locale if you're looking for a well-rounded mate.

FACT

Types (stereotypes) are just simple descriptions of specific groups of people to whom generalizations about basic characteristics (e.g., looks, personality, interests, values) have been assigned. These can be positive or negative. Stereotypes can be used to include or exclude people unfairly. However, when dating, these types of classifications can help you to be more selective and weed out the people you are not attracted to.

Follow Your Heart

It's important to remember that while on your quest to find your match, you should not ignore your own comfort and wishes. Don't put yourself in strange situations or go to places you don't like just to find a particular type of person. If you don't like the places where you're searching for dates, chances are you won't ultimately click with the dates you find there. Shari had to learn this lesson the hard way:

> *I spend every weekend at the golf course, because my mother always insisted that the highest quality men all play golf. I do meet all sorts of great guys but the problem is that they want us to spend all our time playing golf—and I detest this game! (Shari, 28, Junior Executive)*

Shari is not being true to herself by seeking dates at golf courses. There are so many different types of people in the world, why go where people love something you don't? Do what you love, and the dates will follow, including the types of people you want to meet.

ESSENTIAL

Born on June 30, 1901, in Brooklyn, New York, Willie Sutton was infamous for robbing banks. When asked why he felt he had to rob banks, Sutton said: "I rob banks because that's where the money is." Don't follow Sutton's example, but *do* consider his rationale. If you want something, you have to go and get it. To find and "steal" the heart of your special someone, go where the singles are.

Keeping all these lessons in mind, read on and learn all about different types of people and where to find them. If you already attend the events frequented by the group of people you've got your eye on, you're probably on the right track.

Intellectual and Creative Types

Intellectuals are big fans of lifetime learning and are greatly interested in the world around them. The obvious place to find these folks is at institutions of higher learning. However, you can also find them in professional societies, fraternities, alumni clubs, bookstores and book circles, educational travel groups, alternative universities, lectures, museums, libraries, cultural events, and numerous other places.

QUESTION?

What if you love to learn but find intellectual crowds intimidating?
The only way to gain confidence is to practice. If you truly love to learn, you'll soon loosen up and fall right in with an intellectual crowd. If you have been wanting to brush up on your knowledge of modern art, head to a local gallery. Perhaps that's where the date of your dreams has been all this time!

Creative and artistic types may work in creative fields such as art, dance, writing, comedy, or music, or they may just look, act, and think in unusual and different ways. Hone your search specifically based on the type of creative person you are attracted to—visual artists, musicians, dancers, writers, filmmakers, inventors, craftspeople. You can also find creative people in large numbers at craft fairs, cultural events, art galleries, poetry readings, gardening clubs, flea markets, "open mike" nights, associations for creative professionals, special-interest travel events, and other spots. More generally, creative people enjoy museums (especially special exhibits), concerts, and plays. If you're creative yourself but not specifically working in a creative field, exercise your artistic side by taking an arts-related class or volunteering in your local amateur theater, choral, dance, orchestral, art, or comedy club.

FACT

Do you enjoy beekeeping? Would you like to meet strict vegans? No matter where you are in the world, there are others who share your interests. You will find clubs, conventions, associations, Web sites, forums, chat rooms, publications, e-zines, newsletters, and other types of special-interest activities that specifically deal with just about every topic imaginable.

Politicos and Activists

These are often people very concerned about international, national, regional, and local causes. They like to influence public opinion and policy in a direct and personal way. Politically minded people are often involved with politics, work for nonprofit organizations, and/or act as volunteers, and they love an audience. Every town has local politicians and community organizations. Call or write their offices with a "cause" and work with your politicos and community leaders to promote it. Become active in general with your community and citizen advocacy groups (e.g., the local community board, the recycling advisory committee) and you are bound to meet politicians and political activists in great numbers. After a while, you might consider running for office yourself. To meet more regional and national politicos, support more sweeping causes and get involved in your political party of choice.

Getting involved in any cause you believe in will give you a sense of purpose as well as introduce you to like-minded individuals. That's what happened to Bernard, though not in the way you'd expect:

> *I always loved kids, but never clicked with the right woman to have any of my own. I was feeling lonely and bored, so I thought it might be fun to volunteer as a Big Brother for children who really needed love and attention. Bradley was one of the kids assigned to me. I admired his spunk and intelligence, and we spent lots of happy afternoons together playing ball, riding bikes, and even going to cultural events. One day Bradley appeared with his mother in tow, and suggested that we go out together for ice cream. How could I refuse? Over hot fudge sundaes, Lisa told me that her husband had been killed in action overseas. Now she was working*

two jobs and didn't have much time to spend with Bradley anymore. She thanked me profusely for being such a giving person and a good role model for her son. I was embarrassed! As we talked, I realized that Lisa and I had a lot of the same qualities, and I was actually quite attracted to her. I obviously already liked her son a great deal. We're dating regularly now and all the signs point to wedding bells down the road. (Bernard, 46, Chef)

Participating in a regional or national campaign is exciting, and full of opportunities to meet political types of people. Read politically oriented magazines and newspapers to learn where political debates, lectures, and events are being held where you live. You will also meet a lot of these politically oriented singles in volunteer organizations, at parades, government centers, marches and demonstrations, rallies, not-for-profit organizations, and conferences and seminars.

Youthful Dates and Senior Singles

You'll find "young at heart" types with youthful lifestyles in the same places that children and teens congregate: at amusement parks, playgrounds, carnivals, candy stores, and video arcades. Depending upon your own interests, you might also enjoy meeting these types at amateur talent contests, raves, rock concerts, karaoke bars, and "challenge" events, such as eating or drinking contests.

Sun lovers may find these types surfing, as fixtures at ski resorts and beach hotels, and hanging around the scene at Spring Break. Just beware: Eternal Spring Breakers are usually men who are often not only seeking the young-at-heart, but usually also the actually *young*.

At the opposite end of the spectrum are the older singles. Men and women are living much longer today, and middle-aged and golden-aged singles are much more vibrant, youthful, and accessible than they were even a few generations ago. Seniors like to match up friends, and personal introductions are frequent among the over-sixty-five set (especially in retirement communities). You can also find older singles at senior-oriented events, dances, clubs, support groups, recreation centers, clubs, travel events, seminars, and parties.

A significant number of men ages forty to seventy are seeking younger women for various reasons. After age sixty, the proportion of single men to women decreases even more, since men don't generally live as long as women. It is therefore more challenging, although by no means impossible, for women over age fifty to find large quantities of quality men close to their own age.

Adventurers and Athletes

Adventurous people usually have a particular passion for an activity or lifestyle. To meet this type, you may have to enjoy, and be willing to take, some of the same risks they enjoy. Good bets are exotic or extreme vacations and expedition or eco-travel. This type likes the danger of extreme sports and excessive speed as well.

The milder activities that attract adventurers are volunteering for activist causes, gambling and playing the stock market, and dining at restaurants that serve exotic cuisines. If you are attracted to the "wilder" types, try social events, clubs, and bars that cater to the more unusual special interests, such as biker bars and tattoo establishments.

Athletes are generally interested in health and fitness, as well as the great outdoors. You will find them participating in, and watching, all types of sports events and sports-oriented challenges. If you enjoy working out, there are several places you might look. You'll find plenty of athletes at health clubs and participating in out-of-doors activities, such as running, biking, hiking, skating, sailing, camping, golfing, and playing tennis.

You'll also find outdoor types participating in activities concerned with environmental and wildlife conservation and in community gardening programs. Spot nature lovers at botanical gardens, on hiking trails, in parks and open spaces—everywhere. If you are an athlete yourself, sign up for any of your company's sports teams, or get involved in other amateur sports teams. Learn new techniques at sports clinics, especially tennis or golf camps. Visit a sports hall of fame, spend a weekend at a dude ranch, go camping, or just watch the "weekend warriors" do battle on public courts, playgrounds, or ball fields.

QUESTION?

What if your date is into something you just can't handle?
If someone suggests a dating activity that frightens, upsets, or disgusts you, speak up. For example, you shouldn't agree to an arduous bike trek if you haven't been on a bike for years. Be honest and suggest an alternative that you can both enjoy. If you can't find one, that's a sign that you are probably not right for each other.

Even if you're not a great athlete, don't be afraid to try something new. When Joe did this, he didn't find a new favorite pastime, but he did end up with a date that would change his life:

> *I'd never tried climbing before, so when a buddy of mine suggested a beginner's group, I thought it might be fun to give it a try. I didn't realize until I was halfway up the mountain (actually, it was more like a big hill) that I actually have a fear of heights. I made the mistake of looking down and I simply froze. One of the women in the group saw me clinging to the cliff, and coaxed me through the rest of the climb. Then she stuck close to me all the way down. I was never so grateful to anyone for anything in my entire life! I asked if I could show my gratitude by taking her to dinner when we were back on terra firma. I didn't know much about her but she was lean and athletic and had a great smile—just my type. We had a great time and after two years of dating, we got engaged. Obviously, climbing isn't a shared passion, but we have lots of other things in common. (Joe, 32, Police Officer)*

Individualists

It's hard to pin down this type to a probable place, precisely because individualists do their own thing, are likely to think outside the box, and could enjoy recreating in all sorts of interesting places. Look for offbeat and unusual activities, "bohemian" parts of town, experimental art, film, music, or theater, or performance art. Anything out of the mainstream is a likely target, as well as lectures and events of special interest—e.g., sci-fi conventions, mystery weekends, stargazers clubs, trapeze school, etc.

Velma, a movie lover, decided she wanted to find a similar individual to date:

> "I collect and sell movie memorabilia, mostly online, and I really enjoy designing and updating my Web site. I live in a rural town so it is hard to meet singles who share my passion. I was working on my Web site one day and realized that I might be able to use it to locate like-minded singles. So I added a page with my photo, some basic information about me, what I was looking for in a partner, and a new e-mail address from a free mail provider (movieluvr@....) so men could contact me without sending love notes to my personal or business e-mail. I linked this page to my main site with an eye-catching red heart and a caption that read: "Movie fan seeks same to audition for the role of leading man in her life." It might have been a bit corny, but it worked. One of the men who responded was Barney, who lived within a reasonable commute of me. We corresponded first by e-mail, then by phone, and our first "date" was at a movie memorabilia show not too far from where we both lived. We've been together four years now. I'm glad I took a chance and tried this more unusual, but effective, way to find love. (Velma, 35, Movie Memorabilia Collector-Seller)"

Family Folks and Single Parents

Family-oriented singles, especially those with more conservative family values, will be attracted to religious services and events, conservative political events, prayer meetings and vigils, and children's rights causes. If you attend religious services or events, you may already know a few family-oriented singles.

If you don't have children but are seeking a single mom or dad, be aware that many single parents prefer to date people who also have children. People who are already parents may be more tolerant of, and better equipped to deal with, the restrictions and responsibilities that a child, or several, place on dating.

Chances of finding single parents increase at Laundromats, grocery stores, and any place where children play with other children (e.g., parks, playgrounds, play groups). You will find plenty of parents, although not necessarily single, at PTA meetings. Support your child and meet other, possibly single, parents by getting involved as a chaperone or a volunteer for your child's extracurricular activities (Little League, day camp, etc.). Go shopping at children's stores or attend child-friendly cultural events (young people's concerts, Holiday on Ice) and you'll find plenty of single parents. Take a cruise on a family-friendly cruise line such as Disney Cruise Lines to theme parks where single parents are out in force, especially on weekends.

Here's a word of caution about dating single parents if you do not have children: Dating a single parent is not the same as dating any single person. Single parents may need extra support—both emotionally and with day-to-day tasks. If you date a single parent, be prepared to put the needs of the children above your own. When Kevin met Sally, he realized that he would have to wait until Sally and her children got through some rough times before they could work on becoming a solid couple:

> *Sally had just gone through a terrible divorce when I first met her, and she was terrified that the split was having a negative effect upon her kids. We were a great couple, but she was just too fragile to make a new commitment. I stuck with her because I loved her and felt that she had the potential to develop real feelings for me. I also put in the back of my mind that if Sally didn't start moving our relationship forward within the next*

year, I would leave. Luckily, Sally decided on her own to seek therapy for herself and for her family. As I suspected, she just needed more time to get over her losses and let her children put the past behind them. It was worth the wait. We have been together eight years now. (Kevin, 39, Fireman)

As you can see from Kevin and Sally's experience, it sometimes just takes a bit of extra effort, compassion, and patience. If you can get through the hard times in the beginning, chances are you can see things through as a couple.

Animal Lovers

If you have a dog, let your furry friend help break the ice with other animal lovers by making a "love connection" with other dogs. If you don't have a pet but are ready to take on the responsibilities of ownership, you could adopt an animal or volunteer at the local animal shelter. Obviously, you can find animal lovers with their pets at the veterinarian or animal hospital, but they may be more worried about Fluffy's respiratory infection than about being social.

ALERT!

Before you adopt a pet to impress an animal lover, be sure that you really want, and can handle, that pet. If you have allergies or don't really have the time or interest to love an animal, your true self is sure to be revealed in no time flat. In order to be a responsible pet owner (and a good date!) you have to be honest about who you are, first and foremost.

Dog, cat, horse, and other animal shows are great places to meet animal lovers, and so are country fairs, and even pet stores. If you are an activist and believe in their causes, join a local chapter of an animal rights group or get involved in national and international groups via the Internet. The zoo is also a good place to find animals and animal lovers. It's a sure bet that lots of singles will be there (especially weekend moms and dads with their children), looking at the lions, tigers, and bears—and maybe at you.

Dating Perfectly for Your Personality

Doing things you enjoy is the best possible way to meet people. One way to learn about singles-oriented activities that particularly appeal to your interests is to use the Internet. If you don't know where to look, start with any search engine (*www.google.com* or *www.yahoo.com* are two popular sites) and type in a key word or phrase like "single skiers," "single in Chicago," or "singles travel." If you have a very special interest, try "single parent" or "gay singles" or other combinations of key words that interest you. Your screen will instantly be filled with links that you can click right onto and explore. Surf the sites until you find one that is perfect for you!

Activities that you enjoy most are a big clue to the types of people you may enjoy being with. But even if you do something you enjoy and you don't meet the love of your life, the experience wasn't for nothing. Every experience is valuable, and who knows: your perfect match could be just a connection or two away.

FACT

Dating is a perfect way to try new things and get new experiences that you might not have considered before. Placing a personal ad, attending a film festival, taking folk dance lessons, or trying a new sport could be all it takes to find your match. There are a lot of new and exciting things—and people—out there just waiting for you to discover them.

If you have little success searching on the Web, use other tools as well, such as the library, the phone book, newspapers, and magazines. Also ask around to discover where your types might congregate. Don't forget to let people know that you are single and looking and would appreciate them keeping an eye out for people of your type whom they could introduce you to. Maybe your next-door neighbor's second cousin is your next princess charming!

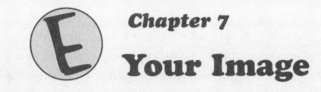

Chapter 7

Your Image

Of course you want to be loved for who you are inside, but your outside image is a powerful tool that can help you on your dating journey. Creating a positive, powerful image is important in your quest for confidence, happiness, and a romantic match—and it's easier than you think! In this chapter you will learn some easy ways to enhance your image while still staying true to who you are.

The Power of Image

Your visual image is an essential part of your entire package. Everyone from your neighbor, to your boss, to sales and service personnel (who will decide how to treat you) makes assumptions about you, based on your appearance. Nadine's story is one example:

> *I went for lunch at a trendy new restaurant, dressed in casual clothes. I had a reservation, but was kept waiting for twenty minutes, then ushered to a terrible table in front of the kitchen. I silently fumed every time the wait staff bumped into my chair. Not long after a friend (who dresses in the latest fashions) and I (similarly attired) lunched there again. We were immediately whisked into the main room and given a great table in the best location. (Nadine, 45, Public Relations)*

But what does all of this have to do with your search for love? Everything! Initially, it's your outside image that's going to reel them in. It would be great if you were identified just by the content of your character, but in the real world, people have distinct biases and preferences pertaining to appearance that subconsciously make them behave more positively or negatively toward you. If you doubt this, consider how you would be viewed if you showed up for work with uncombed hair, in dirty, smelly clothes. How interested do you think your new neighbor would be in getting to know you if you always looked dirty and sloppy? How you look *does* count, not just in dating, but in everything you do.

Keep in mind that you don't have to be perfect to be successful in the dating world. In fact, a few flaws might help. You might believe that singles, especially men, want someone with a perfect body and movie star "assets," but you'd be wrong. Many people enjoy looking at beautiful people on the covers of magazines or at the movie theater, but when it comes to making a relationship, they tend to seek out someone with looks that are on an equal scale of attractiveness with their own.

While creating your image, don't aspire to look like a celebrity or model. These people employ teams of stylists, trainers, and makeup artists to help them maintain their image. Check them out when they're doing real things such as shopping, traveling, and gardening—not just standing motionless and airbrushed in a photo, or fresh from a limo ride or a walk on the red carpet. They rarely look so great in person!

Make an Assessment

If you are not fashion-conscious by nature or don't work in a field where a trendy image is a must, you probably don't update your image very often. When you are on a dating journey, however, an image assessment and update can be essential to your success. Have you ever seen an adult sporting a "look" that is very obviously out of date, unflattering, or otherwise inappropriate? You may think this person is strange or out of touch and wonder why she doesn't realize it. Most are aware to some degree how they look, but they consciously look different, on purpose. Others are too lazy, frugal, or clueless to care. Still others may insist: "I've looked this way since the '60s and everyone thought I looked great back then." Perhaps you did look great back *then*, but everyone has grown up and moved on. People are much more likely to be attracted to someone in tune with today.

An image assessment and mini-makeover can not only help you look and feel great, but also help you attract the types of people you want. It's essential if you have recently experienced a major life change, or if you are feeling less than confident for any reason. Of course, "makeover" doesn't mean drastically altering yourself to be like someone else. Then you would be only a poor copy, and you are already an original!

When you are dating, you are a commodity in the singles marketplace. You are, in fact, a product! Other singles are products, too. Everyone is buying—and selling. You consider a potential partner's total package (internal and external attributes) much as you would any product—even a car or a can of peas. As a consumer, if you have an array of products to choose from, you first look at the different types and narrow them down to the best ones. If the remaining choices are equal in quality, it is their outside packaging that tips the scale in favor of one over the other. When you are shopping for a relationship, you are actually going through the same process of selection and elimination. Image counts, though it's still not everything. Here's Marsha's story:

> *I wanted to make a dramatic statement about my new life after my divorce, so I dyed my hair blonde and cut it in a new, chic style. I began wearing brighter makeup, and exchanged my running suits for body-conscious clothes. I felt great, but my son didn't like the attention I was getting, especially from men. I explained that even though I had made some outward changes, I would always be his devoted Mom on the inside. He finally accepted my new look and admitted that I looked great. (Marsha, 38, Secretary)*

QUESTION?

How much should you seek to change your look?
The last thing you want to do is cover up your natural beauty with heavy makeup and hide your personal sense of style behind a trendy outfit. A true image assessment and makeover should simply consist of discovering which qualities make you truly unique and beautiful and enhancing those features in subtle but significant ways.

Your Look: Love It Or Leave It?

Most people dislike one part of their body or another, but some image issues are more emotionally difficult to deal with than others. The time commitment, cost, and emotional turmoil associated with making big physical changes can be quite stressful. On the other hand, updating your clothing or changing your hairstyle is far less challenging than losing twenty pounds or getting plastic surgery. Still, achieving even these small goals can bring you closer to an updated, pleasing image. So don't worry about costly procedures and time-consuming workout regimens right now. For now, just focus on simple things you'd like to change and easy ways to change them.

What Does Your Current Image Say about You?

Look at yourself in a full-length mirror. Are you generally pleased with what you see? Are your makeup, hair, and clothes appropriate for your age group and relatively current, or do you appear to be stuck in the past? If you don't know the answers, have some fun by people-watching.

To get a better idea of what age- and body-appropriate images are, go sit in a public park, an outdoor café, or a popular mall and watch the passers-by. Pay particular attention to people who are in your (relative) age group. Do their clothes fit properly? Do the colors they're wearing flatter their skin tones? Do you recognize any of your own mistakes in the people you see? While you're people-watching, you should also look for people you are attracted to and people you are specifically not attracted to. What are the differences between them? How important to you is your *date's* image? Like Mary, you may find that it's more important than you first thought:

> I thought Marvin cared about his appearance until the night I went to a local diner. I saw a man with serious facial stubble and greasy hair, who was wearing a ripped shirt, faded shorts, and plastic sandals. When he approached, I realized it was Marvin! He muttered something about how dressing up for dates is stupid, and how I should get used to his real look. I knew right then that Marvin wasn't right for me. (Mary, 37, Sales Representative)

Also, do "research" by watching fashion-oriented television programs to learn helpful tips. Read fashion magazines to get ideas of what's hot and help you decide what you might need to update your look. Keep in mind that most models wearing ultra-trendy styles are often extremely young and unat-tainably thin. Your goal is to get ideas, but not to exactly copy what you see.

Taking Inventory

If you dress in the same styles your mother liked, or you constantly borrow your teenager's clothes, you may be stuck in a rut. Just because you *can* fit into your prom dress from twenty years ago doesn't mean that you *should*.

Taking personal inventory is more than just updating clothes. There might be aspects of your appearance that *aren't* wardrobe-related that you should consider. If you are starting a dating journey, maybe you will want to get a clean bill of health from your doctor, or start an exercise program, or make some changes to your diet. While you still can't change your height or shoe size, medical technology *has* made it possible to fix broken blood vessels and blotchy skin, eliminate coke-bottle glasses, and even whiten yellowed teeth—virtually on a lunch hour! These types of image enhancers require trained professionals and they can be expensive, but consider saving for them if you think they will help you look and feel better. *Everything* you do is an investment in yourself and your success and happiness.

An image is worth a thousand words. Clipping photos from magazines can help you decide what you like and what works for you. You needn't become a clone of the people in the images, but having the photos with you when you visit a salon or when you shop can be a helpful guide.

Be Cautious about Cosmetic Surgery

It may appear that everyone these days has had some cosmetic "work" done. However, the decision to surgically alter your body is a very personal one. Too many people become addicted to plastic surgery in lieu of enhancing their own natural looks. Looking real and aging gracefully is not only acceptable, it's *preferable.* However, cosmetic surgery might be something to consider if you are very unhappy with some aspect of your appearance and it is affecting your outlook or behavior.

Just keep the following in mind: Expensive and often painful and risky procedures such as facial peels, Botox injections, facelifts, breast implants, liposuction, rhinoplasty (nose jobs), tummy tucks, and other modern surgical procedures may enhance your looks on the *outside,* but they will not change how you feel about yourself *inside.* Cosmetic surgery is not an option you should choose expecting happiness or love to result. In fact, if you are *very unhappy* with your image, professional counseling might do more good for you than all the facelifts and chic clothes in the universe.

Your Sense of Style

Style is fun. It also tells people who you are. Your signature style will attract others who have similar styles and interests. For example, you can usually tell athletes by their workout gear, lawyers by their suits, and artists by their colorful clothes and jewelry. You probably know someone with a signature style, such as the friend who only wears jeans, T-shirts, and baseball caps, or that coworker who only wears the same dress in different colors. Perhaps you are known for the capes you wear all winter, or the overabundance of rhinestone jewelry you'd never leave home without.

Chances are you can wear different "looks" and feel good in all of them, depending on the day, your mood, and the circumstances. When you are on a dating journey, however, you will want to ask: "What kind of person do I want to attract?" And: "What kind of person do I want to be attracted to me?" When you are dating, you need a flexible wardrobe that can work for different activities. If you normally only wear sweats and jeans, you will need at least one dressy outfit for parties and dining out. If you are at work all the time and only wear suits, you will need good casual clothes for sports, picnics, and other informal activities.

FACT

Some common wardrobe turn-offs are: too much of anything (clothing layers, makeup, jewelry, perfume, accessories); too little of anything (too little fabric to cover your body); colors that clash; clothes that are stained, ripped, or faded; visible panty lines and bra straps; and anything overly sheer.

If you have body art, piercings, or unusually dyed hair, you are probably already aware of their effect on others. If this is your preferred style, you should be aware that your look will likely attract others of a similar description. "Mainstream" looks are most acceptable, but that doesn't mean you can't be an original. If you're a woman living in a place where everyone wears cowboy hats, for example, consider dressing yours up with feathers, rhinestones, or beads. If you're a man who is limited to wearing conservative suits to work, why not build up a collection of unusual cufflinks? These are hints of style that you can display in simple, appropriate ways.

Select a Makeover Coach

In some popular television shows, men and women are dragged before a style judge or image consultant by concerned friends or family. These reluctant victims are remade by the end of the show. Sometimes they really do look much better. However, their "after" body language often shows their discomfort. Often you will see them forcing a smile but sagging their shoulders, tugging at their new clothes, and staring at the floor. This is not the behavior of a confident person!

Image experts are talented people who, for a fee, can advise you on everything from finding your most flattering hair color, to updating your entire wardrobe, to advising you on better body language. Image consultants will help you work out an overall plan for image improvement that suits your personality, lifestyle, and goals, so you not only look great but feel great, too. Not everyone needs this kind of assistance. Often you can just enlist the services of a friend with good taste as your makeover coach. This person can help you assess and update your image so that you feel "new and improved." Choose your makeover coach carefully. If you love your best friend but hate her taste in clothes, you aren't going to feel comfortable accepting her image suggestions.

ALERT!

Never choose a family member to be your makeover coach. Such close relations can't be objective about you. Instead, pick someone you feel will be relatively unbiased and honest. It won't do you any good to find out that your coach never mentioned your chronic bad breath or your weird penchant for boots with marabou feathers because she didn't want to hurt your feelings.

Arlene's story is a perfect example of why you should *not* choose a family member as your makeover coach:

> *I asked my teenage daughter to help me select an outfit for a dinner date. She produced tight jeans and a skimpy top from her own closet and suggested my hot pink pumps with four-inch heels to complete the look. I didn't want to hurt her feelings, but had to say that her outfit would look adorable on HER, but it just wasn't appropriate for me. She didn't agree and was upset, of course. (Arlene, 55, Homemaker)*

Once you've selected a willing makeover coach, communicate to her what you want to accomplish. Start with your head (hairstyle) and go straight down to your toes (shoes). As you make decisions, continually ask: "Does my appearance accurately project my personality, status, and intelligence level, and convey who I am to those who meet me? If not, what else do I need to adjust my image in positive ways?"

For men: If you don't think "bald is beautiful," be cautious when selecting a method for disguising bald spots. Even multimillionaire Donald Trump is the subject of jokes for his obvious comb-over. A bad toupee is even worse. Baldness is a sign of virility and is nothing to be ashamed of, but if you feel that a bald spot doesn't suit you, consider a hair transplant over a conspicuously false "do."

Addressing Wardrobe Woes

When it is time to assess your wardrobe, your coach needs to ask (with conviction): "Do you really want or need that thing?" and "Is that helping you to create the image you want?" You may feel as though you are eliminating everything from your closet. However, items that you haven't worn in years, those that don't suit you, and things that are just taking up precious space aren't useful. You will honestly feel better when you finally toss items such as:

- The "Care Bears" T-shirt someone gave you as a joke
- The ski jacket that didn't even fit on your ski trip in 1980
- The designer shoes that give you blisters just looking at them

- The lucky hat that also has a few (unlucky) stains
- Anything that must be tailored (but alterations will cost more than the item itself)
- Anything that makes you feel ugly or depressed
- Old bridesmaids dresses (you really *can't* wear them again!)

By yourself or with your makeover coach, take everything out of your closet and decide on an item-by-item basis whether to toss it or keep it. Use the following statements:

- I haven't worn this item in a year or more. (Toss, trade, or donate it.)
- I dislike this item and rarely wear it. (Toss, trade, or donate it.)
- I like this item but it's not fixable. (Toss, trade, or donate it.)
- The style is outdated or unflattering. (Toss, trade, or donate it.)
- I like this item and it fits me well. (Keep it.)
- I like this item, and I can alter it to make it fit better. (Keep it.)
- The color is flattering on me or it works well as an accent. (Keep it.)
- This item is in good condition and I wear it often. (Keep it.)
- The style of this item is classic or current. (Keep it.)
- This item has sentimental value but I don't wear it. (Keep it, but use it in another way; for example, cut up a shirt to make a patch for a quilt.)

After you've separated out the obvious TOSS and KEEP items, turn your attention to what's left and see if there's anything else you can part with. For each item ask yourself:

- Do I really like this item and do I feel great in it? (If not, toss, trade, or donate it.)
- Can I coordinate this with several other pieces in my wardrobe? (If not, toss, trade, or donate it.)
- Is this item consistent with the image I want to portray? (If not, toss, trade, or donate it.)
- Does this item require extensive (and expensive) alterations? (If so, toss, trade, or donate it.)

Clean or mend everything before you put it back into the closet. Purchase real hangers; don't use the wire ones from the cleaners. Have your makeover coach help you coordinate and organize all your clothes by color and function (work clothes, casual clothes, date clothes, dressy clothes) so that they will be ready to wear at a moment's notice. When you get that last-minute invitation, you'll be glad you did.

ALERT!

Protect your clothes by reading the care labels, but use your judgment. Some materials that claim to be dry-clean only can be safely washed by hand, saving you money. If you're not sure, play it safe and send it to the dry cleaner.

Find Your Colors

Colors evoke emotions. They have the ability to inspire confidence, friendship, anxiety, agitation, joy, suspicion, and excitement. A vibrant red can make your pulse race; lilac and light blue can calm you. Politicians, for example, often wear yellow ties because yellow is considered a "friendly" color for both men and women. Everyone has favorite colors and some they dislike. Without realizing it, we often select the colors for our cars, clothes, and surroundings because they suit us and make us feel good.

What's Your Season?

In the 1980s, the four-season concept of color typing was so popular that instead of "What's your sign?" as a pickup line, it was common to hear "What's your season?" The fad has faded somewhat, but the idea is sound, and is very helpful when doing an image makeover. The main concept is that each person is born with a predominant skin tone that corresponds most closely to tones in nature. These are "cool" Winter and Summer (blue-based) or "warm" Spring and Fall (yellow-based). Once you find the colors and intensities of color that flatter your natural coloring, you will look your best.

Nearly every person can wear nearly every color; it's just a matter of choosing the right tone and intensity. You can go to an image consultant or color-typing workshop and learn your "season," but you may already have a wonder color or palette of colors that seem to invite compliments. Chances are you choose these based on seasonal approach without even realizing it. For example, the freckled strawberry blonde with blue eyes may wear a lot of ivory and peach, but when she chooses black or hot pink (best on blue/cool-toned Winters) her skin suddenly looks ruddy and blotchy. The muted Summer who looks beautiful in mauve turns sallow and pale in orange or bright yellow.

FACT

Basics for choosing color using the "seasonal" approach are as follows: Cool—Winter: silver, platinum, white gold, white pearl, gray pearl, diamond, garnet, emerald. Cool—Summer: rose/white/gray pearl, silver, pewter, platinum, white gold, diamond, opal. Warm—Spring: gold, cream pearl, topaz, tortoise shell, coral, turquoise, jasper, wood, jade. Warm—Fall: gold, brass, copper, wood, bronze, cream pearl, carnelian, citrine, amber.

Color and Emotions

Color can be used to evoke emotion and send subtle messages to potential partners. Here are some of the most common colors and a description of the emotions and connotations associated with them:

- **Red:** The color of love, anger ("seeing red"), blood, and the heart. Red is an attention-grabber. It can make your pulse race, or it can be threatening, depending upon amount and intensity. Red is the color of good fortune in some cultures, but loss in others. "In the red" means an overdrawn account.
- **Blue:** The color of sea and sky. It is generally a calm color. Light pastel blue is associated with male infants and young boys. Blue can be stodgy ("blue blazer set") but it is also associated with status and rank ("blue blood," or "blue ribbon"). Blue can signify sadness ("feeling blue") or entering into the unknown ("out of/into the blue"). It can also mean hope ("blue skies").
- **Yellow/Gold:** The color of our life-sustaining sun, and a very happy color. Yellow promotes optimism and friendship but it is also

associated with cowardice ("being yellow"). Gold is a color of rank and good fortune. "Being golden" means to have it made, "gold standard" is the top measure of excellence and quality, and "gold star" is top honors.

- **Orange:** A mixture of red and yellow, this is a happy and energetic color. The wrong tone of orange can instantly turn cool-toned complexions sickly. It is best used as an accent unless you have a warm-toned complexion. Orange family colors are happy, energetic colors that can be found in nature, especially in fruits.

- **Pink:** A mix of red and white. Pink is generally considered a feminine color although men wear it well in shirts and accents. Light pink is often associated with female babies and young girls. Pink is a romantic color and generally a happy one (e.g., "In the pink, tickled pink").

- **Green:** A complex color with both positive and negative associations. It is linked with nature and embodies growth, luck, money, and new beginnings (e.g., "going to greener pastures"). Green is associated with action (green light = "go") but it is also associated with jealousy ("green with envy") and illness ("green around the gills") and with lack of experience ("greenhorn").

- **Turquoise:** A blend of blue and green and the name of a popular mineral.

- **Purple/Violet/Maroon:** Mixtures of blue and red, these colors are associated with wealth and nobility, since the dyes that create them used to be costly and rare. Lilac, rose, and mauve are popular variations and are calming colors.

- **Black:** Black is the color of finality and death. It is somber, but conveys sophistication and mystery as well as sadness. Black has negative connotations—e.g., "black moods" and the color of the hat worn by bad guy in movies—but it also has a positive meaning ("in the black") indicating financial solvency. Black is the classic choice for evening wear.

- **Gray/Silver/Pewter:** Associated with power and in business. Silver and pewter are precious metals and symbolize wealth, although they are less precious than gold. Silver can be nostalgic (e.g., "silver screen") and "silver-haired" reflects aging gracefully.

"Silver-tongued" describes an eloquent speaker. The negative connotations are dull, dingy, or depressing.

- **Brown:** Warm-toned brown signifies hearth and home and honesty. Other variations are tan, taupe, beige, or cream. Brown conveys warmth and wholesomeness. It is most popular in clothing in the Fall and Winter and mostly for casual clothes.

- **White:** a color associated with purity, goodness, innocence, and youth, and therefore associated with new beginnings, brides, graduation, and newborn babies. Pearly white is considered pure. White is also associated with doctors and can look sterile. It is best blended with other colors. Ivory is a yellowed, more subdued version of white.

Chapter 8

Your Attitude

Sometimes it isn't a lifestyle change or a new wardrobe but a real change in attitude that can make you feel new and improved. No matter what you look like or what personal objections you have about your appearance, your external image should never undermine your confidence or hinder you from meeting a potential partner! This chapter will discuss the most common image objections and challenges that singles say they have, and offer ideas about how you cannot only look great but feel great, too!

Attitude Is (Nearly) Everything

Without a positive attitude you aren't going to get very far in your dating adventure. If you're letting a few spider veins, some back hair, knobby knees, or a bald spot keep you from going out and having fun, you're not even giving others a chance to judge you—you've already judged yourself unworthy of their interest. It's a shame to let such worries about image paralyze you and sabotage your chances to meet someone special.

We all have body parts we'd like to swap for better models, but happy adults accept themselves as they are. If your feelings about how you look are hampering your dating journey, an attitude adjustment is even more important than a physical makeover. If you want others to think you are attractive, *you* have to believe that you are attractive. What you think about yourself is radiated to others. If you think you look beautiful, others will agree. If you act unattractive or undesirable, others will consider you that way, too. The next time you get ready to denigrate yourself, think twice. If *you* don't appreciate yourself, how can you expect anyone else to do so?

Image-conscious and youth-obsessed people are not the norm. For most of us, growing old is something to embrace. A mature person who is happy and confident is far more attractive than an ill-at-ease youngster! Sporting a positive outlook is more flattering than trendy clothes or facelifts. It's unfortunate that the media sends the message that only the young are sexy and that older women are viewed not as vibrant love interests, but more often as grandmothers. In truth, most people seek partners close to their own age for the common ground that they share.

Part of your attitude toward dating derives from your level of self-esteem. If you don't believe in yourself you will appear nervous and quirky to potential partners. Fortunately, many people have a special place in their hearts for nervous types, but it will make you feel better to gain some confidence and a positive attitude before going out. Here's what happened to Brad and Gerri:

> *I met Gerri at a luncheon. I was so nervous that I said "Goodbye" instead of "Nice to meet you!" I immediately realized how stupid I sounded, but I just continued talking about other things like it didn't happen. Gerri later told me she didn't remember what I said because she was so*

nervous, too. She just remembered that I seemed friendly and chatty. If I had panicked, I'm sure she would have eliminated me from consideration by the next course." (Brad, 39, Philosopher)

FACT

There is no such thing as being too old to meet a new partner. Singles of every age find love every day. If you doubt this, look at the social calendar in a retirement home. No doubt it's full of engagement parties and weddings, and none of the brides and grooms are likely to be under sixty-five.

Do More with Less

If you really want to change the way you look and feel, but don't have a savings account bursting with expendable cash, you need to look at other options. Start asking yourself some questions:

- What do I already have that I can use?
- What could I borrow or barter for?
- Are there places where I can discount-shop?
- Are there places where I can get a high-quality service for less (free make-up application at a department store, for example)?
- Is there anything I absolutely must purchase new?

Save on transportation costs by walking, cycling, or car-pooling. The savings you put into your makeover fund will help you get physically and *fiscally* fit! Take the change out of your wallet every day and dump it in a large jar. You'll be amazed at how quickly the jar fills up and creates enough for a splurge. Clip coupons and use rebates. Bring your recyclables back to the store and save the planet as well as some money. Put the money you would have spent on nonessentials (e.g., junk food or cigarettes, since you are trying to quit) into an image-improvement fund and soon you'll have money to look better as well as feel better. Sell your vintage stuff (or whatever you don't need) on eBay (*www.ebay.com*) and pocket the cash for something you really *do* want.

Not into Internet commerce? Bring unwanted items to consignment stores or flea markets, or donate them to charity for a tax deduction. Hold swap parties or a stoop sale with friends, family, and neighbors. If you having something to barter, get started. Bring breakfast, lunch, and snacks from home instead of buying them at the coffee shop—put the savings in your fund, and eat healthier, too. Join a warehouse shopping club, or split the membership with a friend and split bulk items in two parts so you'll both save.

ALERT!

Something that *sounds* too good to be true—such as a designer handbag that retails for $850 being sold for $35—usually is too good to be true. This is particularly likely when you're shopping online or through mail order where you can't see the actual item. Read the product descriptions and the fine print of the return policy very carefully.

If finding what you need at thrift stores and outlet malls is not a skill you've developed, bring a friend who knows the ropes. Make sure you have completed your self-image assessment and have done some comparison-shopping before you go. Be sure to factor in the cost of cleaning and altering when considering the purchase price. If you are unsure of your style (or are still developing it) or you are on a limited budget, your best bet is to purchase clothes that are:

- A classic style, or modern but not overly trendy
- Flattering to your body type and well fitted (or that can be appropriately altered)
- Comfortable to wear (test them sitting, standing, walking, and bending to see if they pull, chafe, bind, itch, or poke)

Only buy items that make you feel confident and happy with your image, in flattering colors that coordinate with other things you own or plan to purchase. Get the best quality material and construction you can afford. Be aware that when bargain shopping, there may be defects in the items or they may be used—that's why they are reduced. Some things, such as a spot of dirt or a pulled thread, are easily fixed, but bad stains, holes and tears, and unusual missing buttons are not. A shiny spot on a wool suit or pills on a blouse or sweater means that it's worn out. "Irregular" can mean a minor defect you won't notice, but it can also mean something significant—e.g., the tag size isn't the standard size or the pieces are mismatched.

Think twice before you expand your wardrobe by borrowing from friends. Everyone borrows something from time to time—perhaps a cup of sugar, a hammer, or a book. However, borrowing has led to the ruin of many a friendship. The chance that someone else's clothes or shoes will really fit you well is very small, and why add the stress of worrying that the borrowed items may become damaged?

Try items on and resist impulse buys by not shopping when you are tired or hungry, or need something at the last minute. Most discounters don't make repairs or clean dirty items, and may insist on all sales being final. Know the return policy before you buy and don't buy unless you are sure you really want to keep it.

Dressing for the Occasion

Getting ready to go out is a ritual that stresses out both men and women. Many people might be surprised to learn just how little attention had been paid to their carefully chosen outfits because their potential partners were more focused on their facial expressions and the conversation (as they should be). On the other hand, being appropriately dressed does boost your confidence level. If you are going to meet potential partners, ask the organizer, the hostess, or a savvy friend what style of dress would be suitable. If you're going out on an individual date, ask for the destination and the suggested dress code.

If you haven't a clue what to wear, the outfit that works best for nearly every occasion in business also works well for your social life: a suit or a jacket and tie for men (you can always remove the tie and jacket if everyone else around you is very casual) and a pantsuit for women. If you find that you are more formally dressed than most people, you can always say you came straight from the office, or you had to attend a business event, wedding, or funeral. In general, you can assume that an informal get-together, such as a backyard barbecue or a trip to the amusement park, requires casual clothes.

Dressing appropriately for a date can be challenging, especially if your date says "It's a surprise" or "Let's figure it out when we get together." But on your dating journey the worst thing that can happen is occasional, momentary embarrassment. If you have dressed for dinner in an expensive outfit and high heels, but your date planned a night of fishing on his boat, you may have to ask him to suggest a different activity. If you are at a party or public event where you are dressed improperly, the best thing to do is shrug off your discomfort and don't call attention to yourself. If that's impossible, make an excuse and leave.

ALERT!

Always "test drive" new clothes, products, and accessories at home before you wear them in public. Those new shoes may hurt your feet after fifteen minutes, that new fragrance may cause you to break out in hives, and the pants you had hemmed but didn't try on may actually be too short. It's far better to know what you are facing in advance, rather than when you are rushing out the door or already on your date.

Formal functions take a bit more planning. If you are invited to a wedding, someone's formal work function, or a black-tie event but you don't have a tuxedo or a gown, men can get by with a dark business suit, black (polished) dress shoes, a white shirt, and a conservative tie. Women can usually manage a dressy-enough look with a quality cocktail dress and very sparkly accessories and shoes, or a long skirt with a dressy blouse or sequined/beaded sweater. A few pieces of sparkly jewelry, some shimmering makeup, and strappy sandals can take even a business suit from boardroom to ballroom, in a flash.

Dressing "Sexy"

The definition of "sexy" is highly subjective. What looks sexy to you might be a tacky turn-off to your potential partners. Some people really enjoy dressing in attention-getting clothes. But before you indulge in clothes that are super-tight, shirts open to the navel with tons of gold chains (à la the '70s) or anything that leaves little to the imagination, be sure you know what you want to accomplish with that look. Like over-the-top flirting, there is a fine line between "sexy" and an aggressive come-on. You will get looked at, but you might also send the message that all you really want is someone to come home with you that night. If you are looking for a romance to last a lifetime, save the overtly sexy clothes for when you are just having fun, not when you are looking to meet someone or on a date.

Dressing in a sensuous manner is another story. Sensuous clothes are sexy, but not over the top. What's sensuous dressing? Luxurious clothes that drape nicely on your body in fabrics that are inviting to the touch (e.g., soft cashmere and rich velvet) are sensuous. This style hints at more to come, without revealing everything now. Sensuous clothes fit well. They are never shirts so tight that the buttons are straining, or pants that leave absolutely nothing to the imagination. A small hint of cleavage is sensuous, as is a backless top with a jacket thrown casually over the shoulders. For men, a sensuous outfit would include a cashmere jacket worn over a silky, high-quality cotton dress shirt and soft wool trousers.

Here are a few tips for looking sexy, successfully:

- Always wear soft, inviting (touchable) fabrics (e.g., velvet, silk, angora, cashmere).
- Always wear clothes that hint at the shape of your body, without displaying all of it.
- Don't wear anything that might offend or embarrass your date in public.
- Let the wrap of a blouse, a slit in your skirt, or high heels show your sexy side.
- Whatever you wear, make sure it fits.
- Don't overdose on fragrance or aftershave. It should only be noticeable when up close and personal.

- Mix something sexy with something conservative. Only reveal the "sexy surprise" later on.
- Sexy is a state of mind. If you don't feel sexy, you won't look sexy, either.
- Go for clean lines (no bulging bra, obvious undershirts, or panty lines).
- Avoid embarrassment by keeping a pin in your wallet or purse, just in case.

To remain sophisticated while looking sexy, only show a hint of skin and choose colors and fabrics that compliment you. The last situation you want to end up in is one like Erica's:

> *Kurt invited me to his sister's wedding. I purchased a designer dress with a cutout in the midriff section (to show off my abs), and a slit up the side (to highlight my legs). When Kurt saw my dress he was horrified. His parents were very conservative and he felt my revealing dress would offend them. He gave me his jacket and told me not to remove it. He suggested that I tell people I was cold. I was mortified! (Erica, 34, Receptionist)*

It's Not Only about Clothes

Your image extends beyond your body and the clothes you wear. Your car, your workspace, your home, even just your couch, can speak volumes about you and your attitude. These things also can tell you a lot about potential partners, too.

Assessing Cars

If you live in a large urban area you may not drive, but in many places cars are essential. Chances are you will eventually ride as a passenger in a potential partner's car, and you'll learn several things about who this person really is when you do. First, note the make and approximate age of the car. Newer cars often suggest wealth. However, they might also just be a huge splurge to celebrate a new start in life. Inexpensive cars or clunkers (*not* vintage) could mean a tight budget, but it could also just mean the driver is frugal or chooses to spend big dollars in other ways.

Two-door cars, brand-new cars, and sports cars suggest that the driver is young or hoping to attract someone young. They could also mean that the driver is having a midlife crisis or a second childhood, too. Four doors suggest a practical person or someone who has others to drive around (perhaps elderly parents or children). A station wagon or mini-van or a car seat shouts "I am a parent." Sports utility vehicles (SUVs) appeal to people who like to carry things (e.g., gardening tools, antique furniture, sports equipment). Trucks appeal to outdoor types who typically use them for work or recreation. Someone who drives a Hummer or a "muscle car" is usually a macho man (or trying to be).

Note the color of the vehicle as well. Flashy or unusual colors suggest that the owner is flashy, too. On the other hand, maybe that was the only color for that model left at the clearance sale. Note the condition. Is it in good shape and fairly clean, or does it look like someone has lived in it for months? Are there dents or rust? Are the doors held on with duct tape? It's possible that your date has just had an accident and is waiting for parts, but she just might not take care of material possessions well.

What is the interior like? A showroom-pristine interior indicates a neat, perhaps compulsively neat, owner. A dirty car—one that smells, has a covering of pet hair, or a jumble of junk inside—probably indicates that the owner is a slob or at least didn't care enough to clean up for you. Are things hanging from the rearview mirror or sitting on the back shelf? Bumper stickers? People who decorate like to express themselves in public ways.

Look Around the House

Someone's abode will tell you even more about him than his clothes or car. Although you won't want to look inside a potential partner's home until you know the person fairly well, you will gain a wealth of information from your first visit. If you are *never* invited to visit your potential partner's home, it's a sure sign that he is hiding something (maybe a significant other or children?). That's what happened to Hannah:

> *When we had been dating six months, I asked Tom why I had never seen his car or his apartment. He responded that he was a spy for a secret government agency. I would be in danger if I was seen in his home or car, since both were under surveillance. This seemed ridiculous, but he seemed so sincere and I liked him so much I accepted it. I eventually dumped Tom when I could see that our relationship wasn't going anywhere. I subsequently learned from another woman who dated him that Tom had a wife and three small children. No wonder he never let me near his home or car! (Hannah, 43, Attorney)*

A couch is a prominent fixture in most homes, and the first place you are likely to be invited to make yourself comfortable. A couch says a lot about its owner. Is it a style radically different from your potential partner's usual style? It could mean that something is out of balance in terms of personal life. Is it an expensive designer model or a credible copy? That might mean your potential partner had someone else do the decorating, has megadollars, or is just a savvy shopper who knows where to find style at a decent price. A vintage piece could be something passed down through the family, but something that looks so old it could be from a thrift shop or off the street might indicate a lack of funds or a temporary living space. Ditto if there isn't any couch at all!

Also note personal objects and photographs. Lots of family photos will reveal a very family-oriented person. Lots of bookshelves clogged with books will indicate an avid reader (or someone who wants to appear as such). Houseplants indicate that you're in the home of a horticultural hobbyist. Use all these tidbits of information to generate conversation and to figure out how much you have in common.

ALERT!

Many people like animals, but very few enjoy sitting on a couch covered in cat hair. Before you invite someone to visit, be sure to use a pet-hair remover. You might not mind Fluffy's fur on your clothes, but your dates probably will. Old stains and smells should also be treated and removed before your date has to come in contact with them.

At the Office

There are several things to look for if you are invited to visit your potential partner at work. How organized and clean is her workspace? Does she have an office or a cubicle, or just a desk? Are there mementos and photos? Is there a plastic pen holder instead of a fountain pen in a marble base? Is the calendar part of a desk set or a freebie from a local business? Are there large piles of papers? Flowers or plants? Promotional items from conventions and trade shows? Yesterday's half-eaten sandwich? Business magazines or a paperback novel? If your potential partner works at home, is there a dedicated space for work, or apparently just the dining room table? Is there clutter everywhere—even in the bedroom? Finally, what do these observations suggest to you, and how well do you think you click with your potential partner having made them?

FACT

Where you live and work is a very important part of who you are. If you are never invited to visit your potential partner's home but you have been dating more than a few months, there's probably a reason for it. Perhaps the person is worried about disappointing you or lacks time to clean due to a rigorous work schedule. Remember: Honesty is the key to a successful relationship.

When to Call In an Expert

The problem with assessing and updating your own physical image and your living space is that it's hard to be completely objective about yourself. If you actually do have some significant image issues that you can't seem to conquer on your own and can afford it, consider consulting an expert. Designers and image consultants usually focus just on your personal style and wardrobe, while a personal public relations consultant addresses voice, poise, culture, and even social skills. You can opt for a single consultation and make a plan to guide you, or go for a complete image and home overhaul.

Designers and image consultants also offer personal shopping services and can refer you to various specialists. There are even consultants who coach you to handle your nervousness, perfect your personal ad content, or create your online profiles. You don't always get what you pay for, but you always pay for what you get. If you want to hire a professional, be sure to ask for references, and view a portfolio if possible.

ALERT!

Go for makeup consultations during special store events when the company brings in their best makeup artists. You might even get a bonus with purchase. Be sure to describe what kind of look you want (e.g., daytime, work, evening). Ask questions about how to apply the products and note the colors used. Ask for color swatches. Buy unusual items from that specific brand, but substitute budget brands wherever possible.

If all you want is a quick color analysis or some new makeup ideas, you can get these for free (or nearly so) at most department stores. The big ones usually offer personal shopping services and have good makeup counters. In most cases, you won't pay for the consultation but you will be expected to purchase at least some of the items that the consultant suggests. Expect these to be pricier than what you would normally select.

Alternative universities also may offer image update seminars because they are so popular with both men and women.

Melanie's story exemplifies what an expert can do for you:

> *I signed up for a wardrobe workshop because I wanted to attract a wealthy man for a serious relationship and they weren't "biting." The consultant suggested I swap my bright makeup and body-hugging clothes for a more conservative, sensuous look. At first I didn't think I'd attract any attention, but I actually attracted exactly the type of men I wanted to meet—and they asked me to dinner, instead of to their bedrooms. Now I know that the right image can work wonders. (Melanie, 28, Nanny)*

Chapter 9

Making First Contact

You make contact with new people all the time—at work, through friends, at parties, at the gym, while running errands—just about everywhere. Most of these connections are made so naturally that you don't even think about them. But when it comes to dating, singles say that making contact with a potential partner is more stressful than making initial connections in any other situation. This chapter will teach you how to appear cool and confident when you meet new people—even if you don't feel that way.

Be Approachable

If you really enjoy meeting people but tend to get nervous in social settings, there are a few things you can do to improve your situation. Above all, you must generate a positive attitude about it. If you think of socializing as stressful and difficult, others will sense that and be reluctant to approach you. Transmit confidence with positive body language and facial expressions. Stand up straight—don't slouch. Make brief eye contact (not a blatant stare) instead of turning away or looking at the floor. If you get nervous, encourage contact and conversation by carrying a prop such as a book or magazine or an eye-catching accessory. Such an item will give others with common interests a reason to come over and talk to you.

ALERT!

Nervous people tend to sag their shoulders, lock their arms tightly around their bodies, stand rigidly, and stare at the ground or dart their eyes around. Confident people have an open stance, make eye contact, and lean toward the person they're talking to. If close enough, they often show interest by lightly brushing your arm or shoulder to make a point.

Another way to be approachable, even if your heart is pounding with anxiety, is just to breathe deeply and smile. It's hard to feel negative when there's a smile on your face. The smile is a universal symbol of friendship and it draws people to you. Smile often and (as the old song says) the whole world will smile with you!

The following two lists include body language that either turns people away or invites them to approach you:

Negative Body Language
- Lack of eye contact
- Continual throat-clearing
- Covering mouth with hands
- Tugging at clothes

- Jingling things in pockets
- Fidgeting with accessories or clothes
- Hand-wringing
- Frowning or grimacing
- Stepping backward or away

Positive Body Language
- Steady eye contact
- Smiling
- Leaning toward a person
- Sitting on the edge of a chair
- Periodic hand-to-face gestures
- Moistening or licking lips
- Watching someone else's mouth as he talks
- Arms at sides, as opposed to crossed
- Brief physical contact (nonsexual)
- Pointing arms, legs, or feet or all of the body toward a person

Avoid Drugs and Alcohol

You've probably seen movies where a character gathers up his courage by downing a drink in one gulp. In real life, drugs and alcohol—the two things many people often think will help them to become more sociable—are actually the *least* effective. If you are so nervous that you need to dull your feelings to handle a social situation, drinking will only make things worse. Even one drink makes it more difficult to control your words and actions. If you doubt this, consider the times you have seen someone act like a drunken fool when he believed he was the "life of the party." Carla had the unfortunate experience of being that person at her friend's wedding:

> *I was really depressed that my friend Jane was getting married to someone I loathed. I decided to dull my dismay by having some martinis before their wedding ceremony. I had several more during the cocktail hour. I had some wine at dinner, too. When Jane gathered us all up to*

catch the bouquet, I passed out on the floor in front of the horrified bride and all her guests. Two ushers carried me away and called a doctor. I was fine, but my friendship with Jane wasn't. (Carla, 38, Nurse)

You pay a high price when you lose even a little bit of control due to drug or alcohol use. The time to pay up is usually the next day when reality sets in and you've already said or done something you wish you hadn't.

Anyone who pressures you into consuming alcohol when you don't want to isn't someone you want to be with! If you do want to accept a drink, take it directly from the bartender (drugs can be easily concealed in your drink when you're not looking). Avoid fruity drinks that can be consumed too quickly. Instead, order something "straight up" (with no ice) to sip, not guzzle.

If you *do* drink too much, it goes without saying that you should never drive. Leave your car where it is and take a taxi or public transportation. Even better, if you know that you are going to be drinking, go with a designated driver in the first place. If you are nervous when you go out, don't drink. Reach for this book instead of a drink, and review the tips for boosting confidence and reducing stress.

What to Say (and What Not to Say)

You've dressed up, gathered your courage, and arrived at your social destination—be it a party, dance club, or restaurant. Through the sea of faces, one in particular catches your eye. Could this be the special someone you've been waiting for—your soul mate? Your pulse quickens. You smile. Your eyes meet. Your smile is returned! Now what? If you ever want to know what happens next, you now have to make real contact and say something. After planning, anticipating, and hoping to meet someone, it's show time.

The best way to craft an opening line is to use what you see around you. It doesn't have to be witty, it just has to break the ice. If there is a band playing, you might say: "I just love this music. What do you think?" Or you can bring up the food being served: "I didn't see any sushi on the buffet table. Would you mind telling me where you found it?" Make a comment about the moment (e.g., "Wow, we have both been on this checkout line for at least ten minutes. How long do you think it'll take us to get to the cashier?"). Or, note something that clearly interests the other person and might stimulate further comment (e.g., "I see you're wearing a Syracuse University shirt. Did you go to SU?" Or "That's a colorful drink you have. What is it called?"). Try to think of something that forces the other person to respond with more than a yes or no answer. If your mind goes blank just say something to get the ball rolling.

FACT

The easiest way to break the ice with an opening line is to keep it simple. Your goal is just to get a response—to exchange a bit of information and see if there might be a reason to get to know each other. What you say depends upon your personal style. For example, if you're an amateur comedian, your signature greeting might be a joke or amusing anecdote, though not everyone would feel comfortable with this approach.

Just as there are great things to say when you first meet someone, there are also things you should *never* say. When you meet someone for the first time it's nearly impossible to correctly judge her feelings or know her values. Avoid comments that could be misinterpreted and those that are not politically correct. You may think your one-liners are great, but if they resemble any of the following, it's time to retire them:

- "I seem to have lost my number. Can I have yours?"
- "If I could rewrite the alphabet, I would put "U" and "I" together."
- "Is it hot in here? Or is it you?"
- "Are you Miss Tennessee, because you're the only 10-I-see!"
- "I hope you know CPR 'cause you take my breath away."
- "You know what would look good on you? *ME*!"
- "If I said you had a beautiful body, would you hold it against me?"

Of course, someone who uses lines like these isn't necessarily just a jerk. Often, insecure people say things like this because they lack confidence. If you hear a bad opening line, consider that first impressions can be very wrong. You might pass up the chance to meet someone very special. You'll be able to tell fairly quickly if you've met your dream-come-true, or a true toad. If it's the latter, you can always tell that toad to hit the road.

QUESTION?

What if your opening line is ignored, or worse, rejected?
First, give yourself points for trying. Consider, too, that if someone isn't interested in meeting you or is actually rude enough to turn away, there may be an unrelated reason for his behavior. The person may have just been dumped, had a fight, or experienced a family problem. Learn to accept this type of rejection as part of the process. Move on to the other people in the room.

The ABCs of Small Talk

You've gotten past the first line and a few moments of opening conversation. Where do you go from here? Your aim is to keep the person interested enough to continue the conversation. A subtle compliment is not out of line at this point; something like "I really like your tie," could easily do the trick.

Small talk should never consist of a heart-to-heart or a political debate. Choose lighter, noncontroversial topics like the weather, a movie you have seen recently, or a new exhibit at the art museum. Has he seen the exhibit, too? How did he like it? Local community issues are safe bets if the person lives in town and as long as you don't push your point of view too hard. Does she think the new recycling regulations are a pain or a plus? What does she think of the remodeling being done to the town hall?

With luck, the person you have just met will pick up on one or more of these topics and comment on them, adding new information about himself. When you know the person a little better you can direct the conversation to his interests as well. Does he collect fine wine? Does he love a certain sport?

If things go smoothly, it wouldn't hurt to learn something about his preferred wine or favorite team for the *next* conversation.

If you're still feeling nervous and having trouble getting words out of your mouth, don't worry too much. An insightful person who has something in common with you will pick up on your inner qualities and likely ask to meet with you again in a less daunting setting. And if you're the person noticing another's nervous twitches, give him the benefit of the doubt. Maritza is glad she did:

> *Larry and I had plenty to say when we met, but during our first date he spoke in monosyllables. When I got home there was already a message from Larry on my answering machine, apologizing for acting like a zombie. He said he really liked me and admitted that he was just really nervous about dating. He asked me to give him another chance. I reluctantly agreed to just drinks. This time Larry showed up with a perfect, pink rose and a new attitude. We've been together nearly a year. Larry still isn't a big talker but he's learning to open up. We are both willing to take it slow. (Maritza, 43, Salon Manager)*

FACT

Great topics to discuss during a first conversation are books you are reading, restaurants you enjoy, a trip you've just taken, or your interest in a hobby or sport. You can talk about your job as long as the information is general and you are not whining about the long hours you work or revealing that your boss is part of a love triangle.

Stressed to Impress

The conversation is going well. You've talked about movies, your last vacation, and the band. You've had a few laughs, but now there's dead silence! First of all, don't panic. Being a good conversationalist doesn't mean filling every second with chatter. The silence may seem like it's going on forever, but it will probably be just a few seconds while you both think of something to say to get the conversation flowing again.

Write down the main points of your conversation with each potential partner in your dating diary, and note what topics could be of interest to chat about in the future. Do this right after the date or you'll forget the details by the next day. This trick will help you wow your dates with perfect recollections of what they said the last time you met.

A few moments of dreaded silence during a first conversation can seem like a lifetime, but whatever you do, don't stretch the truth to impress the person or to fill a lull in conversation. Many singles do this, but what's the point? When the deception is realized (and you *will* be found out eventually), you lose the respect, trust, and interest of the person you wanted so much to impress in the first place. On a dating journey, the key to success is being honest about who you are, instead of creating a fantasy character. The following are common "boasts" that singles confess to making:

- Saying you have a certain skill you don't actually have (e.g., gourmet cooking, surfing, painting)
- Offering to obtain tickets to an event when you can't
- Saying you know people you have never met
- Claiming to be wealthy when you are not
- Boasting of false family connections or titles
- Lying about your age, health, or marital status (some people get away with this, but rarely indefinitely)

> *Minutes after I met Thomas I boasted that I could get tickets to any play he wanted to see. Thomas immediately suggested a sold-out show. I said "No problem," but I knew I couldn't get those tickets. Rather than admit I lied, I avoided Thomas and lost out completely. I've since promised myself never to stretch the truth again to get a guy interested in me. (Keema, 39, Dental Hygienist)*

Filling silence in a conversation with lies is definitely a big problem, but filling it with too much truth can be bad, too! You may meet someone with whom you feel an immediate connection—as if you've known each other for years. Just remember that you haven't known this person for hours, let alone years, so you need to keep the conversation light.

It's never appropriate to bare your soul right away. It's fine to share a few details (Sinatra songs make you cry, you love cold pizza for breakfast, etc.) but no intimate confessions. A brand-new contact really can't process your deepest fears, the details of your recent biopsy, or information about your semi-suicidal friend. Telling troubles too soon is a total turnoff to someone you have just met! If you are feeling needy and want to talk, go home and call a close friend. After a few dates it will be appropriate to deal with more serious subjects and reveal some intimate feelings. By then, you'll no longer need to rely on just small talk.

Flirting

Flirting can be lots of fun, or very dangerous. It all depends on how you do it, when you do it, and with whom you do it. Using subtle methods to tell someone that you are interested is fine, but over-the-top flirtation is not. Start by signaling interest with a genuine smile, strong eye contact, and open body language, including leaning slightly toward the person you are addressing. Women often twist their hair, play with their jewelry, or lightly and casually touch their ears or neck. Both men and women can boost positive vibes further by moving slightly closer than normal, fluttering their eyes, or licking their lips.

Indications of overt sexual interest include blushing, raising or lowering the volume of one voice to match the other, winking, heavy breathing, putting a finger near or in one's mouth, touching one's chest or thigh, crossing and uncrossing one's legs, or rubbing any part of one's body. Flirting isn't for everyone, nor is it appropriate in all social situations. In general, flirting is a bit of trickery. If you think it's fun, flirt gently. You don't want to send a harmless "I think you are attractive" message that is mistakenly received as "Let's get naked later on!"

Saying inappropriate things in an attempt to flirt could backfire just as easily as overtly sexual body language or physical contact. If you get too daring with your words, you could accidentally insult, embarrass, or otherwise upset your conversation partner. Though it turned out all right in the end, Paulette almost made this terrible mistake:

> I met Paulette at a how-to-make-small-talk class. We were each sup-posed to interview one another for three minutes and then report what we learned. Paulette didn't seem to get the exercise, because instead of talking about herself she kept saying, "You are so hot . . . you are so hot!" At first I was flattered, but by the end of our three minutes she had worn the expres-sion out. When it was Paulette's turn to report her "findings," she blurted out: "He is SO hot! Don't you all think he's hot?" People were laughing, and I was SO embarrassed! During the break, Paulette came up to me and admitted that she had a hard time dealing with social situations—that's why she was taking the class. Somehow I could see that behind her strange behavior was a nice woman I might like to actually get to know. I gave her the benefit of the doubt, and we went to get coffee after class. Now we have coffee together every day—in our apartment—and we joke about the day she almost turned me off for good. (Tony, 33, Computer Tech)

Remembering Names

Some people have amazing memories for names. They remember the full names of people they met years ago. However, many adults forget names minutes, or even seconds, after they've been introduced to people. It can be especially difficult to remember the name of a person you're meeting if you're nervous and are focusing entirely on saying the right thing and pro-nouncing your own name correctly.

QUESTION?

What should you do if you draw a complete blank on a name?
Be honest! You are better off sheepishly admitting that you don't have a clue who you are speaking to than to spend an entire conversation fran-tically trying to figure out that person's name. Make a lame excuse if you must—you just had a "senior moment," or you are sleep-deprived from your trip to Taiwan—but don't be afraid to ask for the name again.

One thing's for sure: Pretending you know a person's name when you don't could get you into a lot of trouble:

> *I met Alice at a party, but couldn't remember her name when I met her again. I didn't want her to think that I didn't care enough to remember so I didn't say anything. When I suggested getting together she said, "I'm in the phone book." I couldn't look her up because I didn't have a clue who she was! I had to finally admit I couldn't recall her name. I felt so dumb that I stumbled through the rest of our conversation. We never did go out.*
> *(Joel, 47, Physician)*

To keep a new name fresh in your mind, use it a few times right away in conversation (e.g., "Hi, Isaac, nice to meet you. Do you come here often? What do you think of the crowd here, Isaac?") If you don't catch a name when it is first said, ask for it again before you feel too embarrassed to bring it up. If it helps, make a mental image of the person and associate his name with something unique about him—e.g., Isaac, big eyes or Donna, dancer. Luckily, at many social events you will be given a nametag. Many people dislike them, but for singles they are lifesavers. All you have to do is look at the tag and reinforce the name with the face. If you are given a nametag, do everyone a favor and wear it properly on the right side of your lapel. If you place your nametag on the left side, someone shaking your hand has to turn his head to the right to catch your hand, while trying to read your name off your left lapel.

Chapter 10

The Art of the Date

Dating shouldn't be drudgery. Sure, a first conversation or first date is bound to be a bit awkward, but it's all part of the experience. Having a successful date doesn't have to be difficult. As long as you keep it simple, interesting, and lighthearted, it will never be a complete waste of your time. This chapter suggests easy ways to spice up usual dating ideas and make your experiences more fun and memorable. You'll also find tips and hints to guide you through the practical side of dating.

Phone Do's and Don'ts

How you behave on the phone can help or hurt your relationships. When you are dating, it's even more important to be adept at phone conversation. What the other person hears will reinforce any initial positive or negative feelings she may have about you. This is especially important if you have connected through online dating, personal ads, or a blind fix-up where you have not yet met in person.

FACT

Chatting when you are preoccupied will show in your voice and cause you to be distracted. You won't discourage someone who wants to talk to you by being honest and letting him know that now isn't a good time. To show your interest, be sure to suggest a specific time when you will call back.

Here are some basic phone do's and don'ts:

Do's:
- Answer the phone with a simple greeting. Wait for the caller to respond before saying anything else, even if you *think* you know who is on the other end. If not, you might end up like the book and movie heroine Bridget Jones who casually answered her phone with: "Bridget Jones, wanton sex goddess," only to discover that her *mother* was on the other end of the line!
- Pay attention to how you sound. Speak in a moderate, calm, pleasant tone that is easy to understand. If you aren't sure how you sound, tape yourself, or ask your makeover coach and friends to critique you and offer suggestions.
- Keep a pad and pen nearby for jotting down messages, names, phone numbers, addresses, or other information that you might want to refer back to.
- Leave short, uncomplicated voice mail messages in a tempo slow enough for the listener to write down information. Instead of a rambling, five-minute explanation, just say, "Sorry I missed you" and

leave your name, the date and time, the reason for your call, and a time when you will call back or when you can be contacted.

- If you are making a date, be sure to write down the person's phone number and get as much information about the date (e.g., when and where you will meet, directions).

Don'ts:

- Don't put someone on hold for longer than thirty seconds. It is very rude to make someone "hold" as long as you want him to. It's better to call back when you can talk. If someone puts you on hold for longer than you'd like, you are justified in hanging up and letting that person get back to you.
- Don't talk if you're not ready. Your caller can't know that you are suffering from a terrible migraine, or that you are in the middle of something you need to finish right away. Admit that the call has come at a bad time and promise to call back. Suggest a specific time and confirm it with your caller.
- Don't leave intimate phone messages. A parent, sibling, friend, or coworker might get to your message before your intended recipient does! This will *not* be appreciated.
- Don't carry on two conversations—one on the phone, the other with someone in the room. If you have to talk to someone else while you are on the phone, put your caller on hold for a second, and ask the person in the room to wait a few minutes. If she can't wait, excuse yourself to your caller and promise to call back as quickly as possible.
- Don't drink, eat, smoke, chew gum, or perform any other audible tasks while you are talking on the phone. Callers really *can* hear you shuffling your papers, blowing your nose, typing, or washing dishes. Remember that the phone intensifies these noises. Use the "mute" button on your phone or call back at a more convenient time.

Learn from Suzette's story:

> *Two of my friends were hanging out at my place when Vladimir called for the first time. I should have told him right away that I had company and it wasn't a good time to talk, but I wanted to speak to him so much! My friends were acting stupid, giggling and making loud kissing sounds. I was so embarrassed because I know Vladimir heard them. (Suzette, 30, Masseuse)*

Is It Really a Date?

The big question is: How can you tell if it's a date as opposed to a casual "get-together"? The answer is pretty simple. When you meet for the purpose of getting to know each other better and possibly start a romantic relationship, it's a date, even if it is just a walk in the park. Dating by its very nature is a more formal, couples-oriented activity to determine whether you want to go from being just acquaintances to something more. Dating definitely can be fun and entertaining, but dates are not the same as casually hanging out with friends. On dates, you are expected not only to be social, but also to be on your best behavior.

ESSENTIAL

If you don't really like traditional "date" destinations such as restaurants or the movies, then a more casual date might be right up your alley. For example, if you and your date share a particular sporting interest, like boating, why not rent a rowboat and bring some wine and cheese along, instead of sitting rigidly in a restaurant? If you both like to read, browse the shelves in an antiquarian bookstore, or attend a poetry reading.

First dates are fact-finding missions that should be short and inexpensive, such as an outing for coffee, lunch, or after-work drinks. Furthermore, a first date could happen without you even knowing or planning it. If someone eating alone in a café spies you eating solo and asks you to join him, you've just been invited on an impromptu date. These spur-of-the-moment events can be even more fun than the planned kind. In Miranda's case, a surprise date took the place of one that never came to be:

> *It was a bitterly cold night, and I'd been waiting for my date for nearly an hour in front of a nightclub in a less-than-posh part of town. I couldn't imagine why anyone would care so little about me that he'd leave me standing there, but I knew that I'd been stood up. As I walked away to find a taxi, a man tapped me on the shoulder. "Excuse me, miss," he said. "I saw you standing all by yourself, and I just have to say that any man that would leave a beautiful woman like you waiting is crazy. I am not usually so forward but I can't let you walk away without enjoying your night. The jazz trio you came to see will be starting the next set shortly. Would you consider coming in to hear it with me?" I was so stunned by this that I agreed. That was fifty years ago. We're celebrating our fiftieth wedding anniversary soon. (Miranda, 80, Retired Teacher)*

How to Ask Someone Out

So you're ready to take the plunge and ask someone out for a date. That's great, but how do you ask? Asking someone out can be surprisingly stressful, but it's a lot easier if you have a plan in mind. Thinking about what you are going to say and what you might like to do beforehand will help you ask with confidence.

Perhaps you're wondering who should ask who out. The answer is that there is no hard and fast rule. In years past it was more common for men to ask out women, but in today's world, it's acceptable for either to do the asking. And there's no set criteria you have to meet before asking someone out, except that you should feel comfortable and safe. If you've been having friendly conversations with a neighbor for weeks and finally feel ready to take the plunge, go for it! And if you happen to see a friendly, appealing face on the train during your daily commute, why not strike up a conversation? That's what Ida did:

"I'm a widow and I'm not getting any younger. I don't have the patience to wait for a man to ask me out. For weeks, as I commuted, I was attracted to a man who seemed to be about my age. He was always alone, and often carried a bag of take-out that couldn't have held enough for two. Also, he didn't wear a wedding band. I hoped he'd notice me and start up a conversation, but I finally decided that if I wanted to meet him, I was going to have to break the ice. I was scared, because I didn't know what he would think. In the old days, a man who was interested would have asked first. But this is the new world of dating, and so I got up the courage and asked him about some article on the front page of his newspaper. To my surprise, he was friendly. By the end of the trip home, we were chatting like old friends. He later told me that he was impressed that I had the confidence to make the first move, and grateful, too, because he was shy and figured a beautiful woman like me wouldn't be interested in him! (Ida, 60, Pharmacist)

When you ask someone for a date, be sure to suggest that the two of you meet at a specific time for a specific activity. If you just ask, "What are you doing on Saturday?" it leaves the other person wondering if it's an invitation for a date or just general curiosity. If asking the question "Will you go out with me?" seems too daunting, try something more casual but still direct, such as: "I didn't know you liked bowling. So do I. In fact, I was actually thinking of going this Saturday afternoon. Would you like to come with me?" Once you've asked, pause and give the person a chance to answer you. You can use the great first-date ideas in the next three sections if you get the "I'd love to" you're hoping for.

On the other hand, if someone rejects your invitation, that doesn't necessarily indicate a negative reaction to *you*. The person might be involved with someone else, or not really interested in dating. "I'm busy" might mean "I'm not interested," but it could also mean that he has to take his dog to the vet. Maybe she has to do something personal and doesn't know you well enough to explain. Whatever form it takes, a rejection is just part of every dating journey and not a big deal. Pat yourself on the back for asking and move on to the next potential partner.

Short and Sweet First Dates

If you're not sure whether there is much chemistry between you and your date, keep the first date short and inexpensive. The situation could quickly become awkward if it's a bad match and you're wearing dressy evening attire at a five-star restaurant. Quick and easy first-date ideas are going for coffee, lunch, or after-work drinks.

For a lasting impression, bring a "little something" for your date such as a photo frame. Take some pictures on your first few dates, and you'll have a ready-made excuse to get together again to view them together. Be sure to print a copy of the best photo for your date to put in that frame. It will serve as a reminder of the lovely times you've had together.

A short date also gives you a way to retain some "mystery" for the next time—if you want there to be a next time. Or, if the first hour goes so well that neither of you wants to say goodbye, you can always move from drinking coffee at the bookstore to ordering dinner. Adding "stages" to a date also makes you feel as though you are already making decisions as a couple— how exciting!

If you want to keep the first date short but you'd still like it to be a little different than just getting cappuccino, why not try a different approach? The following are some suggested brief but unique first-date ideas:

- **Take a walk.** If the weather permits, why not just take a walk in a pretty setting? Try a botanical garden, an arboretum, or a park or community garden. This will give you time to talk, and things to talk about, as you comment on an unusual tree or a beautiful blossom. For a romantic follow-up, send flowers as a reminder of that rose garden or field of daisies you strolled through.
- **Get drinks at an old-fashioned soda fountain.** If you are lucky enough to have an old-fashioned soda fountain or ice-cream parlor nearby, go there for a lighthearted, first-rate date. Nearly everyone (except

the lactose intolerant and die-hard dieters) likes ice cream. What a sweet way to start a romance!

Classic First-Date Ideas

Perhaps you've already gotten to know your date a little bit through work or through a friend. In this case, you might choose a longer first date, since you already know there's a bit of a spark between you. If you enjoy a classic evening out, you might like to do one of the following on your first date:

- **Go to the movies, the theater, or a live performance.** Movies and live theater are classic first-date choices; just be sure you both agree on the film choice. If you are arranging for theater tickets, make sure you agree ahead of time about how the cost will be handled. Movies and live performances are very entertaining, but such events don't allow much time for chatting and getting to know one another.
- **Dine out at a restaurant.** This timeless option gives you ample opportunities to talk. Choose a restaurant that isn't too expensive, as you may be paying your share or all of the bill. It's good to go where you know the food and service will be good; just make sure the cuisine you choose is acceptable to your date.
- **Go dancing.** Dancing is very romantic, and it's a social activity that allows you to dress up, go out, and have (acceptable) body contact and conversation. Many people enjoy showing off their smooth moves or don't care if they look silly. However, others wouldn't be caught dead on the dance floor, so check with your date first.
- **Visit an amusement park, playground, or zoo.** Playful activities make great dates and show that you're young at heart. However, these activities only work if your date enjoys them, too. Some people are genuinely fearful of amusement park rides or wild animals. Don't pressure your date to go on the roller coaster, pet the snake, or do anything that makes him uncomfortable, even if you really want to do it.

If there's food involved in your date, be sure that *both* of you agree on the selection. A serious food aversion or allergy could really spoil the mood if not discussed beforehand. That's what happened to Evelyn:

> *Ezra asked me to select the restaurant for our date, so I suggested a seafood place. He didn't sound too thrilled, so I quickly suggested something else. But he insisted we go with my choice. It turned out that Ezra hates seafood! I spent an uncomfortable evening watching him pick at his fish, and wondered if he might really get sick in front of me. It was silly for him to insist on going somewhere that obviously wasn't pleasant for him. In doing so, it wasn't pleasant for me either. (Evelyn, 32, Pastry Chef)*

Dating off the Beaten Path

Maybe you're ready for a full-length first date, but dinner or dancing just isn't interesting you. The following funky first dates are great for those with a creative side. Just be sure your date will appreciate your creativity!

- **Look for "Fleas."** If you and your date both like antiques, crafts, or collectibles, a craft show or flea market is the perfect way to get to know one another. You will learn about each other's tastes and interests. A romantic gesture might be to purchase a little token for your date. You might also find the perfect vase for your table. If all goes well, you may receive flowers from your date to fill it soon after!
- **Go for a beach date or a boat ride.** The sea is very romantic, but not everyone feels comfortable in swim gear right away. And some people get seasick just riding in the little boats in the tunnel of love. Ask beforehand. You can always take a romantic walk on the beach instead, and just *look* at the sea.
- **Be tourists together.** Learn more about your community or a neighboring town (and learn about your date, too). Take a walking tour or bus tour of your area, or visit a local monument or historical attraction. Be sure that the subject is of interest to both of you or the time will crawl, not fly.

- **Watch or play a sport.** Watching sporting events is fun and exciting and a good way to get to know someone. However, not everyone is into spectator sports. Perhaps you can enjoy an active sport together, such as roller or ice-skating, bowling, tennis, or golf. Just check first to see if your date knows how to play or is willing to learn, especially if it requires real skill or physical endurance.

If you choose these fun and original options, don't feel you have to cram more than one into your date. A few hours of walking through a craft fair or hitting tennis balls will surely wear you out. Just choose one event for your date and keep the other ideas in mind for your next extraordinary day together.

How to Behave on a Date

First and foremost, you need to know how to greet your date. Once you are at the agreed-upon meeting place and see your date approaching, let your face and body language show how delighted and excited you are. Smile, keep an open stance, make eye contact, and if you feel like it, extend a hand for a handshake or, if you're already comfortable with the person, lean in and offer a kiss on the cheek. Here are some easy tips to make that date great:

- **Be responsive.** Listen to the other person's views and try to understand and be interested in what he is saying. Nod your head slightly, to indicate that you are listening. Try to laugh (or at least smile) at his jokes.
- **Be sensible.** Reveal information about your opinions, values, and beliefs in a respectful, sensible way. Your date is a friendly stranger, but not yet a friend. You can reveal *some* details about important things that are going on in your life, but do it without too much drama. Dates aren't free counseling sessions, even if your date is a therapist!
- **Be responsible.** Never bring your children or anyone else along on your first date. If you are a single parent and can't get a sitter, cancel. Anyone who wants to make a relationship with you will need to understand and accept the realities of raising children anyway.

- **Be agreeable.** Just don't be so agreeable that you do something you'll regret later or give up your convictions. If your date doesn't respect your feelings, she isn't someone you'll want to date again.
- **Be appropriate.** Read an etiquette book to brush up on your manners. Good manners win you points with everyone you meet in your life and career, as well as on your dating journey. The majority of people will appreciate small courtesies (e.g., holding a door open, offering a hand to the elderly or an arm to you when walking on an uneven surface).
- **Be confident.** Don't be afraid to ask for a phone number or suggest a follow-up date, whether you are male or female. The worst thing that can happen to you isn't being rejected—it's letting someone walk away because you are afraid to take a chance.
- **Be respectful.** Don't curse, scream, or spit during your date. It's also best to avoid body contact completely at first. If you put an arm around your date's shoulder and your date pulls away, the time isn't right just yet. There will be plenty of opportunities to make physical contact in the future if you click.
- **Be polite.** You can remove a jacket or tie. However, loosening a belt, pulling up a sock, brushing your hair, picking your teeth or nose, and filing or clipping a nail are tasks that should be done in the washroom.

Who Pays?

You don't have to be wealthy to date, but most activities do involve some cost. At some point, someone is going to have to pay up for drinks, tickets, tip, etc. Younger people are so used to hanging out in groups and splitting the bill or each paying their own share (Dutch treat) that the issue of who pays is not an issue. However, older adults may find the subject more complicated.

The *new* rules are that the person who does the asking also does the paying, or else you can go Dutch treat. This term originally had negative connotations about supposed Dutch thriftiness, but it just means that you each pay your share. If you are a traditionalist, you may feel that a Dutch treat is no treat at all. But consider that when both adult partners have an equal share in the expenses, it puts them on a level playing field.

E ALERT!

You may also encounter some people, usually older men, who simply won't allow a woman to pay for anything. If you meet one of these courtly types, you can always handle it by saying, "Okay, you can get this, but the next time it's on me." If you connect, you'll probably start reciprocating soon anyway in some form, such as with tickets, little gifts, or a home-cooked dinner.

Since the "who pays?" issue can be tricky, it's sensible to begin dating someone new with activities that are relatively inexpensive. If you really want to indulge in a big ticket event, be sure to tell your date and offer it as your treat. This way, your date doesn't end up using rent money to pay for the pleasure of your company, or be embarrassed into asking if the date is "on you" or turn you down due to lack of funds. Consider Joel's story:

> *Sarah, a successful entrepreneur, asked me to an expensive nightclub. I could never afford to go there on my own, but I assumed since she could afford it and had asked me out, it would be her treat. I was horrified when the bill arrived and she handed it to me. I had to admit I didn't have that kind of cash. Imagine my shock when she calmly informed me that there was an ATM near the club and she would have another brandy while I got the money. I walked out and kept on walking. Maybe she was just old-fashioned about dating, but she was horribly insensitive. She knew I was a student with a part-time job. Now I make sure to get the finances straight before going out. I never want to be in that type of situation again. (Joel, 27, Graduate Student)*

Chapter 11

Dating Survival Kit

Think there's no way to be prepared for a date? Think again! There are countless tools and techniques that you can use to be prepared and make every date great. Some are items and ideas so commonplace that you might have overlooked them in the past. In reality, there's no reason to view a stubbed toe or a popped button as the dead end of your date—if you're prepared. This chapter will tell you all you need to know to go from a struggle to success!

Practical Dating Tools

When dating experiences go wrong, it's usually due to something unanticipated and no one is to blame. But that doesn't mean you can't prepare for common problems. For example, if you develop heartburn or a headache, you'll end up feeling miserable if you don't have antacid tablets or aspirin. If you don't bring written directions to your meeting place, you may be lost or delayed, and sabotage the date before it even begins. If you haven't made clear plans, you may be worried about what you're doing instead of calm and confident.

The truth is that even a Band-Aid can be enough to save the day. Hope discovered this on her date with Adrian:

> *Adrian and I went on a picnic. He took out a corkscrew to open a bottle of wine and accidentally shoved it into his finger. It wasn't a deep wound, but was bleeding like crazy. Thank goodness I had tissues, antibacterial towelettes, and Band-Aids in my purse. Adrian was able to fix up his hand and continue our date. He was impressed that I was clever enough to be prepared so our date didn't end in disaster. We're getting married in the same park where we had that picnic. (Hope, 32, Fitness Instructor)*

Here's a list of small, everyday items that can help dates go off without a hitch. Make them standard equipment when you go out:

- Cell phone, phone card, or change for a pay phone
- Phone numbers of friends who will take your call if you need assistance of any kind, along with contact information for your date (in case you're late or you get lost on the way to your destination)
- Phone numbers of roadside assistance, a few reliable taxi or car services, and the local police
- Band-Aids, aspirin, antacids, breath-freshening gum or mints
- Condoms (maybe you're not planning to use them, but just in case)
- Car equipment, such as jumper cables, flashlight, local map, emergency service number
- Prepaid transit card or tokens, and a bus or subway map
- A notepad and a functional pen or pencil

- At least $20 in emergency money
- Tissues or a handkerchief
- Directions to your meeting place
- Your date's cell phone number (in case you get lost or run late)
- On-the-go energy snack

You don't have to tote the following on your actual dates, but these "tools" can help make your dating journey smoother, safer, and more successful:

- An answering machine or an answering service, pager, or voice mail
- A journal (to document dating experiences and information about potential partners)
- An appropriate wardrobe for your lifestyle and activities
- An etiquette book

Dating Buddies

While you won't want to bring your friends with you on dates, it is a good idea to involve a few of them in your dating experience. Dating buddies are people who know your basic date plans, including the name and contact information of the person you are with, where you plan to go, and approximately when you plan to return home. They should be people who are reliable and willing to help you out. And if your dating buddies are also single, you can return the favor.

These people are an important piece of your dating support system. In the *unlikely* event that you don't return home at the expected time and have not phoned with an explanation, your dating buddy will initiate a search for you. Having a dating buddy is particularly important if you are responsible for homebound elderly, minor children, or pets and you are delayed or blocked from getting home. Calling your dating buddy is also a great way to debrief after your date—something many singles do anyway.

Evelyn's story is a great example of how having a dating buddy can really save the day:

> "*After a few dates with Thomas I agreed to go back to his place for drinks. It was fine until I tried to go home. Then he got angry and blocked the door. I calmly told him that my friend Tina had his address and phone number. If I didn't answer her call around midnight, she was to call the police and give them his address and phone number to track me down. Thomas backed off immediately, grousing that I "asked for it" by coming up to his place! (Evelyn, 51, Attorney)*"

Dating buddies fulfill another function, too. If you aren't too sure you are going to like your blind date or that person you contacted through a personal ad or online dating service, have your dating buddy call you about half an hour into your date. You are encouraged to stick out most dates unless they become nasty and dangerous, but if one does, your dating buddy's call is a way to make an excuse and leave.

Dating Cards: Better than Bar Napkins

Business cards are not just for business! These small, slim cards give you credibility and establish your credentials. They also provide your contact information. A traditional business card beats a bar napkin for offering information. However, if you offer a social contact your business card, you run the risk that this person will pay unscheduled visits to your office, send you steamy e-mails, or deliver gifts and flowers that can contribute to office gossip.

So instead of handing out your business card to social contacts, try creating a card just for social purposes. Personal cards are an inexpensive, easy, effective, and fun way to introduce yourself to others. Personal cards are similar to business cards, but they show only your name, telephone number and perhaps an e-mail address. They are less formal in style, and they can save you from frantically foraging for a slip of paper and a pen when someone asks for your number.

Constantine learned the hard way that he needed personal cards:

> "*Bernice asked me for my number. She didn't have any paper and neither did I. Fishing around in my pockets my hands closed around a book of matches I'd taken from a strip club I'd been to for a bachelor party.*"

I pulled out the matchbook and both of us realized that there was a crude photo on the front. This was an obvious turn-off for Bernice, who probably thought I was a pervert. She walked away and I never did give her my number. I blew it with Bernice just because I didn't have anything appropriate to write on. (Constantine, 35, Photographer)

F A C T

You can print personal cards professionally, or make them yourself for just pennies. Be creative but tasteful. A photo or graphic (e.g., a sailboat, a cat or dog, running shoes) reminds people of your interests, but don't try to be too memorable. A photo of your nude torso is a unique approach, but *shockingly* beyond bad taste!

Conquering Nerves

Dating can be a nerve-racking experience, and having some anxiety or nervousness about it is perfectly normal. Appearing a little nervous or saying the wrong thing will not completely blow your chances with a potential partner, but boosted confidence will help you get through awkward moments. Still, someone who is genuinely interested in you will overlook any initial awkwardness and stick around to get acquainted. That's what happened with Iris and Liam:

I met Liam at a networking party and I was so nervous that I began coughing right in the middle of a joke I was telling. I couldn't stop! As I gasped and sputtered, Liam pulled out a roll of mints and handed one to me. When I finally composed myself, I spilled a glass of red wine all over my suit and his tie. Liam just smiled and pulled out his handkerchief to sop up the spill. I assumed he'd never call me again, but he said that my being nervous helped him stay calm because he was so nervous, too. Charming! (Iris, 52, Attorney)

Of course, even the most jittery person can do a few things to look and feel calm. Here are some tips to help you appear cool and collected throughout your date:

- Avoid synthetic fabrics or tight clothes that cause you to perspire.
- Select natural fabrics appropriate for the temperature (e.g., cotton, linen, silk, wool), and wear layers that you can remove if you get overheated.
- Deep breathing automatically calms you. Breathe slowly for a minute, and then take a few deep, cleansing breaths before you walk into a room. Your body will relax and you will feel more in control.
- Feeling so jumpy that you're sure others sense it? Make an excuse to get away for a few minutes—make a phone call or visit the rest room. Visualize a calm place such as a sunny beach or a beautiful garden.
- Smile. Force your face into a big grin before you enter a room. Your smile will stay put for a few seconds to help you look and feel friendly and confident.
- Do a quick self-affirmation. Think to yourself (or say under your breath): "I am calm, confident, and in control." If you *think* it, you can *say* it. If you *say* it, you can *do* it.

Stow Your Baggage

The best way to be relaxed and have a successful date is just to enjoy it in the present. Worrying about what will happen *next* will stress you out, for sure. Hope for the best, but don't raise your expectations to an unreachable level. If you don't click on a date, don't worry. It's hardly the end of the world. Every dating experience brings you closer to your ultimate relationship goal.

There is one thing that can really doom your date: the past. Everyone has experiences and feelings they have developed from prior personal relationships. Most adults can balance these, but some carry a great deal of anger, bitterness, or grief about things that happened in their past. This sabotages not only their dating experiences, but their chances for future happiness. You may feel sad about returning with a new date to a place that you last went to with a former love, or upset that you are forcing small talk with a virtual stranger after being in a meaningful relationship that has ended. Just remember: You are with someone entirely different who hasn't done you wrong.

If you relax, so will your date. You will both have a better time if you remember that you're in this moment together and it's just a date—not brain surgery! Stay in the present. Don't worry about the future or things that may have happened in the past. Stow your baggage and enjoy a new experience with a friendly face.

Lighten your potentially negative baggage by putting your past away and focusing on the present, at least for now—on the date. This isn't always easy, but you can do it if you realize that you are moving on in your life. This date, today, right now, doesn't have to be the best on record. Your expectation should be for it to be nothing more than positive. If it turns out to be even more, that's a bonus.

The All-Important Etiquette Book

Although dating has changed a great deal over the years, good manners were, are, and will always be in style. Having good manners helps you find success, not just with a romantic partner but in every aspect of your life. The use of proper etiquette is much more than just knowing when to pick up chicken with your fingers, or how to make proper introductions. It also includes abstract concepts such as how to be a generous host, a loyal friend, a good companion, a great guest, and respectful of elders, home, and community.

An etiquette book can teach you almost anything, from how to properly eat an olive with a pit to how to hold your wine glass. Be sure you get an updated etiquette book, complete with useful tips for socializing in today's world.

Proper etiquette is a set of guidelines to follow so that you are confident in any social situation. The concept of good manners mainly consists of the golden rule: do unto others as you would have them do unto you. You'll know when you've met someone with excellent manners, like Mary Claire did:

> *Tony arrived at my parent's house for our first date with a box of pastries for my father, and flowers for my mother. He willingly sat on the couch while my dad gave him the third degree. He stood up when my mother entered the room and asked my father for permission to take me out. He thanked them for allowing him the pleasure of my company! To some people these little gestures might not mean that much, but in my community they do. My parents were thrilled that I had selected a man with Tony's qualities. Tony understood that making a good impression on my family was essential, because if he dated me he would need their blessing. He is a true knight in shining armor. Our relationship has been a true storybook romance. (Mary Claire, 39, Production Manager)*

Even if you know basic etiquette, you may have forgotten the finer points. It is a good idea to purchase an up-to-date etiquette book that has a section focusing on business etiquette as well as general. Small gestures can make a lasting, positive impression whether you are on a date or at a business function.

ALERT!

The most beautiful clothes or the wittiest personality can't make up for bad manners. When you know what is expected in social situations, you are confident that you can handle just about anything. Bad manners or ignorance of basic social etiquette is unacceptable, and will not get your far in your dating journey.

Most adults claim that they know how to behave, but then they lick their fingers, use the tablecloth instead of a napkin, talk with their mouths full, apply makeup in full view of others, or "forget" to turn off their cell phones in public places. They forget simple courtesies taught to them as children, such as saying "please" and "thank you" or acknowledging gifts promptly.

The next time you are out, observe how many people you see indulging in overt public displays of affection, pushing to get through a door or into the elevator, not holding doors, interrupting others, openly picking teeth or clipping nails, or harassing the wait staff. Note the number of people who don't bring a hostess gift, bring additional guests to someone else's party without permission, use the wrong utensils, ignore others at dinner parties, act outrageously, openly belch, refuse to remove babies when they are disruptive, gossip openly about others, tip improperly or not at all, leave without paying the bill, botch introductions, or act disrespectfully. These are just a few of the common gaffes adults make all the time.

Barry had the unfortunate experience of discovering that his date, Arlene, had very bad manners:

> *On my third date with Arlene, I had a chance to watch her in action with others. I wasn't impressed. We attended a dinner party at her friend's house. Arlene grabbed every dish first and loaded up her plate, leaving barely enough for the rest of the guests. She licked her fingers, criticized the food in front of the hostess, and burped openly at the table. She nearly got into a fight with another guest over something she should have just ignored. Arlene didn't even bring a hostess gift and she never even thanked the hostess for dinner! If she acted that way with her friends, I couldn't see her being any better with me. Her behavior that night convinced me that Arlene wasn't someone I wanted to continue dating.*
> *(Barry, 39, Dentist)*

You should now be convinced that the guidelines of good behavior can really help you get success in general, and especially when you are socializing and dating. Etiquette books are invaluable tools to help you win in love and in life. Select updated books, as customs and conventions change over time. The best ones offer advice on adjusting your behavior according to your age or cultural differences, or to fit particular social or business situations. Take it from Francine:

I read my first etiquette book the week I was invited to a formal cocktail party. I often referred to myself as an "amateur juggler" because I nearly always dropped something. Along with advice on social behavior, this book suggested an easier way to handle food and drinks. I got through the event feeling really confident. I'll be able to use this information wherever I go, for the rest of my life. (Francine, 38, Public Relations Specialist)

Chapter 12

Stepping Out—Your First Date!

You now know how to meet potential partners, how to improve your image and attitude, and what you need in your dating survival kit. It's time to put all this knowledge to the test! This chapter will walk you through your very first date, from pre-date preparation to saying goodnight. Even if you are used to dating, there are awkward moments in most dates and they are often handled poorly. Read on to learn how and when to end a date, whether or not you should kiss your date at the end of the night, and how to let your date down gently if no match is made.

Before You Go Out

There are so many unknown elements of a first date—and every date—that it makes sense to reduce unanticipated surprises that can make a date go wrong. You don't have to figure out every detail of your dates in advance, but if you discuss the basics you will have some idea what to expect and can prepare and relax. When you agree to go out with someone, you should discuss:

- When, where, and at what time you will be meeting
- What kinds of activities you will be doing
- Any restrictions on time, diet, or activities either of you has
- If and when you will need to check in at home
- Approximately how long the date will last

Most common dating disasters can be avoided with just this little bit of advance planning. Being completely spontaneous is fine when you know someone well, but it *doesn't* work when you don't. It won't be fun to end up at your date's favorite steak house if you're a vegan, or to end up someplace far away from where you must fulfill other important obligations (e.g., picking up your parent from the senior center before it closes, or picking up your friend from the airport that evening). Also, just knowing that you are going out for dinner is not specific enough. If you dress for a restaurant but find yourself on a chilly outdoor dinner cruise without a jacket, you'll likely spend the evening uncomfortable and kicking yourself for not getting more details earlier.

Dating is a formal social activity that requires you to be on your best behavior. Dating partners are expected to be positive, upbeat, and pleasant company. When you are feeling down or slightly tired you may think about canceling a date. Usually, you shouldn't. Being social and focusing on your motivation will energize you. However, there are times when you *should* cancel. If you are seriously distraught or exhausted, you will be distracted and unhappy during a date of any kind. This obviously won't make a good impression. Tell your date the truth, apologize, and reschedule. Ditto if you are truly sick, especially if it is something contagious. Contracting whatever ails you won't suffice as a memento of your date!

If you are hoping to become a couple, you'll quickly need to learn each other's preferences. If you talk about this in advance of your date, you can find an activity you both will like. Since your primary purpose in dating is not just to be entertained but also to get to know one another, why not discuss together what you *both* enjoy?

Conversation Tips

One of the most common things singles worry about is what to say. This becomes less of an issue if you simply consider your date as just a friend in the making. You don't get anxious talking to friends, do you? Stretches of silence may make you think your conversation is failing, but small breaks are actually good opportunities for you to reflect on what's been said thus far and consider what you'd like to talk about next.

If you are verbal but your date isn't, keep in mind that it isn't enough for you to be a witty conversationalist. It is just as important to be a good listener. Show your date that what she says is interesting and important to you. That means not launching into a lengthy description of your prized pooch when your date has just mentioned that her dog has recently died, or ignoring what she has said completely and moving on to a different subject without comment. If you're lucky, your two styles of speaking will mesh well together, as they did for Maybelline and Garth:

> *When I asked Garth out, he said he wasn't sure if he should accept my dinner invitation because he was afraid he wouldn't have enough to talk about. "Don't worry," I said. "I can talk enough for both of us!" I was right; we're a perfect fit. (Maybelline, 32, Teacher)*

Here are some things to do to keep the conversation flowing (and meaningful) throughout your date:

- Use your date's name every now and then to show you are focused on him.

- Even if your date seems shy, give him defined opportunities to talk about himself. Don't spend the whole night blabbering about yourself.
- Discuss what is going on in the moment. Mention how you feel about where you are and what you are doing.
- Refrain from saying anything inappropriate for your current level of intimacy. If you are pressured to say something too personal, reply, "I'd rather save this for when I know you a bit better." Then change the subject.
- Use common sense, especially early on in your dating relationship. Cursing uncontrollably, going on and on about your ex, using foul language, or harassing the wait staff are surefire ways to end your date early.

Great conversation requires more than conjuring up interesting topics. It also requires consideration and common sense. Always avoid:

- Mumbling, or speaking so softly, loudly, slowly, or quickly that you can't be understood
- Using baby talk, slang, or curse words to make an impression
- Expressing strong prejudices when you don't know your audience
- Mentioning anything intimate, gross, or distasteful
- Continually probing someone with personal questions
- Telling long uninterrupted personal stories
- Using trite phrases to tune someone out (e.g., "Got ya" or "Yup")
- Interrupting, or finishing your date's sentences (or correcting his grammar)

If the conversation starts to lag and you think you've covered all the important topics, why not do a quick status check? Focus on what's happening in the moment and ask your date a specific question. Does he like the pasta he ordered? Is she too cold (offer your jacket) or too warm (ask the waiter to turn up the air conditioning)? Perhaps your question will prompt him to tell you all about the pasta his mother makes from scratch, or how her father turned up the thermostat so high that her family wore shorts at home year round. The conversation will be rolling again in no time.

Dealing with Meals

Of course you know how to eat—you do it several times a day. But eating on a date is a whole different story. You may not think twice about ordering a big, saucy plate of spaghetti when you're with friends, but while wearing a brand new white blouse on a first date, tomato sauce might not be the best choice.

Of course, avoiding greasy, saucy, or otherwise messy foods can't always save you from disaster. If an accident does happen, don't be embarrassed. Running off to the bathroom in tears will only make things worse. Handle the situation calmly, as Carlotta did:

> *Brian invited me to lunch at an Italian restaurant. A waiter with a heavy tray lost his balance and as plates clattered to the floor, red sauce got splattered all over me. Everyone was staring and I was embarrassed, but I calmly wiped my jacket off as best I could, called my office and quickly went shopping for a new jacket before my 4:00 meeting. Brian told me later that he fell in love with me right then because of the confident way I handled myself. (Carlotta, 41, Public Defender)*

It's also smart to select foods that are easy to cut, chew, and swallow. If you are served something difficult to manage, eat slowly and carefully. An etiquette book will show you how to appropriately deal with shells, bones, and other meal obstacles. After all, you want to avoid a display like the one Marika witnessed:

> *My new boyfriend asked me to join him for dinner with his new boss and some coworkers. The first course was escargots in the shell. I was SO glad I had read up in my etiquette book about how to handle challenging foods. The man next to me didn't know what to do, and he sent a slippery, garlicy snail flying right into the boss's lap! I was grateful it wasn't me! (Marika, 26, Executive Assistant)*

When it comes to eating out, many singles have questions. Should I only order an appetizer if my date does? Can I have another glass of wine even if my date doesn't? What if I want something on the menu that is expensive? Dining isn't rocket science! The best thing to do is try to enjoy your meal and eat a reasonable amount. When it comes to ordering alcohol, follow your date's lead. If he orders a drink, you are free to do so as well. If he orders wine and you don't want any (or don't want more) just say so.

Stuffing yourself is greedy and unattractive, but eating like a bird to appear "dainty" or "cute" isn't smart either. If the date continues for another few hours, you might find yourself hungry again but too embarrassed to suggest another meal.

Make an Impression

Being impressive doesn't mean driving a flashy car or spending lots of cash. It is the little courtesies that people really appreciate. For example, being on time for your date is among the simplest and most effective things you can do. Of course, if your date is late, be understanding. If you have a sense of humor about things, you'll gain your companion's gratitude and respect.

ALERT!

Be enthusiastic, but avoid over-the-top flattery. It's obvious and cheesy. Your date will know you're being insincere, and may be quickly turned off. Here's a rule of thumb: Think before you speak, and if you don't mean it, don't say it.

Other ways to make a great impression on your date include focusing on the one you're with and using positive body language. Don't make excessive comments about other people, and don't slouch, frown, wrinkle your eyebrows, or make other negative gestures. In addition to this, don't "make eyes" at the waiter or any other people nearby. Even if there's no real spark between you and your date, you still owe this person your full attention.

On the other hand, you don't need to be overly attentive. No one likes to be pawed. Even if you are a "touchy-feely" type, keep your hands off your companion in public and make sure your date is comfortable before you start getting physical. Keep cosmetics and fragrance light and smudgeproof so that you don't mark up your date's clothes.

Be mindful of your date's—and your own—finances. Never order the most expensive thing on the menu even if you can afford it. Indulge another time when you are out with friends or you are splurging alone. Likewise, speak up if your date suggests an activity that is beyond your budget. You won't have a good time if you go along but spend the entire time wondering how you are going to pay your share.

It seems obvious, but many people need to be reminded that loud belching and other bodily noises are total turn-offs. Use antacids to keep gas under control, and excuse yourself to the restroom if you must. If you are feeling a little sick but think it will pass, keep quiet about it. If you feel *really* sick, speak up, apologize, and go home.

By all means mention your family and friends, but keep your chatter about them to a minimum. Your companion may not think the play-by-play of your kid brother's last softball game is that interesting, even if it is fascinating to you. You are there to learn about your date—not just babble about yourself. Also remember that dating isn't a substitute for therapy. Life's too short to dump on your companion about how depressed you are or how your last love did you wrong.

Finally, be a good sport. Be willing to try something new even if you're not certain you'll like it. If you haven't tried roller-blading or seen the opera before, you can't know for sure that you will dislike it—you might be in for an eye-opening treat. However, do speak up and suggest an alternative if you are asked to do something you really loathe or that makes you very uncomfortable. You not obligated to do anything that will upset, frighten, or otherwise discomfort you.

Part of being a good sport is being flexible. If you miss the movie you really wanted to see or can't get reservations for that dinner theater, try not to show your disappointment. You are supposed to be getting acquainted with a potential partner, not just have someone to hang on your arm as you cruise the newest nightclub or restaurant in town.

When to Call It a Wrap

Ending a date can be awkward if you're not sure what to say or do, or when to do it. The best way is to wait until your last planned activity ends, look at your watch, and say, "This has been great! But it's getting late and I really should go home now." If your date argues that the night is still young, you still aren't obligated. Casually mention that you have to get up early for work, or have something you must do at home, or just that you are tired. Anyone who pushes you isn't showing any consideration for your feelings.

FACT

Never expect a follow-up call right after your date. Your date could be thinking about you but busy, or maybe just not wanting to appear too eager. If *you* make a follow-up call, don't pressure the other person to make another date right then. Part of a dating journey is managing anxiety about what will happen next—but that is part of the excitement, too!

Most dates range from just okay to really great. However, there may be a few times when you and/or your date are having such a bad time or you feel so compromised that you must end things early. In general, it's best to stick out a date until its logical end. But if you really must leave, the best way is just to be forthright and say you want to end things. If you are really desperate, here are some drastic measures that some singles have used—but only in truly terrible situations:

- Tell your date that you "just remembered" you had to be somewhere. Check your watch and act horrified—you told your friend that you'd pick her up from the airport twenty minutes ago!
- Introduce your date to someone else or engage him in a group conversation. When his attention is diverted from you, quietly leave.
- Say outrageous things (with conviction!) such as: "I believe people shouldn't kiss until they're married." Or demand an extravagant gift the next time you see the person—a diamond necklace, a new Jaguar, etc.

- Keep a photo handy of a group of children that *could* be yours. Make sure there are at least five (for shock value). Show the photo to your date and exclaim, "My poor babies. They really need a new (mommy) (daddy)!"
- Call your ex, a friend of the opposite sex, or your dating buddy, and invite her to join you and your date *right now*. Make sure your date hears you say that you'll both happy to wait until she arrives!

While escape tricks like these are handy, honesty is really the best policy. It is acceptable in truly offensive circumstances to simply say you don't want to continue the date a moment longer and you are leaving. It is possible that your date really doesn't know how bad his behavior is, but anyone who can't sense your discomfort isn't someone you want to see again. In any case, if you've had enough of a date's genuinely rude, offensive, or otherwise horrible behavior, you might simply call him on it, like Sandra did:

> *Michael seemed nice enough when I first met him, but on our first date, he was a different person. He sneered at my dress, berated my movie choice, and denigrated me by saying nurses were people who couldn't make it as doctors. I somehow managed to stick it out through dessert and coffee. But when the check arrived, Michael made a big deal about how he had to pay. I'd had enough! I snatched the check and said: "'When I'm with someone I like and expect to see again, I always let him pay because I know I'll be reciprocating another time. In your case, just tell me how much I owe!" (Sandra, 40, Nurse)*

It's not fun to be dumped on a date. But if it happens to you, remind yourself that dating is a process of elimination as well as selection. Not everyone will appreciate you. If you are dumped mid-date you need to consider why it happened. What could you do differently next time? Write down your feelings in your dating journal to work through the problem.

Here's one final warning: If you find yourself in a situation where your date wants to get closer to you than you'd like, be careful. Rejecting unwanted advances can hurt your date's ego, and sabotage an otherwise potentially good relationship. Get clear in your mind before you go out just how far you want to go. Let your date know if he crosses that line, but do it with courtesy and respect for his feelings. If you express yourself well, your date will understand that he passed your comfort zone. Your potential partner should quickly rebound from this type of rejection and allow the date to continue pleasantly.

ALERT!

The "Dear John" letter dates back to World War II. "John" was a generic name for a man. Many sad servicemen got "Dear John" letters from lovers back home announcing they had been dumped. You can send a modern version of a "Dear John" letter by e-mail, but it's not a nice thing to do.

The Question of Intimacy

Kissing is a common occurrence—people do it all the time. But kissing a date is different than kissing your cousin, your grandmother, or your best friend. The urge to kiss a potential romantic partner is based on physical attraction and values. You are not expected to kiss a date if you don't want to, but you may experience some tension at the end of the night if your date is expecting it and you don't deliver!

Most kissing on first or second dates are goodnight kisses. If you want to avoid them, end your date in a public place so that there is less opportunity to get into a lip lock. Reinforce your feelings with body language, such as crossing your arms and keeping some distance between you and your date. If your date misreads or ignores your signals and moves toward you anyway, you can turn your head at the last minute so she gets your cheek, or you can initiate a light hug so that she can't connect with your lips. As an alternative, you can offer a handshake, but that sends the discouraging message that you feel no physical attraction whatsoever.

If you *do* want to kiss your date, send the signal by moving closer. It's a positive sign if your date doesn't back away or show closed body language. Move in closer and closer until your lips meet! And what if you and your date want to do *more* than kiss? For most adults, physical intimacy is a gradual process that builds as two people get to know one another, develop trust, and attain a certain comfort level. For some people, physical intimacy is no big deal. For other people, it's something to consider only when you are truly committed to each other. And for others, being intimate is just something that "happens" when they are carried away in the moment.

FACT

An unkind but common practice today is to ignore someone you've recently dated until she gets the message to go away instead of personally ending things. Silence is confusing and mean-spirited, even if it is effective. It might be easier to refuse e-mails or phone calls than to personally address someone, but if you don't want to see this potential partner again, the least you can do is give her the courtesy of some closure.

You may not think you are the type who could ever become *so* smitten that you could be swept away by passion. But don't be so quick to assume—it happens all the time! Still, how you act on it is up to you, as you alone are responsible for your actions and their consequences. If you are feeling torn, consider this: If you feel this passionate *right now*, shouldn't you also expect to feel that way in the future when you know each other better? If so, then what's the rush? Whatever you decide, just make sure that the decision is mutual and that your actions are safe and responsible. Never agree to have sex to be accommodating, and remember that anyone who pushes you doesn't care about you.

If You Don't Want Another Date

Even if you are incredibly tempted to tell that toad to hit the road—here, now, in person—think twice. Doing so will only make that bad date even worse. Chances are if the date was that horrible, the feelings are mutual and you probably won't go out again. If you don't want another date, don't end with a trite, throwaway phrase such as "I'll call you" or "Call me" or "See you soon" if you don't mean it. These types of remarks raise expectations and are a common reason for many awkward misunderstandings.

The person who used the throwaway phrase wonders why he is being hounded for another date. The person doing the "hounding" can't understand why she is being rejected. After all, didn't her potential partner say "We should do this again some time" or Call me"? If you are sure you'd rather eat live worms than see this person again, the best way to end your date is just to offer a handshake (your date knows no kiss will be offered) and say, "I had an *interesting* time" (not *fun*, or *nice*) or "It was nice to meet you." These statements are sincere, but promise nothing and offer no encouragement for another date.

QUESTION?

What if you get vibes that your date isn't interested, but you don't want to give up?

You may feel compelled to keep trying to win the interest of someone you are attracted to, but in the end, the best thing to do is respect your date's wishes. And truthfully, you don't want to force someone to date you—it has to be mutual. Though you may be frustrated and wonder why this person doesn't want to see you, rest assured that there is someone better out there for you who will enjoy your company as much as you do his.

Sometimes it turns out that a single simply isn't ready to embark on a dating journey, even though he'd like to. When this happens, the best policy is to own up to the fact that the timing isn't right. There's no purpose to giving your date hope that you could fall in love if you're still not over your ex, your father's recent passing, or a job-related bout of depression. Get your issues worked out before you drag someone else into the mix. Otherwise you could find yourself in a situation similar to Greg and Debbie's:

> "Greg, a recent widower, assured me he was ready to date again, but when we went out all he talked about was his deceased wife. At one point he sobbed that he'd never again find anyone as wonderful as his "sainted darling." I was embarrassed and annoyed. I felt sorry for Greg and I liked him, but I knew I wouldn't go out with him again. He might make a great partner someday, but he definitely wasn't ready for a relationship now— and I definitely was. (Debbie, 56, Bank Manager)

Chapter 13

E Challenging Dating Situations

This chapter deals with some serious topics that you might not have considered, from merely difficult dating situations to downright dangerous ones. The material presented here is not intended to scare you; its purpose is just to raise your awareness level in the unlikely event that you find yourself in harm's way. Think of this information as another set of helpful resources in your dating toolkit. The more information you have, the happier and safer your dating journey will be.

The Insufferable Boor

A mismatched couple on a date is like an interview where both the job and the job candidate look great on paper but are clearly a wrong match in person. But still, to be considerate, the interviewer and the interviewee usually talk for just a short while before the interview ends.

A date is really no different than an interview. It's just a romantic "interview" for the "job" of being a romantic partner! As with other interviews, it's polite and the parties are expected to talk pleasantly for a short while before ending the date. In other words, even if you know your date will never be your special someone, you are not really justified in ditching him mid-date unless he is truly insufferable, unstable, wild, demented, or dangerous, like Nadine found James to be:

> James wrote in his personal ad that he was in his early thirties and a successful businessman who looked like Brad Pitt and was a tennis champion. When we met for lunch, it became clear that James was at least twenty years older than he claimed and had none of the other attributes that he had advertised. When I asked him why he would blatantly lie, he sneered, "To get young babes like you to go out with me." I told him that lying to women is dishonest and disrespectful, and it wasn't going to get him a second date with me. To my amazement he replied, "Who cares? You're here NOW, aren't you?" It quickly became evident that James wasn't interested in getting to know anyone, but just to talk "dirty" to them without having to pay for the pleasure! Once I realized this, I could see no reason to stick out the date any longer. I excused myself to the restroom, gave the waitress money to cover my half of the check, and left. I normally wouldn't ditch a date, but this time it was clearly the right decision. I didn't feel the least bit bad about it. (Nadine, 25, Banker)

It's a waste of your time, not to mention a blow to your dignity, to hang around while someone harasses and upsets you. If someone really crosses the line of appropriate behavior, you don't have to be "nice" and take it. Find a way to excuse yourself and leave.

Embarrassing Episodes

Surely you've suffered through some embarrassing moments in your life. They're bound to happen, and the only way to get through them is to be a good sport, chalk it up to experience, and forget about it. Just try to remember that these things happen to everyone, and as long as no serious damage is done, it's best to just acknowledge it and move on. Here's what happened to Christine:

> *I excused myself to the ladies room. My date was grinning as I came back toward our table. I figured he was smiling because I looked so cute in my sexy pants outfit, but before I sat down again he said: "I think you might want to zip your pants up.' I looked down. To my horror, my pants were wide open and my lacy g-string was displayed for everyone to admire! The people at the nearby tables were staring, too. I was absolutely mortified! I know this could have happened to anyone and my date made like it was no big deal, but I can't forget how humiliated I was. I couldn't face going out with him again. (Christine, 22, Purchasing)*

Don't let an experience like Christine's get in the way of enjoying your date with a great person. If you can laugh it off and continue the date unscathed it will show your date that you are a resilient person with a good sense of humor. The fact of the matter is that most embarrassing moments seem horrible at the time but turn out to be pretty funny in retrospect.

If you do have an embarrassing experience during a date, don't run to the bathroom and hide there for the rest of the night. Shake it off as best you can and finish the date. If you're still feeling upset by the time you get home, call a close friend or family member to get it off your chest. After a good chat and a restful night's sleep, the incident will not seem so serious anymore.

Under the Influence

Drug and alcohol use is an individual and personal matter for every adult. If you like to party hard with friends, do it when you're not dating, and take turns being the designated driver. That way you will all be safe, if not all sober. However, when you are dating, drugs and drinking in more than a very limited quantity can be trouble. Not all of your dates may realize this, but at least you will know better than to show up intoxicated for a date.

Handling an out-of-control date is difficult but not impossible. First, get your potential partner away from the source of the trouble. Take charge and get him some coffee. Suggest a brisk walk. If your date resists or won't sober up, help him to find a taxi or ask for the name and number of a person who can come and get him. If your date refuses these suggestions, too, ask a bystander for help or call the police. If none of these tactics work, you have to assume that you've done your best to ensure a safe end to the date and there is nothing more you can do. Do your best to leave your date somewhere safe to sober up on his own. Then leave. In the end, your own safety is paramount.

Here are some basic suggestions for how to safely deal with drugs and alcohol:

- Never leave a drink unattended with someone you've just met. Drink it, dump it, or give it to someone you can trust to watch it.
- Don't share drinks with someone you have just met.
- If you don't know the host or hostess at a party, don't drink from the punch bowl or other communal containers that might be spiked. If anything tastes or smells strange, don't drink it.
- If you are uncomfortable doing an activity when you are sober, you definitely shouldn't do it when you are drunk or high. Drinking and drugs will dull your ability to think with a clear head, so set your boundaries of behavior beforehand and stick to them.

Keep in mind that the tales you hear about one-night stands and waking up next to strangers really do happen. Even the most cautious, conservative person can put her guard down after a few drinks. If you're not careful, you could end up in Janine's situation:

> *I was already drunk when Rudy made a beeline for me. He seemed so witty, sophisticated, and cute. We ended up in his apartment in bed, even though I am not into one-night stands. The next morning I realized that he was not as witty and adorable as he seemed the evening before. We had nothing to say to one another and I felt really awkward. Next time I go out I will stay sober. (Janine, 44, City Worker)*

Violence

Sometimes you can't tell that you are in a potentially dangerous situation, but your gut reaction to people and places can often give you a clue. If you are trying to decide whether to stick it out through a bad date or leave, trust your instincts. If something seems wrong, get out of there.

ALERT!

Date rape drugs are odorless and can't be detected when mixed in a drink. Victims generally become disoriented, helpless, or completely unconscious and often describe the experience as confusing and terrifying. *Never* leave a drink unattended or accept a drink from anyone you don't know other than a bartender.

Many ploys that dangerous offenders use might seem quite commonplace, like someone at a bar buying you a drink. However, if you don't have your eye on the drink from the time the bartender pours it to the time it is given to you, there is an opportunity for someone to add a drug to your drink—to "slip you a Mickey." A Mickey—a Mickey Finn—is a drink doctored with chloralhydrate that, when given in a certain dose, can render a victim unconscious.

You might believe that the types of people you meet and date would never resort to such devious, immoral behavior—but you *could* be wrong. Date rape drugs can make you think that you consented to something, even if you didn't. If you believe that you might have been drugged and raped, you are likely not imagining it and should check it out immediately. Here's what to do:

- Go to the police station or hospital and report it right away.
- Try not to urinate before getting tested for the possible presence of these drugs, as they can leave your system very quickly.
- Don't douche, bathe, or change clothes before getting help or you may erase evidence of a rape.
- Be courageous, confident, and empowered, not embarrassed or ashamed. You are a victim of a violent crime and you did *not* do anything wrong.
- Get support. Call a crisis center and talk with a counselor. Enlist the help of your family and friends.

FACT

The three most common date rape drugs are GHB (gamma hydroxybutyric acid), Rohypnol (flunitrazepam), and Ketamine (ketamine hydrochloride). People who use these drugs to control you are criminals, and date rape is classified by law enforcement as a "drug-facilitated sexual assault."

While date rape is an obvious act of violence that you must protect yourself against, there are also less severe (though not less significant) acts of violence that can occur on a date. If your date does so much as squeeze your arm too tightly, don't stand for it. When a date makes you feel uncomfortable or unsafe in any way, this automatically crosses a boundary. Don't allow violence of any kind, even if done in jest or as a "joke."

Understanding "NO!"

Some people think no means "yes," or "maybe," or "later." But simply put: NO MEANS NO! Regardless of how someone is dressed, or how flirtatiously someone acts, it is unlawful to have sexual contact with a person who doesn't have the capacity to knowingly consent to the act, meaning anyone who is drugged, drunk, or passed out. If you take advantage of someone who is in this state it is actually considered to be a violent crime.

If you think the person you are with might be an abuser, don't wait to find out. Get away. Make no apologies. You cannot afford to wait and give him the benefit of the doubt. Even if it turns out you were wrong, don't regret your decision. As the saying goes, it's better to be safe than sorry.

Criminals come in all shapes and sizes. They may look like your next-door neighbor, a teacher, or even a trusted religious or political leader. Albert DeSalvo, a.k.a. the Boston Strangler, was a good-looking, educated, well-mannered man, but he was responsible for killing at least eleven single women in Boston in the 1960s. All of his victims were respectable working women who voluntarily let him into their homes because he had gained their confidence. He sexually assaulted and strangled each one. Luckily, DeSalvo was eventually identified by a victim who survived, and he was convicted to life in prison.

The incident of the Boston Strangler exemplifies the fact that it's not always easy to know who to trust. However, there are some danger signs to watch for. Be wary if your date:

- Verbally insults you, ignores you, or disrespects your views
- Gets jealous for no reason and interrogates you intensely about where you've been
- Insists that you ask permission to go anywhere or do anything
- Gets drunk or high and pressures you to do the same
- Pressures you to be alone with him or to have sex
- Isolates you from your family or friends
- Gets physically rough with you (e.g., grabbing, yanking, poking, shoving, pushing)
- Sits too close, blocks your path, or touches you even when you have said no
- Has sudden mood swings or gets easily frustrated and angry

- Seems overly interested in weapons and violent subjects
- Admits to being abusive to an ex, but insists that it was the ex's fault

The number one sign that a date has no plans to respect your wishes is if he ignores that all-important word: "NO!" If you tell your date to stop touching you, using harsh language, or otherwise offending you but to no avail, end the date immediately. He does not care about you and does not deserve another moment of your time.

Inviting Dates In

For many adults, being physically intimate with another person at some point in a blossoming relationship is a natural part of being a serious couple. It may seem like a big leap from that first cup of coffee to being sexually active, but you know in your own mind where you stand on the issue. The decision to expand your relationship in a physical way must be mutual—and safe.

FACT

Anyone who insists upon sex from you as a proof of affection or refuses to wear a condom or get tested for HIV doesn't really care about you or your future. Getting tested for HIV and other diseases and then formally sharing the results with a new partner has actually become a modern rite of passage for many couples wanting to take their relationship to the next level.

Dating is an emotional experience, and often couples get swept away on a sea of unanticipated passion. Even if you think you are never going to fall into the arms of someone on a whim, remember that even sensible people occasionally surprise themselves. It may seem too calculated to carry protection, but it's too late to worry about the results of spontaneous, unprotected sex after it's over. Your date may whine about condoms or claim not to have any, but thanks to your dating kit, you will have them and you will *insist* upon using them! Unplanned pregnancy aside, sexually transmitted diseases can seriously affect your health and even be fatal.

You may also come across potential partners who think that if you have been in a serious relationship, were previously married, or are over a certain age, you should be ready for sex because you've already done it before. This is nonsense! Your willingness to have sex should not be based on age or your previous sexual experiences. The right time to have sex is only when both of you are ready, willing, and able. Anyone who pushes you further than you feel comfortable should be immediately rejected.

ALERT!

For some, having sex early in the relationship increases intimacy to a comfortable level. For others, it can cause feelings of rejection and disappointment. Only you and your partner will know what and when works for you. As long as you are mature enough to understand and accept the emotional and physical consequences of your actions, do what you feel is right.

Ending It at the Door

At some point in your relationship with a potential partner you will want to divulge where you live and invite your partner in to see your digs. However, there will likely be an intermediate period while you are getting to know one another, during which you may want your date to accompany you home but not *into* your home. Until you are ready, it's perfectly acceptable to thank your date and say your farewells before you walk in the door. All you have to do is stop short of the door, block it with your body, and say, "Thank you for escorting me home. I'm going in now." Then don't linger or you'll send a mixed message.

Don't let a date talk you into letting him in when you're not ready. Be honest and say, "I really like you, but I'm not comfortable enough to invite you in just yet." Anyone who insists is not someone you want to date, anyway. Give your date a good-night kiss if you want to be encouraging. By the time you are willing to let someone walk you home, if you still don't feel like kissing him it's a possible sign that you are not attracted enough to maintain a relationship long term.

Taking Things Further

The next step is to ask your date in, but not for a sleepover. You probably would not be surprised to know that the largest group of "bad date" horror stories stem from the time when a date enters someone's house for the first time. To avoid problems, set boundaries and let your date know what they are from the start. You might say, "I'd like you to come up for a drink, but just a quick one. I have to get up early tomorrow." Once your date has finished that drink, communicate that time's up. Don't offer more refreshments, play just one more song, or start talking about a subject bound to prolong the conversation. Instead, say, "This has been fun, but I'm very tired and we both should go home and get some sleep." Casually stand up, hand your date her things and move toward the door. You date should follow, but if she doesn't take the hint, reinforce the fact that you want her to leave, now.

Your most effective means of protection may be something readily at hand. If you are attacked, use your fingers or your keys and jab your attacker in the eyes. Kick, scream, and don't be afraid to bite—hard. Carry a small, loud whistle on your key chain to attract attention. Be aware that your attacker can grab a weapon such as a stun gun or knife and turn it on you, so use weapons carefully or not at all.

There are some people who think that you will change your mind if they hold out long enough. Don't allow yourself to be intimidated. If your date is still riveted to your couch after repeated requests from you to leave, affirm in a friendly but serious tone: "I mean it. You have got to go home now. Please respect my wishes." If you would like to see this person again but she still isn't leaving, speak sternly. Hopefully your date will grumble "Okay, okay, I'm going" and leave. If your date doesn't move, there is no use in arguing. Call a neighbor or a friend to come over, go inside your bedroom and lock the door, or simply announce that you are calling the police. In the unlikely case that even these tactics don't work and you feel threatened, leave your date right where he is and go to seek help. Here's how Andrea got herself out of a sticky situation:

> "I invited Robert for a quick nightcap, but by 1:00 in the morning he still showed no signs of leaving. I liked him but I wasn't ready for him to stay the night. No matter what I did or said, he just wouldn't go. He didn't seem threatening, just socially inept. Finally, after Robert resisted all my efforts and had tried my patience to the breaking point I stood up and said: "Robert, if you insist on staying, I can no longer entertain you. I need my sleep and I'm going to go into my bedroom alone—and I'm locking the door. So, see you in the morning." Robert finally got up and left, but it was a real struggle. (Andrea, 41, Pharmacist)

Stalkers

Hopefully, the worst that ever befalls you is an overeager suitor who makes a few too many phone calls before realizing that you are not responding, and then gives up. This is not quite stalking, but it's similar. Most people think of stalkers as obsessed fans of celebrities, but more commonly, stalkers are people with whom you have previously had a relationship that has now ended. Immature and mentally unstable people may try to take revenge if you refuse to date them, from inundating you with phone calls, e-mails, and unwanted love notes and gifts to sitting outside your house, following you, attacking you, or causing harm to your home, property, or person. On the Internet, stalkers may make verbal threats or try to infect your computer with viruses. They may even try to hijack your identity and trash your reputation.

The most important thing to know about stalkers is that they want to be in control. They know how to intimidate their victims so they won't fight back. If the stalking is the result of a failed relationship, you may feel guilty, as though you brought this upon yourself just by being friendly. You haven't! Stalkers are violent abusers and the victim is not to blame. If you believe that you have a stalker on your hands, the first thing to do is let him or her know that you are in control and you will not give in. It is pointless to try to reason with stalkers because, like exhibitionists, they are gratified by your responses. Repeated explanations and contact is exactly what the stalker wants. So just tell the person "NO" and break off all contact after that.

Sometimes stalkers, especially lonely single men, do not have the social skills to understand the difference between being overly eager to gain attention and harassment. The following example is an excerpt from an actual letter sent by a single man to a dating coach:

> *I have never been in a serious relationship with a woman, but I'm turning forty, and I think I'd like one now. I made a good living when I had a job. I met a nice woman in a civic association. She is new in town. I sent her an e-mail, but she didn't respond, so I sent her flowers. At the next civic association meeting, we chatted, briefly, but she didn't accept my offer to go for coffee. I called her a few times after that, but all I got was her answering machine. I kept calling for weeks after that and I don't know why she never returned my calls. I believe in going after what I want, so her lack of positive response doesn't deter me. I sent her lots of romantic greeting cards. I showed up at her house unannounced as a surprise, with gifts. I can't understand why she was upset. I told her that I just wanted to get to know her better. She told me that she had recently gone through a horrible divorce and wasn't ready to date anyone right now but I refuse to give up as I want her to go out with me. I feel that I'm not connecting with her as I should, but I'll keep trying. I am sure that she really wants to be with me and she is just playing hard to get. (Anonymous male, 40)*

FACT

Not all stalkers are psychopaths and murderous criminals in search of victims. Some are just socially awkward people who don't know how to properly pursue a date. However, this doesn't mean they are any less dangerous to you. If you feel seriously threatened, call the police and inform them of the situation immediately.

If you are being stalked, don't ignore it. The situation will not improve on its own. Notify the police and keep notes. Even small things can help to show a pattern of criminal harassment. Note time, date, and place of every e-mail, in-person contact, phone call, or event with the stalker. Screen your calls. Tell everyone that you are being stalked. If you have a photo of the stalker, share it with those who might come in contact with him. If necessary, get a restraining order. Locate safe places to go, other than home, in case you are followed.

Challenging situations are a part of every dating journey. If something bad happens to you on your dating journey that traumatizes you, keep in mind former First Lady Eleanor Roosevelt's wisdom that nobody can make you feel inferior without your consent. "You gain strength, courage and confidence by every experience in which you really stop to look fear in the face. You are able to say to yourself: 'I lived through this horror. I can take the next thing that comes along.'" Eleanor Roosevelt, *You Learn By Living*, 1960.

Chapter 14

Narrowing Down the Possibilities

If you have been following the suggestions given in this book so far, you have likely become much more approachable and confident. You've aced the art of conversation, and you have learned what makes a date great. You've also been dating some possible partners. So now it's time to assess your dates' true potential and figure out which of them might be worthy of a second date—or more. This chapter will tell you how to use your dating journal, your gut instincts, and your common sense to decide whether you should move forward with one special partner or keep looking.

The Ultimate Dating Tool

As you learned in the beginning of the book, your dating journal is your relationship road map. Even if you didn't initially take the suggestion to start your very own dating journal, why not start one now? Your dating journal is among the most valuable devices you have at your disposal during your dating journey. It can be as simple as a spiral-bound notebook or as high-tech as an electronic spreadsheet. Whatever method you use, be sure to keep your journal up-to-date, organized, and coherent. After all, you're going to be referencing it countless times throughout your dating adventure.

You can set up your dating journal any way you wish, as long as the information you include is consistent for each potential partner. This becomes more important as you have more and more dating experiences. Try to enter whatever information you have after a date as quickly as possible before you forget the details. Don't forget the following:

- A beginning investigation and statement of your relationship goals and a note of any changes you make along the way.
- For each person you meet and date, write down name and contact information and any specifics you know, such as physical characteristics, age, occupation, interests, obvious assets, and potential liabilities.
- Record where you met or how and by whom you were introduced to each person, and specifics about your date(s) including where you went and a general impression or rating of that dating experience, along with any follow-ups.
- Keep adding new people and more details for each person. If you stop seeing someone, write down when and why.

Here are one woman's impressions of the experience of keeping a dating journal:

> *I looked forward to writing in my dating journal after each date. It gave me a safe, private outlet to express my feelings without being judged. When my relationship fizzled, I was able to review my dating journal not only to get more insight on what I might do differently this time, but also*

to look up a few former possibilities again. I reconnected with a man that somehow I overlooked as a perfect partner last time, and this time, things are going great. (Olivia, 34, Police Officer)

You will no longer need to record your dating experiences when you've finally found your perfect partner and are no longer dating. But if writing down your thoughts has become a pleasurable routine, you might want to start a *new* journal—of your first year as a couple!

Taking Notes

When you were in school you took notes in your classes so that later on you could remember what was said. Taking notes for a love search has the same purpose—you can remember and refer back to information you may need in the future. If you have already started your dating journal as suggested, the chances are also good that you have recorded your relationship goals, your own assets and liabilities, and your requirements, including the major assets and liabilities, for a partner. You are already taking notes about each person you have met and dated. Your efforts will pay you dividends for a lifetime, not only as an entertaining trip down memory lane in the future, but more importantly, to help you view your dating journey progress in a visible way right now.

If you are honest and consistent about adding information, you can identify patterns and problems. You will see where you might be veering off the path to your relationship goal, and what you are doing that speeds your search for love. At the very least, your journal will give you insight into yourself that you might have overlooked.

Warning!

Safeguard your journal and your notes. They are for your use and your eyes only. Never make dating journal entries at work or leave your notebook lying around. Password-protect your personal entry files on your computer and take other precautions to keep roving eyes off your private thoughts and observations.

Also, don't put personal information of any type on a company computer. Many firms use software that can pry open computer files even if they are password protected, and a deleted file may still show up in a hidden backup, rather than be permanently erased. Do not make your dates public online. You may be tempted to keep a blog or a Web site updated with the names and particulars of your dates, but in doing so you will be compromising their privacy, as well as your own.

Using Your Journal to Move Forward

As your dating journey continues, your dating journal will teach you things you never knew about yourself. It will reveal patterns you may not have noticed regarding who you are attracted to, how you make connections, and what type of dating personality you have. You may find that many of your choices are unavailable (emotionally or otherwise) or that you are in a dating rut—dating too much or too little, or doing the same activity over and over again.

It's not enough to just keep a dating journal—you must be honest about it. First of all, you need to write sincerely and truthfully about your experiences. Stretching the truth in your journal is counterproductive. Also, you must be honest with yourself when you evaluate your journal entries. Even if you don't want to see a negative pattern, you first need to acknowledge it in order to change things.

On a practical note, if things are going well with someone, your dating journal will help you remember information that you might otherwise forget (e.g., birthday, favorite song, children's names) to help you move the relationship forward. Keeping a record of his dating experiences has certainly helped Andrew in more ways than one:

I am a busy person. And I initially didn't think I'd like dealing with a dating journal. However, after bad divorces and a lot of disappointing dates, my "coach" insisted that keeping a dating journal was essential for me. I have been making careful notes on every one of my social encounters for six months now. As I continue my dating journey I find that writing

*actually helps me to feel more positive, productive, organized, and profes-
sional. I like recording information about my dates because it is proactive,
and helps me assess my progress in a tangible way. It is actually adding
enjoyment to my dating adventure. (Andrew, 55, Mathematician)*

Reading Signals

You've finally met someone who's perfect—or at least you think so. But suddenly, your perfect potential partner seems distant and unavailable. You
haven't a clue why—things were going so well! You can't think of anything
you said or did to turn your partner away, and you are confused and upset.
When in this situation, you have two choices. You can either delude yourself into thinking that your potentially perfect partner is somewhere with no
access to phones, computers, or postal service—that's obviously why she
hasn't contacted you. Or you can be honest with yourself and conclude that
you and your potentially perfect partner weren't mutually the best match.

Not everyone handles conflict well. Right or wrong, some people feel
that if they just break off contact, you'll get the message without ever
having to suffer through a painful, emotional ending. Unfortunately,
this method rarely works well. If you have been dumped by someone
who won't give you the courtesy of a reason, you are within your rights
to try and find out. If this former partner won't respond after a few tries,
however, you have no choice but to write him off. Comfort yourself by
affirming that he was inconsiderate to end your relationship without
allowing you the benefit of closure. Then, move on with your life.

Even busy people will stay in touch if they want to be with you. Little to
no contact is a sure sign that the other person is no longer interested. If you
sense something is up and want definite closure, it is appropriate for you
to make a few calls over the course of a couple of weeks asking what's up.
If you haven't made contact or resolved things after that, assume that your
potential partner is telling you she is no longer interested in you. You can

continue convincing yourself that your potentially perfect partner is just "a bit busy this week," and chances are she *is* busy—with someone else! At this point, the reason is not as important as the reality of the message: You have been dumped.

Most if not all of your relationships will begin with some potential. But as you continue to date, you are likely to learn things about some of your potential partners that indicate that you are not a perfect match. Since dating is more a process of elimination than of selection, this is a common dating experience. Most new connections actually are dissolved after just a couple of dates, to up to six months.

Obviously, being dumped or dumping someone is not the most pleasant part of dating. Whether you are doing the dumping or are being dumped, keep in mind that this type of elimination is *not* a failure or a reflection on worth or desirability. The reality of dating is that neither you nor your ex-partner will be the ideal match for the overwhelming majority of people you meet and date.

Do an Investigation

Sometimes your gut instinct tells you that someone is too good to be true. In the old days, you might have checked this person out through personal connections, or a private investigator. Today, with the Internet at your disposal, you can simply search for your potential partner's name in any search engine. If she spends time online, is published, works for a large company, posts on forums or bulletin boards, or is part of a social, professional, or alumni association, you are likely to find at least some references to her in an instant.

Is she claiming to be a big shot at a large company? The corporate Web site will give you easy access to check. Did he say he graduated from an Ivy League school? The alumni association online will shed light on the truth. The more you search, the more you are likely to find. You might also consider using an online investigative service and let them do the digging. They can do everything from a quick search to a full background check and the basics cost less than a modest dinner in many cases. If you prefer to go the more traditional route, you can use a private investigator, or gain your own access to all sorts of public information through the library and public agencies to help you determine if this person is who she claims.

Here's Rosa Clare's story:

" I met Chuck through my church so I didn't think I needed to check him out. Luckily, when another woman in my church (who had dated Chuck) found out, she told me a different story than Chuck did. Chuck told me he was saving his money to put his teenage son through college, so I had to pay for our dates. This other woman confirmed that Chuck didn't even have a son. And his claim that his ex-wife took all his money was also untrue. Chuck was a compulsive gambler who lost all his money and was being targeted for big debts by some loan sharks! When Chuck asked me for several thousand dollars as a deposit on an apartment, I told him that we were through. I also alerted all the single women in my church about Chuck. When he realized he had been found out, he changed churches. I'm sure he's somewhere else, scamming other women. (Rosa Clare, 32, Office Manager)"

If You're Doing the Dumping

If you have decided not to date someone anymore, there is no need to give him a list of all shortcomings or cause him any more pain than is absolutely necessary. Remember: What goes around, comes around. Be kind in your dealings with others and others will be kind to you.

In order to avoid a traumatic end to a relationship, some people choose not to break up in a direct way, but to simply to do a slow fade. Their calls become less frequent. They begin to argue and emphasize all the ways they are unsuitable for the other person. Eventually, unless the person being rejected is totally clueless, he usually realizes what's happening. The slow fade can backfire with someone who just can't take no for an answer. In most cases if you are sure you don't want to be with someone, it's best to let him down gently—but not so slowly that he doesn't get the message and holds onto false hope.

Honesty Works Best

Adults should be able to handle bad news, even if it hurts. Although breaking up with someone in a restaurant or other visible location theoretically should force your newly liberated partner to refrain from screaming, crying, throwing food, etc., in reality public dumping causes public scenes. The kindest way to break up with someone in person is to do it in a private, quiet location. Breaking up with someone over the phone is also acceptable, but only if the relationship has been relatively short. If you are going to break up with someone over the phone, don't blurt it out the moment your soon-to-be ex picks up. Ask if she is alone and available to talk. If she is not, delay the news until you can give her the courtesy of being in a position to handle it.

When you have the person's attention, be firm, clear, and kind. Say that you enjoyed your time together, but affirm that your goal is to find the right partner and you need to keep looking. Be generous. Reiterate this person's good points and avoid as much negativity as possible. Wish your ex-partner love, success, and happiness. Do *not* say "We can still be friends." Maybe at some point you can be, but that's not the right thing to say right now. You may get tears, anger, or pleading as a response. Listen and be sympathetic for a short time, but remain firm in your decision. Taking someone back won't get you (or him) where either of you want to be.

What to Say

Breaking up with someone can be extremely upsetting. You'll probably try to plan out what you're going to say and review the words in your head a thousand times before you finally say them. However, it's best not to obsess over exactly the way you break up with someone, as the message will always be the same. Just be clear, firm, concise, and kind.

Some common "breakup lines" are:

- I think of you as a friend (or brother or sister).
- We have too much of an age difference.
- I'm not attracted to you in "that" way.
- My life is too complicated right now.
- I've got someone else.
- It's not you, it's me.
- I'm concentrating on my career.
- I've decided to swear off men (or women).
- I've decided to stop dating and become celibate.
- We would make better friends.

If You've Been Dumped

Whether you knew it was coming or not, chances are being dumped has got you feeling pretty down. The longer you have been in a relationship and the more emotion you have invested in it, the more it will distress you to realize that it is over. If you have been dumped by someone you really cared about, you may think that she will take you back and see the error of her ways. In nearly every case, you'd be wrong! Whatever compelled your potentially perfect partner to want to end this relationship with you will still be there if you get back together. That was certainly the case for Elizabeth Taylor and Richard Burton, Don Johnson and Melanie Griffith, and Donald and Ivana Trump. They all took their partners back, but didn't make a success of it the second time around, either.

Less frequently, you may be dumped by someone who really does care for you, but upon realizing it, freaks out and bails. Unfortunately, commitment phobias are rarely cured. You will learn more about this in Chapter 16.

Getting dumped is definitely a dating downer, but it also gives you an opportunity to move forward toward your goal if you look on the bright side. You didn't make the match you have dreamed of just yet, but your special someone *is* still out there. Crossing one more person off your list who obviously isn't ideal takes you one step closer to finding the right one—not just *any* one.

FACT

If you are dumped, after the initial shock subsides you may feel angry or vengeful. Acts of angry passion will not change your ex's feelings about you. They will just reinforce the conviction that dumping you was the correct decision. Instead, find consolation in the following wisdom: If you love someone, let him go. If he returns to you, it was meant to be. If he doesn't return, his love was never yours to begin with.

Dive Back into the Dating Pool

If your relationship with someone has ended, it doesn't mean your dating journey has. You must still find a way to continue dating if you hope to eventually meet your special someone. This isn't always easy when you feel hurt or disappointed. You might want to take a short break, and while you are doing so, consider the following: Whatever the reason, the two of you just didn't match each other's requirements well enough. Neither of you are failures or bad people. You just want different things. You have both learned from and been enriched by the relationship. You may be wondering what your former partner is doing, even if you have new romantic interests brewing with others. There may be occasions where you date someone new and that doesn't work out, and you feel you will never reach your relationship goals. Some frustration is normal on a dating journey, but negative thinking won't help you get where you want to be.

Things don't always work out as you plan, and you may not get it right on the first, second, or even third try. But giving up won't get you anywhere. Luckily for her, Velene summoned her courage and took the plunge back into the dating pool after her divorce:

> *I had just gotten divorced and wasn't really up to going out. My friend suggested online dating. I was reluctant, but curious. Leon's profile caught my eye. He seemed so confident, offbeat, and he had an adorable smile. After we'd been e-mailing and chatting on the phone for some time, we wanted to meet. Unfortunately, I broke my leg right before our first real date. Then, Leon contracted pneumonia. It took nearly four more months before we finally got together in person. When we did, we were already close friends and it was instant magic! We eventually bought a house together. The night we moved in, Leon proposed. Naturally, I accepted. (Velene, 44, Web Designer)*

There are plenty more fish in the sea. If you aren't igniting a flame with anyone new, reassess your goals and requirements before you go "fishing" for a new catch. You may be surprised to find that what you *think* you want in a mate has changed. Your new potential perfect partner is still out there, waiting to meet you.

Chapter 15

Beyond the First Date

That date was *great*! You talked. You laughed. You exchanged opinions. You learned more about each other. Maybe this is a mutual attraction! If you think you might want to take things to the next level with a potential partner, you have several options. This chapter will give you fun ideas for follow-up dates and help you handle some not-so-great dating situations. It will also give you guidelines to determine whether you are genuinely clicking with someone, and suggestions for how to express your true feelings.

Great Second- and Third-Date Ideas

During the first date you kept things pretty mellow so you could get to know each other. But now that you have more information about this person, why not make your next dates more exciting? Traditional activities such as movies, dinner, picnics, and theater are always appropriate, but your dating journey will be more fun if you do things that not only let you learn about each other but provide fun and memorable bonding experiences.

Doing something as a "team" on a date helps you create a more meaningful connection. An added bonus is that you'll focus on the fun you're having and stop thinking about the fact that it's a *date*. Here are some ideas to try:

- **For volunteers:** Do some good together. Volunteer at your local park or community garden, deliver or serve meals as a duo at a shelter or senior center, or enter a "walk for the cause" event as a couple.
- **For literary types:** If the weather isn't wonderful, do something indoors. Check the papers for in-house book signings at your local bookstore, or readings by authors at the library. Browsing stacks of books also gives you built-in topics of conversation.
- **For lifelong learners:** It takes two to tango, so why not take a one-session dance class? Or learn a new sport neither of you has tried, such as in-line skating, skiing, or tai kwan do.
- **For outdoorsy types:** Go apple-picking, hike a local mountain, or enter a sandcastle-building contest at the beach. No matter what activity you choose, you'll be enjoying the great outdoors with your sweetie.
- **For house hunters:** Are you both interested in real estate? Spend the afternoon visiting open houses. Take a walking tour of an interesting local neighborhood or take a theme tour (e.g., haunted houses, homes of famous writers, or Victorian homes).

After More than a Few Dates

You've had a couple of dates and no longer feel like strangers. If you think you are ready for (a bit) more intimacy, read on and discover some ideas that will bring you physically closer together, but not necessarily in an overtly sexual way (unless that's where you want things to go). Remember to stop and evaluate your level of comfort before you bring things to each new level.

Bring Your Date Home

Invite your date into your home and try out what you learned in that cooking class you took together. Set a romantic table complete with china and candles. You can buy or prepare all the ingredients yourself first, but cook the meal together. If you want to end the date outside of your home, go out for dessert. It is romantic, less expensive than a full dinner at a restaurant, and you will be saying goodnight in a public place instead of your living room.

You could also invite some of your friends and your partner's friends to an informal gathering—a Super Bowl party, for example. Offbeat holidays such as Groundhog Day and Sadie Hawkins Day are also good excuses to throw a party. Your friends get to meet your potential partner, and who knows? Some might make a love connection of their own with other guests. If a crowd is not your style, invite one other couple over for dessert and a night of board games, or watch a movie. This gives you a chance to see how you both interact with others in a social setting. Obviously, these ideas are best when you are already clicking as a couple.

You can also make a date for an offbeat hour. Fly a kite together in your backyard just as the sun is rising. Your spirits will soar! Or have wine and cheese and get together just to watch the sun set. It's a nice way to end the day.

A fun option is to invite your date to your house for brunch. Add a twist and create a picnic indoors. Spread a blanket on the floor and serve everything from a picnic basket just as you would outdoors. Make the food elegant and be sure to serve bloody (or virgin) Marys from a thermos. You'll have everything for a picnic but the ants!

Are You Really Clicking?

With luck, your bad dates have been few and your good dates many. By now you may have found someone who seems to be the one you are seeking. If so, you may be wondering whether this could become more serious. You might not yet know for sure. Not having a clear sense of how you feel doesn't mean that the relationship isn't good. Love at first sight is a wildly romantic concept, but real feelings take time to develop. If you aren't sure how things are going, just relax, continue spending time together, and don't worry about the future. Eventually, you'll get a clearer sense of how things are progressing.

Will Sex Make the Relationship Stronger?

Ideally, both potential partners will be ready for more intimacy at approximately the same time, but this isn't always so. One day, both of you are mutually likely to feel a certain closeness that you want to act on. However, many new relationships end within the first three to five months, so it's wise to keep the sexual energy to a slow simmer until both of you are sure of each other.

Caution aside, if you have been dating for a few months and one or both of you don't feel much attraction, that is a definite sign that the relationship isn't all you want it to be. If you feel attracted, but aren't sure to what degree this person is the right one for you, check your dating journal. Based on what you've outlined in the past, does this person generally meet your requirements? Ask yourself the following questions:

- Is this a person I respect and admire?
- Is this a person who respects and admires me?
- Is this a person who has similar life beliefs and values as mine?
- Is this someone who shares my vision of the future?
- Is this someone I can really talk to?
- Is this someone who feels comfortable talking to me?
- Am I attracted to this person—mind, body, and soul?

The more positive answers you have, the more positive the potential is! If you answered "no" more often than "yes," you might want to take another look at your match. Something's not quite right, and you need to figure it out. Pamela, for instance, picked up several hints that things were headed downhill in her relationship:

> *After we met, Stan called every day. We talked for hours on the phone. But when I suggested getting together in person, Stan always had an excuse why he couldn't. After four months of talk and only two coffee dates, I realized that Stan only wanted me for "good phone" and he wasn't seriously interested in having a real relationship with me. I told him we would be dating in person from now on, or he could just lose my number, permanently! (Pamela, 37, Architect)*

The fact of the matter is that you can't light a fire without a spark, and if the spark isn't there, a relationship probably won't ever evolve. Be honest with yourself early on and discontinue a dead-end relationship before things get too awkward. In most of these cases, sex won't awaken hidden passions—it will just make things more awkward.

Is It Love?

Lots of adult singles are told that they will just "know" when the right one comes along. That's not always true, as love often takes a long time to develop. Meanwhile, if it is lust you feel and not love, you'll recognize it by the fact that you can't keep your hands off one another but you don't really have the other things that make for long-term relationship success. If it's infatuation you feel, you probably are still in the early stages of your relationship where the world revolves around your partner, but you don't know each other very well yet.

If most of the following statements resonate with your situation, chances are it's probably love:

- This partner has told me that he has deep feelings for me, and I feel the same way.
- This partner makes me feel special and good about myself.
- I trust my partner and do not feel jealous with regard to him.
- I would never consider betraying this partner or hurting his feelings.

- I feel secure and calm when I am with this partner.
- When I fight with this partner, we usually make up quickly.
- I feel confident that I can be honest and express my feelings openly with my partner.
- My partner never pressures me to choose between our relationship and my family or friends.
- I feel more able to be myself with my partner than with any other person.
- I can envision a romantic life with this partner, beyond friendship.
- I do not see that this partner has any major liabilities.
- I see this partner as being the possible father of my children.
- My level of physical intimacy with this partner is by mutual desire and consent.
- My relationship with this partner has been tested by differences of taste and opinion and has survived well.

If you related to many of the previous statements, you probably have a very solid relationship. If you have been dating someone for at least six months, the answers to the following questions should further help you to clarify your feelings:

- Would I be willing to let him go if I believed it was the best thing for my special someone?
- Would I still feel this way if my partner gained weight or developed a serious disability or disfigurement?
- Would I be willing to put some or all of my own dreams and goals on hold to allow his dreams to come true?
- Do I really respect and admire this person?

If you answered "yes" to all of these questions it is an indication that you have made a relationship that is based on much more than just chemistry. If both of you feel the same way and you have chemistry too, you have the basics that can turn your relationship into true love.

Saying the L Word

As a wise woman once warned her granddaughter: "Once you spit, you can't pick it up." What she meant, of course, is that once you say something, it's out there forever and you can't take it back.

Loving someone is a precious gift that you can't buy, borrow, rent, or steal. If someone says "I love you" to you, your relationship with this person is forever changed. If you feel in your heart that you are in love with someone, you have found out something wonderful about yourself as well as your special someone. You know that you have the capacity to give and receive love, and that is an amazing feeling.

Who Says What, First?

At some point in every relationship that is moving forward, one or both members of the couple will start realizing that they have deepening feelings for the other person. If it turns into love, one of both of you will eventually want to tell the other. But who says what, first?

Being the first one to say "I love you" is risky. It's a bit like being in a business negotiation where the one who quotes a price first weakens their negotiating position. But love isn't a business deal, and if you feel strongly enough about your feelings, you won't want to hide them for long.

One way to let your partner know how you feel, short of going all-out and declaring "I love you," is to say, "I'm developing really strong feelings for you." This signals your partner that it's safe to reciprocate with a declaration of strong feelings, too. Chances are that by the time you get to "I love you," both of you will already know how the other feels, but it is still a thrilling moment in your dating journey to hear or use this simple, three-word phrase!

How to Say "I Love You"

Don't say "I love you" unless you really mean it. If the words themselves are just too much for you to handle, consider that actions speak louder than words. You can certainly show how much you love someone by what you do. If you love someone, you'll brave a blizzard to bring your sweetie hot chocolate and cinnamon buns fresh from the bakery (or the oven) early on a weekend morning as a surprise. You'll give up front row seats to the final game of the year or a sold-out concert to be your partner's escort to her kid sister's birthday party. If the words don't roll off your tongue, at least go ahead and *show* how much you care.

You can also show your love in abstract ways. For example, be honest and trustworthy. Do *more* than is expected. Get genuinely excited when something good happens to your special someone and genuinely feel pain when things don't go well for him. If you do decide to use the L word, make sure that you present your special, precious gift—the declaration of your love—in a thoughtful way and in a quiet setting. You don't want to scream it out during the final moments of the championship game so that your partner says "Huh?" instead of "I love you, too!" For instance, the way Gabe said those three special words to Carmella really confused her:

> When I met Gabe, I knew right away he was my special someone. One night, after a particularly intense session of sex, he screamed "I love you!" just as we were finishing. I froze! The words I had wanted to hear for so long ended up being said in bed! I didn't know how to respond. I didn't know if he had said "I love you" in the throes of passion, or because he meant that he was in love with me! (Carmella, 29, Real Estate Agent)

Here's a much more successful "I Love You" story:

> My boyfriend and I were both afraid to be first to say "I love you." He broke the stalemate by using the L word in conversations. First he said, "I love your smile." Then, " I love your laugh." Then he looked at me and said, "Actually, I love everything about you." He paused, looked directly into my eyes, and said, "I guess that means—I love you!" It was SO romantic! (Sarina, 29, Harpist)

If It's Not Mutual

Some people fall in love easily, and some people fall in love easily and often. But others need lots of time to sort out their feelings and even more time to declare them formally and out loud. If you are the latter type of person, you should know that you are never obligated to reciprocate with "I love you, too" if you're not sure you feel the same way. Likewise, you should not expect your partner to instantly respond to your declaration of love with the same. Your special someone will respond, when (and if) the time is right.

Love is a precious gift. If someone says "I love you" and you don't feel the same just yet, but you possibly *could*, don't say you do when you don't! Let your partner know that his feelings mean a great deal to you, but that you need more time to know for sure how you feel in return. Your partner may be disappointed, but at least be reassured that you expect your feelings to grow, if more slowly than his.

If you already know that you will *never* love this potential partner, the kindest thing to do is to tell the truth. The chances are that a person you are this close to has already sensed the truth—but the truth still hurts. Elimination of potential partners is part of dating, and both of you gave this relationship a chance. Both of you deserve to find the right partner, not just *any* partner.

All good things take time. That is particularly true of personal relationships. At this point, you may find yourself wondering where your special someone is, or why you continue to meet people but no sparks are flying. This is not the time to be discouraged or to slack off or give up. You have been working toward your goal and you will get there. Now, more than ever, feel confident that you will reach your goal. Every dating experience brings you closer, and you have the resources you need to write a happy ending to your own love story.

Chapter 16

Relationship Trouble Areas

If things are not going well in your relationships, there's likely a good reason for it. You've been getting used to each other's preferences, quirks, and pet peeves, but perhaps things aren't quite clicking. This chapter will help you decide whether a particular relationship has the potential to go the distance (despite occasional bumps in the road) or whether a match is about to fizzle. If you fear the end is near, read on. This chapter will suggest ways to get back on the path to your goals.

Possible Obstacles

If you have a dating journal full of potential partners, but none are standouts, you may be consistently looking at something the wrong way or repeatedly making the same mistake. Some possible reasons for your lack of success thus far are:

- You aren't sure, or haven't clearly defined, what you are seeking and why.
- You aren't being honest about your real needs and desires.
- You are being influenced by outside sources.
- You are looking for the right person but in the wrong places.
- You aren't dating actively enough.
- You are dating so much that you are burned out.
- Your expectations for a partner are unrealistic or unattainable.
- You don't recognize how your behavior affects others.
- You don't know how to communicate or ask for what you want.
- You come across to others as desperate, angry, upset, closed, and/ or bitter.
- You are not ready, or available, for the relationship you say you want.
- You select others who are not ready, or available, for a relationship.
- You are still the "walking wounded" from a previous romance.
- You can't adjust to someone else's routines, needs, and desires.

If one or more of the statements above could apply to you, it's likely that you just aren't in a personal place yet where you are ready for a special relationship. Again, review your dating journal and consider your progress so far. What is blocking you? Could you be subconsciously avoiding the right people? Are you very upset about being single and transmitting your distress so others are afraid to approach you? Are you dishonest about your goals? At this point it would be helpful for you to revisit and redo the goal-setting exercises in the beginning of this book and ask yourself the following questions:

- Am I still sure I want a relationship?
- Have my relationship goals changed? If so, how?

- Am I still attracted to the same types of people as at the start of my dating journey?
- What is the primary appeal of these types, then and now?
- What qualities and/or factors might be causing me to reject people and them to reject me?
- If I have had a few recent relationships that have ended, what caused the breakup?
- Could I be attracted to people who are afraid of commitment?
- Am I looking in the wrong places?
- Am I displaying a positive attitude or do I come across as being negative?

Not all of these questions have easy answers. If all this soul-searching and reassessment seems like too much work, consider that if you don't want to spend the rest of your life searching, you need a clear vision to help you move forward to your goals with less frustration, time, and effort. Until you find the person who is right for you and vice versa, everyone you meet will be a "miss."

Come to an Agreement

Every couple faces major decision points. Should you move forward? Keep things as they are? End the relationship entirely? Ideally, both of you will be sure of what you want at the same time but not every couple is always in sync. You may be with the right person, but at the wrong time. One of you may be ready to make a commitment but the other isn't. You may have irreconcilable differences. You and/or your partner may not be financially, emotionally, or legally ready to move forward. One or both of you may be ambivalent. No matter what, you have to find out.

Signs that your relationship has run its course include:

- Your once hour-long nightly chats are down to five minutes.
- Your partner is too busy to see you on the weekends.
- You and/or your partner aren't interested in physical intimacy.
- You and/or your partner avoid talking about the future.

- Your partner wants "space" or "needs to experience other people."
- Your and/or your partner avoid eye contact.
- You and/or your partner avoid physical contact.
- You fight frequently.
- Your and/or your partner "forget" birthdays or other special days.
- You and/or your partner arrive late for dates or end them early.
- You and/or your partner take up a new interest the other doesn't share.

If any of these occurrences are happening in your relationship, it's time to discuss things with your partner. Perhaps your partner really doesn't notice any change, or perhaps it's time to end things. Either way, a decision must be made between the two of you. Drawing out an unsuccessful relationship is a waste of time and effort for both of you.

Fear of Commitment

Most people enter a relationship wanting to be part of a couple. However, sometimes they like the idea but not the reality. Some adult singles become very set in their ways or become fearful of losing their solo identity if they're in a couple.

Even if your relationship is going well, the reality of becoming part of a twosome is both exciting and frightening. You or your partner may just need some extra time to get in touch with new feelings. Here's Gillie's story:

> *My relationship with Thomas was fine until someone introduced him as my boyfriend. He freaked! That night, he told me he wasn't ready for a serious relationship and wanted to date other people. I had no choice but to agree, even though my heart was breaking and my hopes were dashed. Over the next few months I made an effort to go out with friends, to do volunteer work, and to just keep busy. I was happy to hear from Thomas when he called, and went out with him when he asked, but I didn't push. I guess Thomas must have thought about what he was risking, because he came back and said he couldn't live without me. We eventually got engaged and married several years later. (Gillie, 42, Counselor)*

Luckily for Gillie, Thomas just needed some time to adjust to the relationship and realize that he could retain his identity *and* be in a relationship at the same time. However, sometimes it's not that simple, as in Karen's case:

> *John lost his wife and child in a tragic car accident. We met several years later, but John was still the walking wounded. Every time he looked at me, every time we made love, every time we talked about the future, I know his wife and child were on his mind. We dated for more than two years but John couldn't find a way to put his past in a special place in his heart and open the rest of it to me. I was heartbroken to break up with this wonderful man in whom I had invested my hopes and dreams, but after more than two years of waiting, I knew it was time to move on. (Karen, 35, Health Practitioner)*

If you or your partner is reluctant to commit, set a time limit, as Karen did. If things don't resolve, you have no choice but to cut your losses and find someone else.

The Real Deal with Commitment-Phobes

Commitment-phobes can be charming, but they are toxic to your heart! They will insist that they love you, but they don't have the capacity to give or accept real love. They love the thrill of attraction. Once someone shows true feelings for them, however, they flee.

It isn't always easy to recognize a true commitment-phobe, but a tipoff is the way they pursue you. Most relationships develop in a gradual progression, but commitment-phobes pursue vigorously, in an immediate, overwhelming, and overly enthusiastic manner. They fill your home with flowers. They write love poems to you every day. They profess undying love before they really get to know you. Once you are smitten, they run.

Check It Out

You can tell a lot about whether your partner is just slow to commit or is a true commitment-phobe by looking at her past relationships. Has she had many partners, but no serious relationships? Does she have few friends? Has she suffered a serious trauma that might cause her to shut down emotionally? Is she *unusually, overly* devoted to her mother, or her pet? Does she always cite her partners for the reason the relationship ended or can she not cite any substantive real reasons for these breakups? These are common traits of commitment-phobes.

Marian had the unlucky experience of falling in love with a man who was afraid of commitment:

> "*Gene was the most beautiful, romantic man I ever met. He filled my apartment with flowers. He told me I was the most wonderful woman in the world. He serenaded me from the street below my balcony. He wrote me endless love poems. He gazed deeply into my eyes and never let go of my hand. Gene had a string of past lovers but had never gotten serious with any of them. He said none were "right" but he couldn't say why. The day I told Gene how much I loved him he got the strangest look on his face. He smiled, but he didn't say he loved me back. Then he stopped calling and returning my calls. I had NO idea what I had done to make him reject me! Not long afterward, I read a description of a commitment-phobe and realized this was just like Gene. Our relationship was doomed from the beginning but I didn't recognize it. It took me a long time to get over Gene. I finally got married, years later, but Gene is still single. (Marian, 59, Interior Decorator)*"

Breaking off a relationship with a commitment-phobe is a painful experience. If this happens to you, console yourself with the fact that at least *you* have the capacity to love and be loved. The commitment-phobe will likely never experience that joy.

If Your Date Is Not Free

You might meet someone who seems great at first, but then find out that this potential partner isn't currently free to be with you. The reasons may be that he is married and cheating, or just not yet divorced, but he could also be dealing with complicated career, health, financial, family, or practical or legal issues that block him from getting closer to you.

If you are attracted to a potential partner who isn't free right now but soon *could* be, there is no harm in waiting a little while. Be sure to set a specific time limit to minimize your risk, however. If things don't improve by the deadline, you will have to cut your losses or you could possibly spend the rest of your life waiting. Here's Ernestine's story:

> "Bill told me he was nearly divorced but after I had fallen for him he told me that he hadn't even filed his separation papers! He said he was "busy" and would get around to it eventually. I had no intention of being the other woman. I told Bill that I wouldn't go out with him again unless he filed those papers. When Bill called to tell me he had filed the paperwork, I demanded proof since he had previously lied to me. After that, I had to wait two years for his divorce to become final, but I knew it would. I took a calculated risk and stuck with Bill. Now we are married. (Ernestine, 32, Music Teacher)"

Fighting and Making Up

In romance novels, it's common for a terrible row between lovers to break them apart, only to be reunited many years later. The couple realizes that it was a silly fight and that they never stopped loving each other. They live happily ever after, of course. Real life, however, can be quite different.

QUESTION?

What do dreams about fighting signify?
Fighting with strangers in a dream usually represents an internal struggle, but fighting with familiar people may be an extension of real life. In general, fighting in dreams usually symbolizes anger and confusion that comes about in times of change. If nothing is changing in your life, it may be a clue that a change is needed or that there is something about yourself that you want to change.

In real life, a fight, even an awful one, doesn't usually end a loving relationship. A certain degree of discord and disagreement is to be expected (and can actually be healthy) in every relationship as you learn how to negotiate and resolve differences with one another. On the other hand, chronic fighting with no resolution can signal serious relationship trouble:

> *Brad and I had been dating for nearly three years. I wanted to get married and start a family but Brad kept saying he didn't want children, and he wasn't even sure he wanted to get married. He also couldn't seem to hold a job for more than a few months, which worried me. As the weeks and months dragged on, I began to lose patience and hope. While Brad was still trying to figure out what he wanted from life, I had figured it out. I was tired of waiting. We began fighting about everything. The night we finally broke up it was over something really stupid—the right way to cook chili. After I stormed out of his apartment I realized that I could never fix what was wrong between us. The fight was just an excuse to leave for good. (Madelyne, 28, Designer)*

Constructive disagreements can help you clear the air and negotiate solutions to problems in your relationship, but it's not always easy to fight fairly when you are angry. Here are some suggestions to keep in mind:

- Choose your fights carefully and remember what's *really* important.
- Ask yourself: Is the problem really significant, or are you just overreacting?
- Delay your emotions long enough to consider whether the time is right to fight.
- Fight in private. There is nothing more humiliating than knowing the world is watching you bicker. It's rude and inconsiderate to the onlookers, too.
- Remember that it's just a temporary disagreement. Hold your partner's hand to remind you that even though you're angry, you care about one another.
- Clearly define the problem or situation that is upsetting you and stay on topic.
- Tell your partner how *you* plan to be part of the solution—don't just make demands of him!
- Don't interrupt or get defensive. You may completely disagree with everything your partner is saying, but he still has the right to say it.

- Never use threats or sex to get what you want. If you say you are going to end the relationship over an issue, be genuinely ready to follow through.
- Compromise is key. Once you make an agreement, make sure you affirm to each other that you are okay with it.

Dealing with Really Bad News

Imagine this: You've been going out with your partner for some time now. Tonight at dinner, he says, "We need to talk about us." You know what is going to happen next—he is about to *propose*! He fishes around in his pocket. Your heart is beating faster than a hummingbird's wings. He takes something out of his pocket. *It's a ring*, you think. Then, as he opens his hand, you realize that it isn't an engagement ring—it's the key to your apartment. He is breaking up with you to get back together with his ex.

Most of your dating disasters won't be as devastating as *this*. Even so, be comforted that human hearts, including yours, are amazingly resilient. Few breakups are total surprises—you can sense them before they happen. Your partner's attitude might suddenly change. She may become evasive, unavailable, distracted, or hot and cold. She may suddenly be very anxious or busy. She may pick fights with you over nothing. This behavior may be due to worries about work, family, health, or other significant problems. Perhaps a former love has returned or she has just received some shattering news, like a medical diagnosis, that she is afraid to share with you for fear of rejection.

If you think something is up with your partner, be direct in expressing your concern. If you sense something is wrong, you are probably right, and you will need to deal with it. Your relationship is heading for the skids if your partner:

- Is uncommunicative
- Keeps secrets
- Avoids spending time with you
- Is geographically distant and doesn't want to change the situation
- Never asks for commitments from you and never makes any of his own
- Doesn't want to move the relationship forward

- Tells you everything is fine, but his body language and actions tell a different story

No matter how bad the news or how much it hurts, breaking up and moving forward to find someone new is better than being in a confusing holding pattern. You can and will love again!

Heartbreak Hurts

Some problems aren't fixable no matter how much wishing, hoping, and waiting you do. If you discover serious issues that may not be resolved, set a time limit on how long you will wait or risk ending up like Nanette:

> *Charlie didn't tell me eight years ago when we first met that he was married. By the time he confessed, I was in love with this very married man. Every time I tried to break away, Charlie would insist that I was his true love and that he would marry me as soon as he could get free from his wife. That was always "any day." As the years went by, there was always an obstacle: his daughter needed surgery; his mother died; his cousin died; his business was in trouble; they were moving to a new house, etc. I desperately wanted to marry Charlie and start a family, so I tried to be patient. I finally realized that Charlie liked having a wife and a mistress "on the side" when he told me he couldn't leave his wife because his car wouldn't start! I had wasted eight years of my life. I knew we would never be together no matter what he said. I am nearly forty and alone. Charlie is still with his wife and they are expecting another child. (Nanette, 39, Secretary)*

Breaking up feels bad, maybe even horrible. But if you must end things, focus on the fact that if you don't, you will be missing out by staying with someone who can't satisfy your needs. Give yourself credit for having the ability to love, the wisdom to heal, and the courage to try again. Wish your former partner happiness and your good feelings will be reflected back to you. Stay firm in your belief that you will find the love you seek. The next time it will be even better, because you will be with the right person.

Chapter 17

A Fresh Start

At this point in your dating experience, you've probably found at least one partner you really clicked with and started a serious relationship with. You may also have experienced the sting of a breakup, whether it was initiated by you or by your partner. It's certainly difficult to bounce back after an unsuccessful match, but it's not impossible. This chapter will offer practical and constructive ways to feel better, gain a fresh perspective, and try again after dating disappointments.

Dealing with Rejection

Uh-oh! You're at that point in your dating journey where you've hit a snag, a disappointment, or a breakup. At this point, your positive dating journey may feel like a giant dating downer, but don't despair. Negative experiences are part of life—and part of everyone's dating experiences.

In time, you can and will get past the bad feelings, but first it helps to know what you're about to face. There are four basic stages from grief to healing: denial, depression, anger, and acceptance. Depending upon how invested you were in the relationship, the healing process may take weeks, or it may take months. Try to look at this setback in a positive way. You took a chance on a relationship that didn't work out, but you have learned from this experience and it has put you that much closer to finding the right person.

Meanwhile, put your emotions and efforts into things that make you feel good and keep you too busy to feel bad. Reconnect with the people, such as family and friends, you may have neglected when you were busy with your partner. They'll understand, and give you support, too. If it helps you, get spiritual support and positive vibes from working for social and political causes. Don't be afraid to try some self-affirmations such as " I will be fine without _____" or "I will find the right one for me." Thinking and saying positive things has a strong, cumulatively uplifting and empowering effect. You will find more information about them later in this chapter.

Negative experiences aren't worthless; they give you an opportunity to view life with a fresh vision. And even if they leave you reeling with despair, remember: The feeling will pass. Never forget that you are worthy of happiness and you can get it if you want it. Embrace *all* of your experiences, good and bad.

Surviving a Dreadful Night

Life hasn't been kind to you lately. You feel horrible and you can't sleep. You are upset and alone. Things may feel hopeless, but you must remember that there's always light at the end of the tunnel. For now, you just need to focus on making it through the night. Reading this book instead of reaching for the sleeping pills or the cookie jar is a good start.

ALERT!

When you're trying to find ways to get through a lonely night after a breakup, *never* just lie in bed in the dark and contemplate your situation. Do anything else—read, go for a jog, or watch your favorite TV shows. Replace gloomy thoughts with other, lighter ones. Soon you'll tire yourself out, and awake to a brand new day—and every new day brings with it new possibilities.

Here are some quick-fix ideas to get you through a horrible night, especially if it's romance-related:

- Tell your pet how you feel. Any ear will do right now, but especially the one that belongs to your loyal pet-friend. Don't have a live animal in the house? Tell your troubles to the stuffed variety.
- If you live on the East Coast, call someone on the West Coast. It's three hours earlier there. If you live on the West Coast, call someone in another country where it's not so late.
- Write down your feelings in your dating journal. You'll find that the process is habit-forming, especially when you are feeling down. Think of it this way: Your next entry is guaranteed to be a happier one.
- Wash your hair. It's a cleansing experience, literally and figuratively. Don't like showers? Tubs are another relaxing option. Light some candles. Sit, soak, relax! Push out sad thoughts by thinking of things you love.
- Work it out. If you've got equipment or tapes at home, get moving, no matter how late it is. Exercise produces a chemical reaction in your body that elevates your mood. Or just move your body to whatever music moves you.
- The surf is always up, online. Wander through cyberspace surfing for outrageous sites that you can forward to your friends in the morning.

Even better, visit some relationship advice sites and resources for singles (see Appendix A for suggestions).

- Turn on the TV or a movie and temporarily turn off your pain. Entertainment takes your focus off your misery.
- Turn on all of the lights: This *automatically* makes things look brighter!

Unfortunately, these rough nights don't always come in singles. You may have several of them back to back, and the misery may last for weeks or even months if the breakup was especially traumatic. In that case, you'll need some longer term pick-me-ups and strategies to feel more positive. Start wearing cheerful, bright colors to lift your mood. Sign up to be a volunteer for a worthy cause. Reconnect with people, take up favorite hobbies, and fix problems at home and at work that you put aside because you were so focused on your partner. Need tangible proof that good things can happen? Plant some seeds and wait for new growth—in the flower pot and in you.

Curbing Depression and Anger

You know it's finally over. Maybe the breakup *was* for the best, but you can't remember the last time you were happy. Oh—yes you can . . . it was with *him* (or her). Welcome to the second stage of grief: depression. You may be totally obsessed with getting the relationship back. Every song you hear reminds you of your ex. Everyone in the world seems coupled up except you. Movies, books, even television commercials with happy people make you feel sad. Everyone knows you are miserable, from your best friend to the guy at the deli down the street.

This stage may pass quickly, or it may linger. Give yourself permission to feed bad—for a little while. Meanwhile, get a reality check on your feelings. Once you are no longer depressed, you may feel angry and wonder how anyone could do something so cruel to nice, wonderful you! Strange as it sounds, you are actually making positive progress—moving to the third stage in your healing process.

Anger is a hard emotion for many people to handle appropriately. Even if you are normally level-headed, you may find yourself reveling in revenge fantasies about destroying your ex's property or reputation, or sabotaging his or her new relationship. Don't even *think* about it! You will end up feeling ridiculous, and the only person you will hurt is yourself.

If your level of anger is off the charts, this is a definite sign that you should seek professional support. If counseling isn't something you've ever considered before, don't be afraid of it. Therapy is useful for anyone who wants to gain a better understanding of his feelings, get control of a situation or situations, and be guided to make good decisions that improve his life. Anyone in transition or facing a challenge can benefit from just a few sessions with a great therapist. Most people who go to counseling do so because they want more success, not because they are losers or lost souls. Whether you choose online counseling or in-person assistance, make sure that the person you choose is qualified. Get personal recommendations and check credentials. Be sure to ask the therapist questions about costs and procedures before you agree to begin counseling.

FACT

It's true: Living well is the best revenge. The best way to get back at someone who broke your heart is to make yourself happy. If your ex ever inquires, you can assure her that you're doing well—even better, you're doing GREAT!

Anger-Reducing Techniques

If you want to purge your relationship-oriented anger, make sure you do it privately and safely. Violent displays will get you nowhere (except maybe behind bars). Here are a couple of safe agony reducers:

- Write down all the things you hate about your ex. List every nasty thought. Be brutal. Then build a campfire and burn the list to embers. Watch all your anger float away with the smoke.
- Put a photo of your ex on the bottom of your shoe and walk on him all day. Then, literally scrape the remains of this person off your shoe and out of your life!

Take a Break

If you have had a few major disappointments or bad breakups, you might start to think of dating as a hopeless chore. If you feel that way, or you are beginning to feel bitter or upset because you haven't met the right person yet, you need to take a break. A vacation from dating for a few weeks won't hurt you, especially if you feel better afterward. However, unless you want to wipe your social slate completely clean, tell the people you are seeing that you are taking a social sabbatical for a few weeks. You hope this will help you gain a better perspective on your life. Meanwhile, consider sending an occasional "thinking of you" message by phone or e-mail so your potential partners know you are still interested in them.

If taking a vacation from dating doesn't make you feel better, how about taking an actual vacation? There is nothing that better helps you adjust your view of life than being in a different location, whether it's Boston or Bombay. If you can't get away, rearrange the furniture in your home, or change your routine. If you have been going to a lot of singles parties or places where there are large crowds, try something like online dating or personal ads, where your social interactions will be one-on-one. If all you've been doing is making connections one at a time, try a singles social or speed dating, to see what it's like to be with a lot of people all at once. The pressure is off since you're just trying something out, but you are actually *more* likely to meet someone when you're not looking.

Here's what Mary did to help herself move on:

> *When my relationship ended I was so discouraged that I stopped dating entirely. But I kept going to the dance studio where I met my ex, because I really like dancing. A few months later I met Wally at a salsa class. I almost turned down his offer for a date, but decided to take a chance. That was fourteen months ago. Tomorrow we're picking up our wedding rings! (Mary, 34, Cosmetician)*

Self-Affirmations

Self-affirmations seem so simple you may be tempted to write them off as New Age nonsense. They are a classic, time-tested way for people of all ages and goals to handle challenging tasks. Positive thinking and self-empowerment are the driving forces behind the success of self-affirmations. If you can think it, you can believe it. If you can believe it, you can say it. If you say it, you can do it . . . and you *will*. Self-affirmations use personal statements to remind your brain that if you don't quit, you can channel your own inner resources to make your dreams a reality.

Self-affirmation works well for every aspect of your life, not just your dating journey. From work to relationships to just helping yourself to feel confident and great every day, the sky's the limit to what you can accomplish with this form of positive reinforcement.

You simply write out one or more self-affirming statements that have meaning for you, and put them where you are likely to see them often (e.g., on your bathroom mirror, in your car, on the refrigerator, on your computer). Sticky notes are particularly good for this purpose because you can stick and unstick them practically anywhere. Every time you see one of your self-affirming notes, you repeat the message (aloud is better, but you can say it mentally). Repeat your selected affirmation(s) more often if you're getting ready to go into a potentially stressful or difficult situation or time.

The statements can be anything you want them to be, from "I am confident" to "I will find the love I want" to anything that helps you manage an emotion or situation. Ideally you'll make up your own, but here are a few dating-related samples to get you started:

When you need confidence:
- I am worthy.
- I deserve to be treated well.
- I believe in myself.

When you feel disappointed:
- Everything good takes time.
- Every day holds new opportunity.
- I will reach my goal.

For times when you feel you might not meet your special someone:
- My special love is out there.
- I will attract the love I want.
- People are drawn to me.

For times when you feel hopeless:
- I will find love, happiness, and success.
- Everything I do brings me closer to my goals.
- Things are looking up.

Dating Support Teams

Most singles seek support from their family and friends, but these sympathetic ears are too close to you to be impartial. You might also not want to drive them crazy with your distress, or divulge your intimate details or feelings.

Dating support teams are a great way to get support with collective brainpower. These groups offer support, but they're a far cry from group therapy. In actuality, support teams are most commonly used by business executives. The focus isn't so much on dealing with emotions as with generating positive action and results. The members of a *dating* support team are on their own dating journeys. You will all pool your collective experience and wisdom to help each other.

How to Organize a Team

In a dating support team, all members get equal time by dividing the amount of time available by the number of participants. Some groups hire a moderator/timekeeper to make sure the session begins and ends on time, to contact members if there is a change in time or location, and to make sure everyone gets equal time to talk. In most groups, the members just take turns. If this is the case, a member serves as the moderator; he takes his own turn to talk and participates actively in the session. The moderator also provides a two-minute and a final warning to let each member know that his or her time is up, but the group can opt to give additional time to someone who needs it.

FACT

The four most common types of support you will find in support teams are: (1) Brainstorming—asking the group for ideas about how to handle a specific problem; (2) Barn-raising—asking the group to help with resources, information, inspiration, contacts; (3) Role-playing—using the group as a test audience to rehearse a presentation or provide feedback on written materials; and (4) Sympathy—asking the group to act as a sympathetic "ear."

You may use your time any way you wish. If you're late, you join the group in progress. There is no backtracking for latecomers! When it is your turn, be prepared with a purpose or goal for that session and ask the group for the type of support that you require. You will also be encouraged to report your progress from the previous session and to advise the group as to your next steps to reach your goal. After your time is up, you listen and interact honestly and freely with the other members in the group as they request or require.

Start Your Own Group to "Get a Grip"

You can join a group in progress (check bulletin boards, newspapers, and the Internet) or start your own group. You need at least four, and no more than ten, adults who are actively pursuing a relationship journey. Their romantic goals, ages, lifestyles, or professions needn't be the same. Select a regularly scheduled time to meet for an hour to two hours on a regular basis. Bimonthly is the standard. Find a quiet, private place to talk. You can take turns hosting in each other's homes or find places that offer rooms for community activities.

This experience worked really well for Jon:

> *When I was ready to look for love again I was pretty nervous about calling the woman advertising the dating success team, but she turned out to be really nice and a single parent like me. Our group was pretty diverse in age and profession. Some were re-entering the dating scene after a long absence, but others had been dating for a long while, too. Our differences were helpful in seeing different points of view. We did gripe some, but mostly we stuck to positive action and support. It was easy to stay motivated because once I told the group I was going to do something, I knew I would have to report on it the next time. We supported one another in practical ways, too. For example, a woman in our group didn't have the money to pay a sitter so we took turns staying with her kids so she could go out. We helped another member to prepare a romantic dinner for his new love. Some people dropped out as they reached their dating goals, but others joined in their place, so the group remained lively and strong. The group's success was phenomenal. We had two engagements and a commitment ceremony in just the two years I was in the group. Most important of all, I was introduced to my wife by one of the group members. I'd recommend joining or starting a dating success team to anyone who was single and looking. (Jon, 36, Teacher)*

If someone is having trouble, the group should ask, "What can we do to help you?" There are no right or wrong answers. You alone decide what course of action you will take.

A Word of Caution

Privacy and confidentiality are paramount! No one must ever discuss personal details or the particulars of the session with anyone outside of the group for any reason. Also keep in mind that a dating support team is not designed for and does not take the place of professional counseling, group therapy, crisis counseling, or other intensive personal counseling. If you sense that someone in your group is deeply troubled, do not attempt to "treat" him or her. The right thing to do is to urge this person to seek therapy along with the dating support team activities. You have the right to decline offers of unwanted assistance, or any unreasonable requests for help from others in the group.

When to Get Professional Help

In most cases, adults can find constructive, effective ways to handle their negative emotions and problems on their own. Sometimes, however, a problem or situation is too great or complex to handle by yourself. Realize that you may benefit from professional support if, over time, you can't seem to get past your anger, or you are continually depressed, anxious, fearful, or hopeless.

ALERT!

Seeking help is not giving up! On the contrary, it's a move that takes courage, intelligence, and strength of character. Everyone needs help sometimes. Your needs do not make you weak or a failure. Even if you don't believe this now, it will be clear when you're looking back from the other side of your recovery.

The best way to find a good therapist or counselor is to get referrals from reliable sources. Try your doctor, family, friends, support group, hospitals, or universities with psychology departments. Interview each counselor over the telephone. Ask them about credentials, how long they have been in practice, what their specialty is, their fee, and how they might approach your situation. Some therapists are very interactive and some are quite passive. If you don't think you'd be comfortable with a particular therapist, don't agree to see him. If you do and you don't like him, you are not bound to continue. Keep looking until you find someone you can relate to. You might need just a few sessions to clear your head, or perhaps find a support network.

Chapter 18

Your Special Someone

You've come a long way on your dating journey! You might have had a setback or two, but that hasn't stopped you from moving forward. You've learned from your experiences and adjusted your strategies. Maybe you have already found someone special and are wondering how things will turn out. This chapter will help you handle the hurdles you are likely to face as your new relationship moves from early dating to something more.

How Do You Know?

Hopefully you're moving toward the home stretch on your dating journey. If you and your partner are still stalled, you need to think about why. The signs that you might not be quite ready to take things to another level include:

- You're reluctant about the future.
- You notice similarities between your partner and your ex.
- You've chosen a partner who is the exact opposite of your ex.
- You've noticed that your friends and family are more excited about your partner than you are.

If one or more of the above statements apply to you, don't worry. Relationships don't happen on a set timetable. If you are not ready to move forward yet, give yourself permission to take the time you need to learn about yourself, and to get over whatever ails you. You'll make it all the way to the end of your dating journey when you are feeling available, upbeat, and energized.

FACT

If you dream of glue, this may indicate a fear of being trapped in a situation that binds you, such as a partnership or commitment. Dreaming that you are gluing things together suggests that you are piecing together aspects of yourself and you are acknowledging those previously rejected parts.

At some point you will meet someone who is more than another acquaintance, and the two of you will begin to develop stronger feelings for one another. You may wonder whether this relationship is the one you've been searching for. Only time will tell. You need to make it through the stages of just dating, a budding relationship, and then couplehood. Consider it encouraging when:

- You feel happy for your ex when you learn he is with a new love.
- You can appreciate the good parts of your former relationship(s).

- You no longer think about being asked out because you expect to have a steady date.
- You don't see any major liabilities in your new partner.
- You have been introduced to at least some of your partner's friends and family.
- You have pet names for each other.
- You have begun saying "we" instead of "I."
- You consult each other about major purchases such as cars, furniture, and clothes.
- You send gifts and cards as a couple.

Introducing Your Partner to Friends

Your new partner's family and friends can reveal a great deal about how your new partner thinks, feels, and behaves. Family approval is so important to most people that they are more likely to introduce you to friends first. On television comedies such as *Friends*, if the group of friends doesn't like someone's new love interest, or vice versa, that new person is quickly banished from the show. In real life, if your friends don't like your new partner, you aren't necessarily going to break up with her. However, their feelings will impact your social life in your group.

QUESTION?

What does it mean if you have dreams about weddings?
Dreams about weddings most likely signify that you want a partner. But dreaming of a wedding might also mean that you have a desire to have unity or the wish to have inner harmony and balance.

You may be in love with your new partner, but you want to keep peace with your friends. For this reason, you should be sure that you are ready to make introductions and not rush it. You want your friends to be accepting and your partner to feel comfortable with them, but the initial contact is going to be stressful. You may be surprised to find that your high-energy motormouth friend suddenly becomes withdrawn when meeting your new partner. Your new partner may say or do something that turns your friend(s) off without realizing it. No matter how everyone feels, they have something in common: they care about you. If you are lucky, they'll love each other right away. If not, with luck they will be able to like or at least tolerate each other for your sake.

Unenthusiastic Friends

It can be very distressing and disappointing to have people you care about react unenthusiastically to your new love. The reasons could be sound or selfish. A friend might give a thumbs-down to your new partner because she realizes that her relationship with you will change now that you have a romantic partner. This is particularly common when your tight-knit friends are all still single and pal around together constantly. However, knowing you as well as they do, they might also see a potential problem that you have overlooked.

If one of your friends objects to your new partner, ask yourself the following:

- Has my friend proven to be a good and impartial judge of important matters in my life prior to this time?
- Does my friend know me well enough to really judge what might or might not be right for me, or is she someone I mostly hang out with for sports, parties, or volunteer activities?
- Could my friend be jealous of my new relationship because he doesn't have one of his own?

Friends are only human! Even the most loyal friend may consciously or subconsciously feel threatened, be jealous, or have negative feelings about your new love. If a friend asks you for your opinion about a new love, be forthright but gentle and give the new couple a chance. You want your lovestruck friend to know that you care enough to say how you feel, but that you will respect and support his choices.

If your friends know you well and you believe they are acting in your best interests, listen to what they have to say, but don't write off your new love. Give the relationship between your new love and your friends time to click. In the end, you may not agree with their assessments, but a good friend will eventually realize that you are happy and you must do what you think is best. If you decide that your partner is a "keeper" over their protests, they also will realize that if they don't acknowledge your special someone, it is their friendship with you that will suffer.

More than Friends

Your friend may express reservations about your new love because of another reason you may not have considered. Your friend may be attracted to you and want you as more than a friend! People with longstanding friendships sometimes do confuse deep affection, or loneliness, for love. This is common when a longstanding friend finds a partner and is no longer available as a single anymore. This friend might be the soul mate you've been seeking. But more likely, both of you would know by now if there were any romantic chemistry between you. If you are not interested in exploring a platonic-to-romantic possibility, handle the rejection with kid gloves. You care about your friend and will want to protect her emotions. If you like the idea of changing friendship to something more, however, consider the risks. It could be the best thing that ever happened to you, but it could also threaten a precious friendship:

> *We hung out together for several years when neither of us was dating much. We spent so much time together that we even shared a car, fed each other's pets when one of us was away, and spent all the holidays with each other's families. During a particularly lonely time we decided that maybe we should explore being romantic and intimate. We cared a great deal for each other but after a few weeks we realized that we were not attracted in that way. Fortunately, our friendship was strong enough that we could go back to being just friends. Eventually we each married. While we never become romantically linked again, even after being widowed, our friendship has lasted more than thirty years. We nearly ruined something very precious and feel lucky that we didn't! (Grady and Candace, 68 and 70, Retired Schoolteachers)*

Introducing Your Partner to Work Colleagues

Introductions of your new partner to your boss or work colleagues are similar to introductions to friends. The main difference is that your career is involved, and that can be risky. So don't rush the introductions. A company social event such as the annual picnic or holiday bash is a logical way to bring your partner into your work social circle *after* you are a solid couple. When you are ready, it is wise to prepare your partner in advance. Clue him in to your company's corporate culture. Tell him a few things about the significant people he may meet (e.g., Mr. Smith is an avid Asian art collector, Ms. Jones loves fly-fishing, Mr. Brown is very conservative in his views). Your partner's behavior impacts your reputation and your working life. If your new partner doesn't get this, don't invite him to business functions or you could end up in Brady's situation:

> *I invited my girlfriend Sally to last year's company party. She aggressively marketed her home business to my peers and gave unsolicited advice and her business card to my boss. When I told her I didn't think that was proper, she got defensive and said she was just "doing a little business." We argued about this but I could see that Sally really didn't think she had done anything wrong. I didn't want a repeat of last year so this year I went to the party alone. (Brady, 32, Accountant)*

If you know your partner is great at socializing with new people and will know how to behave at a work function, there's no reason not to extend an invitation. In fact, a well-chosen mate can boost your standing in the eyes of others. That's what happened for Ned:

> *I invited Bridget to our annual company picnic. It was very formal. Everyone had pasted-on smiles. Bridget is so sociable, she knows just how to warm up a group. She made a few well-placed, witty remarks and got everyone laughing and relaxed. We all had a very good time. Later, my boss remarked how lucky I was to have such a wonderful woman in my life. I agree! (Ned, 53, CFO)*

Introducing Your Partner to Family

Romeo and Juliet met a tragic end because their families were feuding. In real life, families *can* significantly influence your love life. If the families don't get along any better than the legendary Montagues and Capulets, or a family member disapproves of your new love, keep things in perspective. It will be great if you have a mutual admiration society going, but all you really need is acceptance and for everyone to get along.

Families have biases and can be overprotective in ways you can't control. You may be surprised to find that your usually open-minded family suddenly thinks no one (including your new love) is good enough for you, now that you are serious. Your usually warm sister may give your new partner the cold shoulder or the third degree. Your kid brother may play irritating, embarrassing practical jokes. Your mother may suddenly launch into a story about how much they loved the girl you dated in college and wasn't it a shame that she moved away because you two lovebirds would have surely gotten married.

Neither you nor your partner should take these slights personally. Often, outrageous, inappropriate, or unusual behavior is simply caused by anxiety, but it pulls you between your partner's needs and your family's happiness. Most people will relax and eventually accept each other in time. If it never happens and this is the cause of a huge level of stress in your relationship, you may not survive as a couple.

FACT

In the movie *Guess Who's Coming to Dinner*, Katharine Hepburn and Spencer Tracy are a white couple who meet their daughter's fiancé for the first time. They are surprised to learn that he is an African-American and must quickly deal with their feelings while he is visiting. Watch this movie to get an idea of what this situation would be like if yours is similar.

First contacts between family and your new love are stressful enough without unnecessary surprises. Prepare your partner in advance to meet your family, and vice versa. Suddenly realizing that your new partner is a vegetarian as your mother starts the pig roast festivities will be awkward for everyone. Clue your new partner in about any unusual family rituals, too. For example, the famous Kennedys expected everyone to participate in their touch football games, whether they were athletic and interested or not.

If you are having a large family gathering, such as a reunion or Fourth of July picnic, and you don't have minor children to deal with, such a family gathering can be an ideal way to introduce your new partner. There are lots of other people around to diffuse tension, take part in the conversation, and divert attention away from the two of you. You and your partner may feel as if you are under a microscope, but most of the scrutiny is well intentioned. These people really do want to get to know your new partner and support your choice. And your new partner will get to meet a lot of family members all at once.

Keep in mind that even if things don't go well, you must make your romantic partnership your first priority. Your family may find themselves seeing a lot less of you if they don't like your partner and won't try to develop a relationship with him. They should eventually realize that, as an adult, you know what is best for you and that you have found someone you really believe will make you happy.

Introducing Your Partner to Your Children

Your friends and adult family may not like your new partner and the relationship will still thrive, but if your *children* don't climb aboard your "love train" it could be the end of the line for your budding romantic partnership. Depending upon their age, maturity level, personality, and relationship with you and their other parent, children may be very accepting of your new partner—or not. Most children are naturally possessive about their parent's affection. They may honestly not understand why you would need anyone's love other than theirs. Even very young children can sense when an "interloper" is present and become very protective. If they do make a quick attachment to your new partner, they may feel doubly victimized if your relationship with that person ends. It is absolutely essential that you make introductions of a new partner to a child or children very carefully. Don't even think about it until you are certain you are a couple with serious potential.

If you find that your children are reluctant to even accept the fact that you are dating, let alone that you have fallen in love again, explain that it is natural and important for adults to connect with other adults. Suggest that just as they have very special friends, so do you. Affirm to your children that, as their parent, you will do your best to always do what is right for them, but it is your choice as an adult to make the decisions about your own social life. Of course, when they grow up and become adults, they will do the same.

Are You Going to Be My New Mommy/Daddy?

Make any first introduction to a new love short, informal, and in neutral territory (e.g., a park with a playground, or a pizza or coffee shop). Although family gatherings give your children the comfort of having trusted elders around, they may also be upset and resentful if they see your new partner taking what was formerly their mommy or daddy's place in family traditions. If introduced to family gatherings too early, your partner might sabotage a young or resentful child's serenity at these events and ruin their happy memories.

Be Patient

As with every relationship, the best ones develop over time. It's best to assume that things will not go perfectly when introducing a new love to youngsters. Count on some embarrassing or inappropriate behavior and hostility. All you and your new partner can do is be patient, keep the lines of communication open, and be sensitive to the child's feelings. One thing you should never do is engage in public displays of affection in front of your children at this stage. Even a sophisticated teenager may be upset by the sight of the two of you kissing, or your partner in a bathrobe having coffee at the family breakfast table.

Introducing Your Children to Each Other

If you eventually plan to marry or live together and you are both parents, any children living under your roof will eventually have to meet each other. Assume that even the most mature, open-minded child will have fears about stepbrothers and stepsisters who are virtual strangers and possible rivals for your love and attention. When you know you are going to be blending families soon, start getting your children used to the idea. You might start by casually mentioning the other children in conversation. If both your daughters play soccer, for example, you might say: "Bob's daughter Susie plays soccer, too. Some day the two of you will meet and perhaps you can exchange pointers." Or suggest an activity that your child really likes: "Jane's son Robert is a Jets fan like we are. It might be fun for us all to go to a game together." Even if you get a positive reaction, don't rush to action. Give the kids time to get used to the idea, then make plans.

Blending Families

With luck, your children will like and accept your new partner and any children involved. If they don't, allow them to freely voice their opinions. Don't force them to show affection, but make sure they show proper respect. Consider their feelings at all times. You and your partner chose each other, but the children didn't have any say in the matter. It will take time—maybe lots of time—and patience—lots of patience—for the families to blend. The most important thing to remember is that you are the adults and they are children. When tempers flare, the adults must stay in control. If you can do this, you will be a successful parent or stepparent.

Moving In/Marriage

If you are definitely planning a date to move in together or to get married, your children deserve to know first. By this time, your children have hopefully already been introduced and possibly spent some time with your new partner and her children, if she has any. If you've been responsible and honest throughout the development of the relationship, this news shouldn't come as too much of a shock to your kids.

Calmly outline your plans. Let them know about the other children involved, what the visiting and living arrangements will be, and anything else that will significantly affect them. Be specific about what will change and what won't. For example, you might say: "Mary and her two boys will be living with us after the wedding, but I will still make all of you brunch Sunday. I will still drive you to football practice and you will also have Mary as a bonus parent to take you places, too!" Reassure your children that the thing that will *never* change is your devotion to them. Then it's up to you to live up to that promise.

On moving day, ask children to "help" even if it is just taking some of their toys and putting them in their new room or helping you to open boxes. Older children have more capacity to understand interpersonal relationships, but they may also be more emotional, resentful, anxious, and rebellious than the younger ones. Teenagers and young adults have so many challenges of their own to handle. Dealing with a new stepparent and possibly some new stepsiblings can make them very angry and upset. How would *you* feel if you were uprooted from your home or suddenly had to share a bedroom? How great would it be for you to be forced to live with strangers? How easy would it be for you to accept rules or new ways of doing things issued by an adult you barely know or like? One possible way to handle the emotional strain that you may all feel is to institute a weekly meeting. Here, each family member can safely voice their concerns and feelings and talk about it. If this isn't enough, family counseling is another option.

Stepparenthood

Whether you are both parents or one of you has just acquired an instant family, you will need to compromise and develop compatible parenting styles. You may be uncomfortable with the way your partner lets his teenage daughter stay out until all hours, or you may require your children make their own beds and participate in the housework when your partner doesn't. Now you are a couple. That means being a unified force with equal authority.

ALERT!

Don't make the mistake of being a buddy and relaxing the guidelines beyond your better judgment to make things "easier" on the kids. Kids don't really want a parent to be a chum, they want parents who care about them, keep them safe, and provide boundaries. Do not let any child dictate to you or intimidate you. If a child under your roof disobeys the rules, make it clear what the consequences will be, and follow through.

Getting together as a family is even more difficult if you become an instant parent. Even if you really love your stepchildren they may not feel the same about you. Assume nothing as you start integrating yourself into their lives as a parent. Do it slowly. Never pressure stepchildren to call you "Mom" or "Dad." Suggest they address you by your first name. In time they may come to think of you as Mom or Dad and want to call you that on their own. Introduce your stepchildren like this: "These are my new girls, Sharon and Tiffany"—not "These are John's kids," which makes it seem as though you do not want them. And what if you really don't want them? If you are not open to the idea of raising someone else's children, this is something you must make clear before you start dating a partner with kids. Laura learned this the hard way:

> " I never wanted kids of my own, and never wanted to be a stepmother to someone else's children either, but Stan was so wonderful that I convinced myself that I could handle the biweekly visitations of his two small children. I quickly began to dread these weekends and the way Stan let them act out. When I looked at the notes I'd made in my dating journal I realized that we fought constantly about the kids—even more than we just enjoyed being together. The log made it clear that this wasn't a good relationship for me. Stan was great, but his children were a non-negotiable liability I couldn't live with. (Laura, 31, Broker) "

Introducing Your Partner to Former Loves

At some point you may find yourself bumping into your ex, or having to introduce her to your new partner. If you do not have children, you probably won't be seeing a lot of your ex, and any contact would naturally be quick and cordial. If you do have children (especially if there are visitation and joint custody agreements in force), your new partner is likely to meet your ex more often and at family and school functions. Your ex will always be a part of your life and your children's lives. A new partner has to accept this to be with you and both of you must find a way to keep communication cordial, if not friendly.

FACT

Children are very intuitive. If you are respectful with your ex and his new partner, your children will feel safer and more secure. If you are continuously in conflict, your children will pick up on the tension. Successful blended families are those in which the children know that they can fully love and appreciate all of the adults who love and care for them.

In most cases, biological parents have the final say over the care of their children, but stepparents also require consideration and respect. When your children are with your ex-husband and his new wife, she may allow them to eat junk food, or stay up late, or let them do other things that are not allowed under your roof. You may hear protests of "But Dad lets me do it!" The key to making the relationships successful is to remember that all of you are caregivers and *parents*. It is your responsibility to work out the problems you face for the sake of your children.

Chapter 19

"Firsts" as a Couple

After you have made it through the stages of meeting and dating, the next part of your dating journey is adjusting to the joys and challenges of couplehood. You have been introduced to family and friends and are continuing to become more solid as a couple. However, there are still many important challenges and "firsts" to deal with. These include vacationing together, handling the holidays, and dealing with celebrations and gifts special to the two of you. This chapter will help you prepare for and deal with any difficulties you may encounter as you journey together as a couple through your significant firsts.

Going Away for the Weekend

Good feelings and romance go hand-in-hand with going out of town with someone special. Taking a trip together is also another way to find out whether or not you are compatible on a more sustained basis as a couple with a higher level of intimacy.

ESSENTIAL

Always sort out money issues before you go on a trip with your new partner. Ideally, the person who offers the invitation is also offering to pay for your share of things, but you shouldn't make this assumption. Be sure to discuss—thoroughly and well in advance—travel costs, restaurant bills, and other expenditures you'll be encountering during your trip.

The best type of first trip is a simple overnight or weekend close to home. Make sure that both of you know what you're getting into before you pack those bags. If you believe the purpose of the trip is to get to know your partner better, but your partner thinks it is just a fun getaway and you'll be on your own, both of you will be confused and unhappy. You might also want to get clear how you will handle the sleeping arrangements if you haven't yet been physically intimate or are not intimate on a regular basis and you're not ready for sleeping together just yet. Discussing these important aspects beforehand will help you avoid a situation like this:

> *When Brian asked me to go on a weekend cruise with him, I was so excited! I really thought this little trip would be the thing that brought us closer together. You can imagine how horrified I was to see Brian chatting up some blondes at the bar almost the minute we boarded. When I let those girls know I was with Brian, he pulled me aside and told me in no uncertain terms that he liked me a lot as a friend but nothing more. He said he felt really comfortable with me as a roommate, but asked me along only to avoid the exorbitant singles supplement on the cabin. He actually thought I felt the same way! I was miserable and humiliated. A simple discussion in advance about what we expected would have saved us a lot of pain. (Carrie, 28, Art Therapist)*

Full-Length Vacations

A long vacation with your new partner may sound wonderful, but consider the timing. Don't agree to go away together unless you know you can handle the stress of being a couple, most or all of the time.

In the good old days, couples didn't travel together unless they were married, but situations where someone receives tickets as a surprise gift or gets an all-expenses-paid vacation proposal from a new partner are increasingly common. This may seem generous, but there is no such thing as a free lunch. Perhaps the giver can easily afford to pay for your trip and just wants the pleasure of your company, but is it really a good idea to accept? A trip is an expensive gift. You may just want a week in the sun without any obligations, but the person who is paying for the trip may put demands on your time and person that you are not ready to deal with. Be absolutely clear what the real deal is before you leave home.

E ALERT!

Even if you think you are solid as a couple, keep control of your own tickets, documentation, and passport. Bring a cell phone or prepaid phone card for emergencies. Take a credit card and enough cash to cover your expenses just in case you are dumped, left with the bill, or want to leave in a hurry. Also, be sure that someone at home knows where you are going, when you are to return, and how to contact you.

Whether you are splitting the cost of the trip or being "hosted" by your partner, talk ahead of time about your expectations. You don't want to end up like the woman who thought she was going on a weekend cruise as someone's girlfriend, only to find out that her partner had other ideas! It is also a good idea to arrange some activities (e.g., scuba diving lessons, boat trip) ahead of time so you know there will be things you both enjoy doing together. Perhaps you can spend some time together surfing the Web before the trip to get information about your destination. That helps to build excitement, and as the following story illustrates, it could save your vacation.

The first time we went away together we almost broke up because of poor planning. Tammy envisioned dancing, romantic dinners, and moonlit walks on the beach, but I wanted to play golf every day and was tired by the time the sun went down. Our daily habits irritated each other, too. I couldn't understand why Tammy had to sleep until nearly 10:00 when I wanted to get up early and golf. Tammy couldn't understand why I didn't want to spend all of my time with her. By the time we boarded the plane for home, we were barely talking to one another! We patched things up at home and even eventually got married. To avoid disaster on our honeymoon, we talked in advance about what we wanted to do, and we compromised. Tammy took a few golf lessons so we could enjoy this sport together, but I also played less golf so we could spend more time doing other things. It was a great trip! (Tammy and Bill, 42 and 43, married three months)

A vacation should be fun, relaxing, interesting, and an escape from your everyday routine, but don't expect a reluctant partner to suddenly fall in love with you just because things heat up on vacation. Once you are back home again, your relationship is likely to be less romantic than it was on holiday. Your expectation should be just to have a good time and a photo album full of memories.

Major Holidays

Most people think of "the holidays" as the time ranging from Thanksgiving through New Year's Day when there are many family occasions and parties. Depending on your religious and cultural heritage, you will find yourself dealing with various celebrations and holidays throughout the year. These special events can be joyful, but they can also be full of expectations that are not always satisfied. Families can be unrealistic and demanding. Celebrations can hit a snag just when you most want things to be perfect. Singles sharing these types of special days with a partner for the first time may find that it is exciting, but stressful.

Handling the major holidays with a new partner takes thought, preparation, and compromise. You are going to have to consider your partner's expectations, rituals, and needs as well as your own. What things are most important to you? To your partner? How can you blend them or compromise to make everyone happy? If you can't figure out how to deal with your families and each other at Thanksgiving, or how to celebrate Valentine's Day, how will you deal with even more important decisions?

Here's what Jennie and Brad did to make sure each was comfortable for the holidays:

> *The first New Year's Eve I spent with Brad, he arranged for us to attend a black tie dinner dance. It was a lovely party and I was glad to be with him, but the entire time I kept thinking about the annual family get-together that I was missing at home. Afterward, I confessed to Brad how much being with my family on New Year's means to me. We compromised by celebrating Thanksgiving with his family, Christmas by ourselves, and New Year's with my family. (Jennie, 32, Writer)*

FACT

Romantic gifts don't require a special occasion. If you see something that you think will appeal to your partner, give it now. Unexpected gifts are often the most fun, and surprises can be a great way to put some spark into your relationship. Just make sure your partner appreciates being surprised.

Enhance the Romance

The holidays are great times to give gifts, but a "thinking of you" gift is a welcome gesture that helps fan the flames of love anytime. Here are some easy ideas to enhance romance and make your special someone smile any time of year:

For women:
- A heart-shaped locket
- Flowers of any type
- Stuffed animals
- Books of interest

For men:
- CDs, DVDs, or video games
- T-shirts
- Plants or flowers (men like them, too)
- Books of interest

For men or women:
- A tape or CD of yourself singing, or telling a sexy bedtime story
- A romantic card
- A photo of you or the two of you in a beautiful frame (signed by you "with love")
- A love poem or words of love written on just about anything (try permanent marker on a T-shirt or pillowcase)

Family Pressures

Although you and your partner are quickly becoming a unit, you still both have families and friends who will expect you to incorporate them into your new relationship. You won't always be able to please everyone, equally. It may seem to you that you are working so hard to make everyone happy that you aren't all that happy yourself.

ESSENTIAL

If you are inviting your family to meet your new partner and her new family for the first time, ask some friends to join you. People tend to be at their best when there is a mix of family and nonfamily. This also takes some of the pressure off the two of you as "the couple."

Relationships are wonderful but they aren't all fun and games. As a couple, your first consideration must be for each other. Some of the people around you may feel that things should remain the same even though you are now part of a couple. This is unfair and unrealistic. The minute you couple up, all your relationships change. Even well-meaning loved ones may have unrealistic expectations and make unreasonable demands. This is particularly true for single parents. If you feel real pressure from outside your relationship, don't stay silent. Emphasize to your loved ones how much both you and your partner want to be part of their lives. Let them know that even though you are forging a new bond with someone as a couple, you still love them. That said, you will also want them to know if their expectations and demands are hurting you.

Then assert yourself and negotiate new ways of handling touchy issues. Perhaps now the two of you will open holiday presents the night before instead of in the morning, or have holiday dinners at a different time, or visit your families on alternate years, or consider a blended celebration at your house. Maybe you will just celebrate alone as a couple. Whatever you decide, compromise, flexibility, and the willingness to change as a couple are the keys to your happiness and success.

Making Adjustments

Your first year together is a time to initiate new ways of doing things and create new traditions. Perhaps you will bake cookies together and give them to friends and family. Maybe you will host an annual party on July fourth. It doesn't matter what you do as long as you do it together:

> *My wife Jennie is Catholic and I'm Jewish. At first she insisted that we have a large Christmas tree, but Chanukah is nearly the same time. It never felt right to be lighting Chanukah candles in front of a Christmas tree. After the first few years together, I finally told Jennie how much this bothered me. We compromised first by decorating our holiday tree with universal symbols of the season such as apples, pinecones and candles instead of Santa Claus. Now, we decorate a tree outside in our yard with lights and edible treats for the birds and animals to celebrate the season instead of having a glittery tree in the house. We also invite friends to our annual holiday party, where we serve foods traditional for both Chanukah and Christmas. We feel we have successfully created ways to make both holidays special, retain some of each other's traditions, and not tread on each other's feelings. (Joshua, 47, Attorney)*

Birthdays and Anniversaries

To be sure, there are a few Grinch-like people who don't see any reason to celebrate special occasions, but most people really do enjoy celebrating days that are special to their partners and themselves. The most obvious and important are birthdays and anniversaries. If you've only been going out with someone a short while, you can't go wrong by going out to dinner and giving a card and a token (e.g., book or CD). If you have been dating for a while, however, the amount of thought and the quality of the gift have to be greater. This is especially true for your first year together.

Celebrations are more than just a way to mark time, they're a way to send the message to your special partner that you are glad that he is in your life and you are happy and honored to be able to celebrate special days with him. If you know your partner values such occasions, don't make the mistake of forgetting or otherwise devaluing them:

> *My birthday was coming up and my girlfriend was called out of town on business. She didn't think it was a big deal because she travels constantly. But she didn't call or send a card. That really hurt me. The next year she was also out of town and insisted that we celebrate on another date. Apparently, her family does this all the time to suit their busy schedules. One year they even moved their Christmas celebration! When Jane returned I told her how bad I felt. Now she makes more of an effort to be home for our special days. When this is impossible, we still find some way to "celebrate" even if it's just by telephone. (Dan, 32, Musician)*

What's Good to Give?

You don't have to spend a fortune on parties and gifts, but you *do* have to demonstrate your thought and effort. Maybe a weekend for two in a romantic inn is out of line with your finances, but you can still plan a just-the-two-of-us celebration with your partner's favorite music, foods, and of course, champagne and cake. If it is your first anniversary, present your partner with a "certificate" good for a massage or a complete evening of pampering at *your* house. Start with a romantic but healthy dinner (e.g., shrimp or chicken over greens, with strawberries and champagne), followed by a bath drawn just for your special someone, complete with rose petals and bath oil. Here's Carole's gift story:

> *My husband was frantically seeking a champagne-quality gift on our beer budget for our first anniversary. I have no idea why, but he bought me enamel earrings in the shape of chicken heads. They were ridiculous, but I know he thought I would think they were cute since I love animals. I have treasured them my entire life as they remind me of him and how much we loved each other, every time I look at them. (Carole, 79, Widow)*

A special gift can make you glow with joy and become a treasured keepsake, or keep you wondering what your partner was trying to tell you:

> *The first birthday gift my boyfriend ever bought me was an expensive cashmere head and face mask. I was expecting jewelry or something romantic, and he got me a gift that made me look like a bank robber. It was hideous! He could tell by my shocked expression that I didn't like his gift. He defensively explained that he had selected it because I am always complaining of the cold. Maybe that is true, but a mink scarf, ear muffs, or soft wooly gloves would have been a MUCH better choice. (Alicia, 45, CEO)*

Gift-Giving Failures

If you get a gift you dislike, consider the good intentions of the giver before you get upset. Not everyone "gets it" at first. Some people never develop the ability to understand what others would really like to have. If you give someone a gift, it is theirs to use, discard, re-gift, etc. It is bad manners to insist that a recipient of a gift use it or display it. It's even worse to continually ask about it. This is particularly important to remember if you give someone a handmade gift. Homemade items are gifts from the heart, but beauty is in the eye of the beholder. Make sure the item you have created is not going to make your new love look or feel silly.

If you *get* a handmade gift and you don't like it, remember that someone who cares about you took the time to create something very special for you.

The proper thing to do is to sincerely thank your special someone for the item and then bravely taste, wear, display, or use it at least once. Then put it somewhere visible where your partner can see it—at least for a while. Don't go overboard with fake enthusiasm, however. It's dishonest, and worse: you may end up with a hat and gloves to match that badly-knitted scarf next year!

Unfortunately, even honesty and constant reminding won't always work with your partner. Marianna has had that trouble with Jeremy for years:

> *Although we have been together more than twenty years, Jeremy still hasn't been able to select a gift for me. I have dropped hints, I have pointed out things I really love, and I have gone shopping with him numerous times. By now he ought to know my taste, but he never gets it right. We have even started playing a game where we go into a store and he selects the one item he thinks I would like the best and I do the same for him. I am usually dead-on for him, but without fail, he selects something I would never wear or use. I don't know why he's like this but I have definitely given up ever expecting him to select a gift on his own. (Marianna, 41, Editor)*

Luckily, most people will eventually catch on to your likes and dislikes. However, people can't read your mind. Give your new love some guidance in terms of the perfect gift by dropping a few well-placed gentle hints. For example, in the bookstore point out a beautiful art book and mention how much you love to collect art books. When you are window shopping, reveal to your partner that soft, wooly sweaters are your guilty pleasure, or that you have a thing for big earrings, or anything do to with sports cars. This doesn't mean that you should trawl for gifts or make demands or insist that your partner buy something for you, but it will help make gift-giving easier for him. It also means that you're more likely to get a gift you can be enthusiastic about. You'll both feel happy!

Entertaining Together

During your first year as a couple you may find yourselves entertaining together, even if you aren't setting up house just yet. Entertaining is a great way to introduce your friends to each other and even get your family members together. Entertaining as a new couple can be a bonding experience, or cause serious tension—especially if your party styles don't match. Your idea of a get-together may be one where expense is no object, the food is expensive and lavish, and everyone dresses up. Your partner's vision of a party may be simply opening a few cans of mixed nuts and setting out a few bags of chips while the gang sits on the floor, dressed in T-shirts and jeans. If you find that your styles clash, you will have to find a middle ground and create a new way of entertaining that suits both of you. As with everything, compromise is key. There is no "right" way to entertain. What seems right to you is that way only because it is the way you have done it in the past and you are used to it.

One way to avoid discord when you entertain together for the first time is to do something completely different than what you would normally do. You might consider creating a signature dish together, or inviting friends to a cocktail or dessert party instead of a full dinner, or doing a costume party where the dress code is pure fantasy. Whatever you decide to do, it's the *people* who make a successful event. If your friends mix and mingle well and you are relaxed and happy, they won't care if the liquor is limited or the cheese selection is small. They *will* notice if the atmosphere is strained, or if the guests don't mix well. Prepare in advance, be enthusiastic and generous hosts, and you will have a great time.

Attending Weddings as a Couple

Going to a wedding or another major social event as a couple is often considered a milestone in a new relationship. However, these types of major social events are expensive. Friends who have to foot the bill may not invite the two of you as a couple unless you have been dating steadily for more than a year, or are engaged or living together. If your new partner gets invited to his friend's wedding and you aren't asked to attend, don't feel terribly bad. It is probably not at all personal. Chances are that finances or space considerations are all that has stopped the host or hostess from adding you to their guest list.

If you do end up attending a wedding with your partner, use it as an opportunity to get to know your partner better and perhaps judge whether or not you could end up as a married couple. How does your special someone feel about going to the wedding? Is he excited about the event, or making comments such as "Marriage is an outdated institution" or "I would never get married"? Can you see yourself getting married to this person down the line? How does your partner react to friends and family once at the wedding, and how do they react to her? Watch the event as though you're watching a movie and reflect on it, as Arlene did:

> *My boyfriend invited me to his friend's wedding. You didn't have to be intimately involved to know that the families hated each other and didn't support the union of this couple. The groomsmen kept razzing the groom for getting "hitched" and called the poor bride a "ball and chain" to her face. The bridesmaids were bickering with each other. The music was awful and the singer couldn't hold a tune. The food was served late and arrived cold. Many people left way before the cake was cut and served and no one stayed very late. I felt bad for couple that they had such a sad, tense wedding day. I wonder if their marriage will survive with an initial send-off like that. More importantly, I wonder, if I marry my boyfriend, whether his friends and family would behave that badly on our wedding day. (Arlene, 29, Graphic Artist)*

ALERT!

Proposing to your partner while you're guests at a wedding may seem like a romantic gesture, but don't be so sure. All the attention properly belongs to the bride and groom, and your proposal diverts attention from *their* love on their day. Save the declaration of devotion for another time when the proposal can be all about you and your sweetheart.

Depending upon the strength and nature of your relationship, demonstrating that you are a solid couple at a wedding or major social event could be a good way to let others know that you are serious about your partner. The exception would be arriving with a new love at a family affair when the ink is barely dry on your divorce papers or if your ex might be there, too. Separated and newly divorced people have every right to move on in their lives, but they must always consider the circumstances and the timing. If tensions are still high, keep your new partner out of the picture until things settle down. There will be other opportunities in the future.

Wedding Guest Woes

Beware of the bouquet and the garter toss. These traditions are the scourge of most singles over a certain age who don't want to be on public display as "still unmarried." If you are part of a couple but still single, you open yourself up to repeated choruses of "You're definitely next!" or "When are you two getting married?" This can be embarrassing if you aren't ready yet to get engaged, and downright irritating if you are happy with your single status. However, if you are an incredible romantic or want to advertise that you are single and looking, grabbing the garter or catching the bouquet will momentarily make you the center of attention and your "prize catch" is a conversation starter, too.

Although this type of wedding gaiety might make you cringe, be a good sport if you are called by the bride or groom to participate. Participating in these time-honored traditions honors the couple. Many modern brides and grooms, especially more mature ones, choose not to do a garter and bouquet toss. Instead, the bride offers friends and family members who might realistically be "next" a flower from her bouquet. She also gives her groom a "groom's garter" as a substitute for her personal one that the groom can give to his best man or to another male of his choosing as a memento of the special day.

Of course, the bouquet or garter toss isn't the only thing that can cause discomfort for you as a couple attending a wedding:

> *When Ann was separated but not yet divorced, she asked me to accompany her to her brother's wedding. When we arrived at the house after a six-hour drive, her sister told Ann that I wasn't invited to the rehearsal dinner because it was for family only. Ann refused to go unless I went. I was completely ignored by Ann's family except for a few relatives who thought I was Ann's ex-husband! The next day at the wedding, I was seated in the back of the church while Ann sat up front with the family. As the bridal party made its way down the aisle, Ann's mother took her arm and steered her into the family limo, leaving me to find my own way to the reception.*

We weren't even seated at the same table. Ann should have known her family would be hostile and give me the cold shoulder. She shouldn't have asked me to attend, and I never should have agreed to go with her. Our relationship didn't last much past that wedding. (Michael, 42, Inventor)

An Emotional Experience

Weddings can be particularly emotional for new couples. A happy bride and groom are the ultimate proof that love exists, but there are often hidden agendas in inviting someone as your date to a wedding. You may just be happy to have her there so you don't have to be at the singles table, but your invited partner might believe that the invitation was meant to send the clear message that next time, *you* two should be the ones getting married! Inviting someone you would like to marry won't get a reluctant partner to propose. In fact, it could just push him away. Weddings should always be happy events. Alas, they don't always turn out that way for the bride and groom, their families, or their guests:

We had been officially engaged just a few weeks when my fiancé Frank and I attended the wedding of one of his work colleagues. Somehow, Frank "forgot" to mention that his ex-wife was a good friend of the bride and would be there, too. The introductions were uncomfortable, and worse, his ex apparently didn't realize that Frank had been dating, let alone that we had just gotten engaged. Needless to say, she didn't take the news very well. All night I could see her staring at me across the room, and making comments to her friends. My fiancé could have gone alone or asked me if I was ready to meet his ex. Or at least he should have prepared his ex for our engagement before he introduced us. It was really thoughtless of my fiancé not to consider my feelings, or hers. (Tamara, 29, Dental Assistant)

With any major issue or experience you encounter as a couple, communication will help clear obstacles from your path. Be open with each other about your misgivings before you dive into a potentially stressful situation. Looking back, you'll be glad you did.

Chapter 20

Taking Yourself Off the Market

Your dating journey is almost at an end. If you have found your special someone, you and your partner are now moving forward to a more solid relationship, be it loving companionship, living together, or marriage. This chapter will help you deal with any lingering uncertainties you may feel about your final decision. Once your choice is made, you will find suggestions about how to tell others you are officially "off the market." It will also give you tips for working toward your next steps as a couple.

Anxiety about the Future

Choosing a partner is an important, life-altering decision. If you have had serious relationships that didn't work out in the past, you may be worried about this one, too. By now you have spent enough time with each other to be aware of any major problems in your relationship. Reassure yourself that neither you nor your partner is the same as you were before you met one another. Now it is a different time with a new partner, and a chance to use what you have learned from past relationships to make this one last.

If there are existing issues that are blocking either of you from making a commitment, don't ignore them. Now is the time to face the situation and work on solutions. If your partner has concerns about an aspect of your behavior, reassure him of your willingness to work on what troubles him. Be as specific as possible about what steps you will take to turn things around. Ignoring your partner's pleas for change will not move the relationship forward.

Perhaps you or your partner is reluctant to commit because of education, career, financial, parenting, or eldercare issues. The need to get these situations under control before making a commitment to a partner are often valid. However, they can also often be used as an excuse to delay moving forward in life and in your relationship. Ask yourself. "How long am I willing to wait for my partner before I cut my losses and start a search for someone new again?" Set a time limit and stick to it. If there are problems with *no* solution, you will have to adapt as best you can, or, more likely, end the relationship. Everything changes with time, and not always for the better, as Barbara and Daniel discovered:

> When I moved to Chicago to take a job, Daniel couldn't come with me because he was in his last year of a Ph.D. program. The plan was for him to join me in Chicago in a year, but I was so busy that I didn't see Daniel very often in the months after I arrived. When the time came for him to move, it was clear that we had really grown apart. He loved his New York lifestyle and

I loved my luxurious corporate life. Daniel had also changed his mind about marriage, but I still wanted that type of legal bond. It was sad to let go of our relationship, but time had changed us and we couldn't change each other back to what had once been. Moving on was the right thing to do even though it was sad and lonely for a long while. I finally got married last year and now live in a huge house and have a child on the way. Daniel is enjoying a bohemian bachelor's life with two of his buddies, crammed into a one-bedroom apartment. He says he loves his life, too! (Barbara, 31, Executive)

Burying the Black Book

Are you ready to bury your little black book of possible partners, shelve your dating journal, and tell everyone "We're taken"? Only you and your partner can know for sure if you are ready for this commitment. If you are wondering how long you should wait, keep in mind that there's no right answer. Some people find true love in a day, but most couples take a lot longer to feel confident about a true commitment. You may be excited about moving forward with your partner but still have some lingering doubts. If this describes you, take one last look at your dating journal. Then you and your partner should sit down together to consider the following questions:

- Does this person have the requirements I stated when I began my search?
- How much adjustment will I have to make to make this relationship work?
- Is something or someone else clouding my/our real feelings?
- Are we sufficiently attracted to each other physically?
- Do we find it hard to compromise?
- Do we show a lack of support and respect when we disagree?
- Does one or both of us have a problem sharing our thoughts and feelings?
- Do we share new interests and activities together?
- Have we met most of each other's close friends and at least some coworkers and family?

- Have we discussed the possibilities of a future together and agreed on the basics?
- Do we both feel that we have met the right one?

The answers to these questions will help you validate your choice and support your final decision. If things don't add up, you may have to give the relationship more time to grow. You might also decide to end this relationship and start again.

Relationships with Exes

In the business world, when a finalist for a job doesn't get the offer, his resume is often kept on file in case there are future openings. However, keeping ex-loves around is a different story. If you think you might like to keep an ex in your life, the success of this decision depends upon the reasons you broke up, your level of maturity, and your current romantic situation. Even if you've fallen in love and chosen your final romantic partner, there may be other people you have dated in the past that you still want to keep as friends. Friendship is at the core of every good relationship. Now that you're not heavily invested in being together as a couple, you might be able to just enjoy the positive qualities that attracted you to each other in the first place without the stress of a romantic relationship.

As nice as this sounds, a friendship with a former romantic partner is risky. It's definitely a selfish move on your part if that person still has strong feelings for you. Your continued contact as "friends" still sends false hope to someone who is hoping you will fall in love with him. It also may block his ability to make new romantic connections. If your breakup was over non-negotiable liabilities such as anger, addiction, violence, jealousy, or total lack of compatible values, it is probably not a good idea to try to remain friends. The negative things that pulled you apart will not change and are bound to hurt you again.

If you think you want to turn a former love into a platonic friend, be honest about the reasons. Do you genuinely find that the relationship enhances your life, or are you insecure or unfulfilled, or are you hoping that this person will finally fall in love with you if you hang in there long enough? An *ex* partner should never become just a *sex* partner—but they often do. Are you interested in being with this person because of their physical aspects? Could you handle sex without love?

> *After two years together Terry told me that he couldn't see himself married to me, but that he cared for me and hoped we could be friends. I loved him so much that I just wanted to keep him in my life. He has found someone new, but I haven't. It's really painful to hear him talk about his new girlfriend and how great things are with them. I pretend to be supportive so he will continue to talk to me, but inside I ache to have him back. Being friends is not what I want, but I also can't stand the thought of cutting him loose and never being with him again at all. I feel hopelessly stuck. (Samantha, 37, Efficiency Expert)*

If your new partner has a close relationship with an ex, you may be worried that the flames of passion will grow between them again. This is certainly a possibility, but if you feel you can't trust your partner, then perhaps the relationship is not as sound as you thought. While trust and honesty are essential elements in a serious partnership, if you aren't sure where you stand when there is still an ex in your partner's life or your partner is still highly social with members of the opposite sex, ask yourself the following questions:

- Is your partner suddenly fixated on her looks? Dieting? Buying new, sexier or more up-to-date clothes?
- Does it seem like your partner is always at the office or out of town?
- Has there been a radical change in your sex life?
- Has your partner bought you a very expensive gift for no reason, while picking fights and complaining about you more than ever?

If your partner shows marked changes in behavior and you have "Yes" answers to at least one of these questions, it is likely that your partner is cheating or at least thinking about it. If this is the case, talk about it with her; don't just let your suspicion fall by the wayside.

Ready for the Next Level?

Human nature being what it is, the people who most want to be part of a couple often seem reluctant to leave the positive aspects of their single life behind when they are in a relationship that is moving forward toward a commitment. If this describes you, keep in mind that nothing is all good or all bad. Being single is great, and being part of a couple is great, too—but different.

Your new relationship is a combination of everything you have learned from the past, everything you have hoped for, and everything you will do to make it work in the future. You may have to give up something to be part of a team, but you will get something back in return. With the right person, the price you pay for being part of a couple is a bargain!

ALERT!

Is your partner reluctant to commit? An ultimatum *might* work, but it's risky. If you decide to issue an ultimatum, never do it as a challenge or bluff because you are angry. Once you put it out there you must be prepared to follow through on it. An ultimatum must be given with a clear goal in mind, and a deadline that must be met. Do it if you must, but do it at your own risk.

If Your Goals and Needs Have Changed

Change is inevitable. Sometimes couples who are together for a long time find that their goals and needs change before they make a commitment. When this happens, the couple has to either renegotiate their goals or end the relationship:

> I moved in with Jason because he didn't want to get married but still wanted a serious, monogamous relationship, and I did, too. He'd been married several times and had four grown children. He told me right away that he would never marry again. That was fine, at first, but soon I began wishing for a baby of my own. Jason wouldn't even consider it and we ultimately broke up. Jason had been clear and honest about his needs from the start. I am the one who tried to convince myself otherwise. (Ellen, 38, Physician)

No Right or Wrong Answers

A woman once advised a younger woman afraid of making a mistake that she should not be afraid to make mistakes. According to her, no decision is a bad one—at least not at the moment you make it. If things don't turn out as you planned, you always have a chance to turn things around. "If you live another day, you can make another decision. Where there's life, there's hope," she wisely counseled. Making big decisions takes courage, but if you feel fairly certain that know what you want, the risk is worth it.

> *When I came to America in the early 1900s, I was introduced to Frank, a furrier who came from a nearby shtetl (small town in Eastern Europe). When we had been together a while but he was dragging his feet on marriage, I made the arrangements and said to him: "Frank, I rented the hall—we're getting married Tuesday"—and that was it! We were married over fifty years and had three children. (Tillie Bader, Homemaker, deceased)*

Sometimes couples are pressured by outsiders to commitments even though they are satisfied with the status quo and aren't ready to move forward to another level. If this is happening to you, be firm in your resolve to do what's right for you. Moving forward in a relationship is a decision that you need to make jointly with your partner and *only* your partner. If you agree to make a commitment because people are expecting you to and your heart isn't in it, the relationship will suffer.

Telling Others "We're Taken"

When you choose a partner, it is the logical end of your relationship search. Telling the other candidates that you are off the market marks the end of your current relationship journey. Whether you are moving in together, getting married, or going steady as constant companions, now you'll want to let everyone know!

Moving In

There are an increasing number of couples who are setting up house because of practical reasons and as an alternative to prolonged dating. Unromantic as it sounds, the high cost of maintaining two houses or apartments is often cited as the reason. Some couples want to live together but never plan to marry. Some just view it as a trial period before getting married. Whatever your reasons for moving in together, there are some important things to consider in advance.

First, be clear on your goals and expectations. Don't agree to live with someone hoping that she will fall in love with you or marry you. In fact, living together before marriage does *not* commonly seal the deal. You may not have as many legal ties as married couples, but you will have fewer protections, too. Some couples believe living together will be a never-ending honeymoon. They are disappointed when they learn what life together on a daily basis is really like.

The best way to protect yourself if you are setting up house together is to make a *written* agreement about how you will handle legal, financial, and practical decisions should the relationship end. Even if you remain single, you may eventually be considered as common law married. You may have palimony, child support, and/or custody concerns, too. Should you register as domestic partners? Will you tell your work colleagues? How will you deal with telling minor children and family if the arrangement ends? These are things to work out before, not after, you put your furniture into the moving van.

Trial Before Marriage

If marriage is your ultimate goal but you have decided to live together first, you may want to get engaged but not set a wedding date. However, you absolutely should set a date for when you will make the final decision to either marry or move on. Living together doesn't always enhance a relationship. Protect yourself by putting in writing how you will handle finances, legal, and living arrangements if things don't work out.

Living together before marriage works for some, but not for all. If possible, keep your own apartment or house during this temporary phase. At least you will have a place to go back to if things don't work out, and you can always break the lease or sublet later if your relationship works well and you decide to stay together. Unfortunately, you can't always prepare for these things and may end up losing more than your relationship:

> *When my relationship with Paulette ended, her friends, who had been mine for years as well, refused to see me any more. This really was a shocker, because I expected that I could count on them to support us both through this difficult time. I was completely unprepared to be rejected not only by Paulette but by our friends as well. (Sam, 46, Baker)*

Also keep in mind that live-in arrangements can be especially complicated if you have children:

> *My young son Marc was even more devastated than I was that my live-in arrangement with my ex, Paul, ended. Although Paul didn't want to live with me any more, he did take responsibility as a surrogate father to Marc. He is still active in my son's life and often visits him with his new girlfriend, who Marc likes a lot, too. I am very grateful for this. (Sally, 37, Nurse)*

Getting Engaged

Engagement is news that couples usually broadcast in a public way. If you are getting engaged, you may want to send printed announcements. You may post your happy news in your local newspapers, but only after you have introduced your fiancé to your immediate family (you don't want to embarrass them by making them admit they don't know a thing about the partner their child has chosen!). You may want to have a party to celebrate. An engagement party is traditionally hosted by a bride's parents, but adult couples may host it themselves either at a restaurant or at home.

If you are not getting married but plan to live together, you can also celebrate your news and new status as a couple with a housewarming party. If you are planning never to make your union legal, but you want to make it official to your family and friends, you can announce that you are "going together" at a casual get-together, brunch, or cocktail party. Increasingly, mature adults, many of whom will not want to marry again but who expect to be considered as a committed couple, are exchanging tokens such as a locket, watch, or promise ring, and announcing their commitment this way.

The decision to marry is just one of the many decisions you will make together as a couple. Although in the movies it is almost always a huge surprise when a man gets down on one knee, hearing "Will you marry me?" from your own partner will likely be a natural progression of your relationship, and probably no surprise at all.

ALERT!

An engagement party is a way for people you care about to meet your fiancé. Alas, some couples think this is nothing more than a way to get gifts. While most if not all of your guests will bring a gift, asking for them, or requesting a donation to a charity instead, is absolutely inappropriate and very, very bad manners.

The time between engagement and marriage is exciting, but many couples agree it is extremely stressful. You will not only be working through your own visions and expectations, but dealing with those of outsiders as well. The first decision you will make after you set a date (or agree to wait on the date) is about the most visible sign of engagement—a ring. An engagement ring is not just another piece of jewelry. It has enormous emotional value and is offered in promise of marriage. Sometimes couples exchange rings, but more commonly only the woman wears a ring. She may give her fiancé something personal and of value, such as a watch or cufflinks.

An engagement ring isn't required for marriage. And, despite popular belief, it *doesn't* have to be a diamond. Many brides actually prefer wearing a signet ring with a family crest, their birthstone set in gold, or an anniversary-type band with stones all around it. Three-stone rings (one each for the past, the present, and the future) are a lovely and modern option as well.

An engagement ring is a token given in contemplation of marriage. If the marriage doesn't take place, the giver of the ring has the legal right to demand its return. After marriage, the ring is the bride's property. If the ring is a family heirloom, it is up to the bride whether or not she wishes to return it to the family, but it is still legally hers. Some couples consider an engagement ring to be collateral against possible wedding expenses, and others have purchased their ring from their fiancé after a broken engagement. This is extremely bad taste!

Ladies: If you know that your fiancé doesn't have the money to give you the big ring you want, it's not fair to insist that he go into debt for it. If your family and friends are "old world" and expect you to flaunt a flashy ring, it is your responsibility to let your family know that you are proud of the modest ring you have been given and that you find it totally acceptable (and so must they). You are marrying a person, not a ring.

Preparations for Marriage

The adjustment to becoming a committed couple will create new challenges to your relationship on a literally daily basis until your wedding day. For this reason, in some faiths you may be asked or required to undergo counseling with a religious leader, or attend a retreat or group instruction before getting married. In these sessions you will be guided through discussions about resolving conflict, learning to communicate, and becoming a family. If you are planning to live together or get married, these types of support systems can be useful in helping you to figure out how to manage your new partnership. You can find couples counseling, encounter weekends, and so forth by searching online, looking in the telephone book, and through recommendations from religious leaders.

FACT

Some states have recently instituted a voluntary agreement to couples called a "Covenant Marriage." This document is legal and binding and sets forth more stringent requirements for marriage and divorce than a regular marriage contract. Couples who enter into these agreements may be required to undergo marriage counseling prior to the wedding and there will also be restrictions on the reasons they may divorce.

Family Involvement

Marriage is not just between you and your partner. Your family and friends will impact your relationship, too, with their own values, expectations and feelings. Dealing with family can be especially tricky during engagement time:

> My fiancé and I planned a simple wedding on the beach in Hawaii, but Mark's mother had other ideas. She insisted I wear her daughter's wedding dress, even though I had already picked something else. Then she insisted that the food be Kosher at our reception, even though neither family observed these dietary laws. Things broke down completely when she sobbed that I was robbing her of her dream to walk her son down the aisle, and I was taking her son away from her. When Mark didn't stop her and defend me, we began to argue. He was unable to disappoint his mother, and I was unwilling to bend any more than I already had. I realized that his mother would be trying to call the shots in our lives, and I couldn't accept that. We eventually broke our engagement. I feel sorry for any woman who falls in love with Mark—she will also get the meddling mother-in-law from Hell in the deal! (Annette, 35, Bank Teller)

Wedding Blues

Weddings are particularly notorious for bringing out the "beast" (not the best) in people. You can count on virtually everyone having opinions about what *your* wedding should be like. In addition, you'll be staging an event most likely larger and more complicated than anything you've ever done before, or will attempt again. Even with the help of an etiquette book and/or a wedding planner, there will be things you just can't anticipate.

How you deal with your interpersonal relationships and wedding challenges will reflect upon your future success as a couple. It is easy to say (and harder to do), but remember that the wedding is just one day and the marriage is the rest of your life; don't let any one person or detail ruin your happiness!

> *For my wedding, my mother picked the dress SHE wanted me to wear, the color scheme SHE liked best, and the restaurant SHE wanted. My fiancé and I were happy to be getting married and we were so busy with our careers that we allowed Mom to sweat the details. However, things went too far when we went to pick our wedding cake. I wanted a traditional bride and groom as a topper and my mother insisted, " NO! No bride and groom on MY wedding cake!" Bob and I realized that Mom was completely out of control, and we needed to take charge again. (Alice, 39, Editor)*

The most important thing is that both you and your partner feel ready for and confident about your upcoming marriage. If you have that piece of the puzzle, everything else will eventually fall into place. Families won't feud forever, and droopy flowers or table linens of the wrong color are hardly going to affect your success as a couple. If things don't go as planned, try to laugh them off and just focus on the best part of marriage: your growing love for one another.

Chapter 21

Dating Each Other— Forever!

Now that you've found your permanent partner, you may think your dating journey is over. In some respects, the journey has just begun. This chapter will help you think about how you can nurture the relationship you worked so hard to find. It will help you think about your new partnership in ways that will keep it strong and positive. Finally, it will offer some last suggestions to end your quest for a partner, and point you down a new path as part of a couple.

Dating Doesn't End

A popular myth is that good relationships just happen. They don't! If you plant a seed, water it, weed it, and nurture it, the seed may grow into a beautiful flower. However, if you take it for granted and don't tend to it, it will die. Relationships are very similar. Once you've planted the feelings and they have taken root, you still need to treasure and nurture the relationship or it won't flourish.

A high-profile mogul reportedly said that he picked his fiancé because his relationship with her is "easy." He asserts that since he works hard all day at the office, he doesn't want to come home at night and "work" at marriage, too. This mogul thinks he's worked out the secret to relationship success, but he hasn't. He knows that business relationships are not always smooth and easy and they take effort to maintain. Romantic relationships are no different. Perhaps that is why this famous businessman is equally famous for his two failed marriages!

QUESTION?

How do you keep love alive even after you're done dating and settled?
First of all, don't think of yourself as being "done" and "settled." Nothing is over for you, and there is still a lot to learn and love about your partner. Keep things exciting by surprising each other with gifts and notes, plan fun trips together, and take the time to celebrate anniversaries and other special occasions.

Many couples feel that dating takes so much effort that they "deserve" to relax once they have found a partner. They assume their partner will understand if they are always busy with work or family obligations, or overextended with things other than their romantic partnership. In reality, an understanding partner will accept being put aside occasionally, but if the flame of love isn't kept burning, it will eventually go out.

Now that you are part of a couple, you will find that another passion-extinguisher is the demands of daily life. When you are dating, each time you are together is a special time that you think about, prepare for, enjoy, and savor in memory. When you become part of a couple and are together constantly, the novelty begins to wear thin. Additionally, you will find yourself having to negotiate serious issues that didn't concern you when you were just dating. Even if you are well matched, things will come up (especially in the first year) that you might not have anticipated. Hopefully, you read Chapter 16 and have learned how to disagree constructively as a couple. If you do it successfully, your relationship will ride over the bumps.

Stuck in a rut? Don't complain—communicate! Share with your partner some of the things you'd love to do (e.g., go picnicking, bowling, dancing, antiquing). Tired of television? Cook dinner together. Begin a weekly board game or cards night. Work on crafts or another creative project, or do the crosswords together. It isn't so much what you do, but that are doing it together.

Make Romance a Part of Life

After the formal and often frantic routine of dating, many couples really *do* prefer to stay home and stop socializing. That's okay as long as you balance this with other activities. If you just sit on the couch and never do anything else, you may start to take one another for granted very quickly! The key to relationship success is to never stop dating your mate. Maybe you can't spend hours reading the paper in bed over bagels and coffee on weekends anymore, but you can still reconnect with your partner! Even an hour of uninterrupted time not doing household or parenting chores can be a date. Here are some great ways to add a little excitement to your life:

- Meet for a quick cup of coffee or a drink after work, as you did when you were dating.
- Go in late one day and spend that hour in bed, *not* sleeping.
- Gather a bottle of wine, glasses, and chairs, and go outside late at night to gaze at the stars.

- If you are on a very tight budget, save your loose change and money from rebates and coupons in a "date jar." When you have enough for an inexpensive night out, indulge.
- Dress up and have dinner at your own table using your best china and glassware.

If you are parents, or you have caregiving responsibilities to the elderly, find a family member or friend who can watch the kids while you take some time out for yourselves. It isn't *that* hard! Romance just takes motivation, and a bit of planning.

Be Romantic Every Day

Happy couples share little romantic gestures that help affirm their feelings for one another. These little things can be as simple as leaving "I love you" notes on Post-its where your partner can find them, or placing a real love letter on your partner's pillow. Why not take your partner to lunch as a surprise (check with her work first to make sure you aren't pulling her off an important project or out of a meeting). Do something fun and silly, like cheering him on (with pom poms or hand movements) for a great day as he is leaving for work. Call each other by secret pet names. Say something nice about your partner every single day, such as how adorable she is, or that he is your *hero* and never a *zero*! Encourage each other to share fantasies. Create a romantic atmosphere in your home with candles, flowers, incense. Bathe together. Make a mundane chore romantic with a kiss in the supermarket or by the washing machine. And above all, pay attention to the hints your partner drops about things she might like, as Jeremy did:

> I bought my girlfriend Lorraine a beautiful piece of jewelry for her birthday, but then she mentioned how a book was the most romantic gift a man could give a woman, and let it "slip" that she really wanted a new dictionary. It would never have occurred to me to consider that as a great gift, but I bought it for her (I wrote a love note in the front) and kept the necklace for another time. Lorraine was thrilled! (Jeremy, 58, Engineer)

Another great tip is to think of e-mail and cell phones as a way to leave romantic "thinking of you" messages—not just to find out who will pick up the dry cleaning or the kids from school. Rekindle the excitement you felt when you first met your partner by rereading all the things you wrote about him in your dating journal and by looking at photographs and scrapbooks. Read bedtime stories to each other—even *The Cat in the Hat* is a romantic treat, when read just for you by your partner!

Top Ten Ways to Awaken Passion

Here are ten great ways to liven up your love life when it's down in the dumps. Find the one you think your sweetie would most enjoy and then customize it to his own style and preference:

1. Light candles when the sun sets, and enjoy the flickering flames while you're having dinner.
2. Add romance with a new set of luxury sheets, and replace those threadbare bath towels with thick, soft ones. Then enjoy your new linens—together!
3. Buy some fresh flowers for your home. A ribbon tied around the vase adds an ultra-romantic touch. Also, occasionally send flowers to your partner's workplace as a "thinking of you" surprise.
4. Love to watch TV? Do it differently. Wear sexy lingerie, or make a bed in the living room and "camp out" (with popcorn and sodas) as your favorite program is playing.
5. Have a party to perk up an otherwise ordinary week. Dim the lights, ditch the usual chips, pretzels, and beer in favor of easy, elegant cheese, fruit, crudités and chocolates. Suggest that your guests arrive nicely dressed, even if it's just the usual gang.
6. Couples who physically connect keep warm feelings brewing. Greet your partner with a kiss in the morning, a kiss when she is going out the door to work, a kiss when she gets home, and a kiss at bedtime. Touch often.
7. Take dance lessons with another couple. Learn about wines. Entertain. Take a cooking class—whatever you do, just do it together.

8. Get a pet. Adopting a dog or cat gives your relationship a new dimension as you discover how to be "parents" to your new four-legged friend. If you are willing to take on the responsibility of years of care for your new "baby," you will also have the added satisfaction of knowing that you saved a life.

9. Find the scent you used as a teen or in your early twenties and bring back the old feelings. Bake a pumpkin pie, light a lavender candle, or burn incense and bask in the lovely aromas.

10. Rearrange the furniture. Paint or refinish damaged pieces or find ways to cover them with pretty cloths or pillows. Get everything out of your bedroom that isn't for sleeping or dressing. Keep it clean. Make your space and your life sparkle.

It's All in the Attitude

Keep a romantic attitude. You don't have to be overly mushy if that's not your personality. Be a quiet romantic if you wish. Actions speak louder than words. Don't worry about grand gestures. It's the little things that make your partner fall in love with you again, every day. Give your partner a back rub. Offer to do chores for his children or elderly parents so he can get some "just for me" time. Know what your partner really wants. One person may believe nothing says "I love you" like flowers or a book of poetry, and another may believe a gift marked "14K" is a sure sign of love.

Showing Your Love with Food

Use food to boost passion. Certain foods are very romantic. Take pasta, for example. Who could forget the memorable scene in Walt Disney's *Lady and The Tramp* where the two dogs eat a piece of spaghetti from either end and meet in the middle? Fondue is also a very sensuous food. Yummy items dipped in warm, gooey cheese or chocolate are sure to warm you from the inside out.

Some claim oysters are the ultimate aphrodisiac. They certainly *look* suggestive and slide down easily. Chocolate is an obviously romantic food—in any form. Berries are also a great treat to share with your love. They're tart, sweet, and juicy. They taste even better covered in whipped cream, powdered sugar, or melted chocolate or dunked in champagne. For a full evening of love-filled foods, enjoy an entrée of oysters over pasta, followed by chocolate fondue for dessert.

Celebrate Special Days

When you have finally met your special someone, there will always be a few days of the year that mean more to you two than any of the others. If you are married, this obviously means your wedding anniversary, but it can also be other special days such as the anniversary of your first kiss, or the day you moved in together, or the first time you both said "I love you." Celebrating on a monthly basis doesn't mean you have to spend a fortune on gifts, cards, and dinners (although if you can afford it, this is a nice gesture). Celebrate your feelings all year by celebrating these days if only with a kiss and the affirmation "This is a special day for us—I love you."

If you are married, a private, romantic gesture that some couples do monthly or once a year is to remove their wedding rings and then replace them as they did on their wedding day, affirming: "I choose to marry you all over again." For a more formal affirmation, you might actually renew your wedding or partnership vows in an official ceremony and even indulge in a wedding party.

FACT

Men like receiving flowers as much as women. The most romantic flower choices are the ones your partner likes best, though some flowers have nearly universal meanings: *four-leaf clovers*: be mine; *forget-me-not*: true love; *ivy*: fidelity; *orchid*: beauty; *orange blossoms*: weddings; *rose*: love; *daisy*: loyal love; *dandelion*: faithfulness, happiness; *striped carnations*: I'm sorry I can't be with you.

Other anniversary celebrations can be spiced up with a night in a hotel (or camping under the stars) or just drinking something bubbly with strawberries out of a champagne glass. Consider a second (or third, or fourth, or fifth) honeymoon or just book the honeymoon suite or the "romance package" because it makes you feel romantic. Celebrate for silly reasons, too, such as National Hug Day (January 21), National Teddy Bear Day (September 9) or Kiss Your Mate Day (April 28).

Lianne's boyfriend picked up on her affection for a certain holiday and won her heart:

> *Groundhog Day has always been my favorite holiday of the year. My boyfriend thought this little holiday was ridiculous until he realized how much it meant to me. He decided that every Groundhog Day he would make me a special Groundhog Day card (there aren't many commercial ones available). Now I look forward to receiving these little cards more than anything else! (Lianne, 39, Artist)*

How Old Relationships Evolve

Now that you're part of a couple, you can help other singles who are available and looking by making introductions and perhaps recycling some of your still-single ex-partners. Before you do this, however, consider the individuals involved very carefully. If an ex wasn't right for you but is basically a stable, nice person, and (you think) he might be a good potential match for someone else, then it's okay to try matching them up.

ALERT!

Unless you and your partner are extremely open-minded and agree on open sexual contacts with others, keeping up sexual relations with anyone else, and especially with your ex, will obviously put your new relationship in jeopardy. Ask yourself: Are you willing to risk losing your new partner for this reason?

On the other hand, don't suggest an ex to someone else if that ex has obvious liabilities that would impact another relationship as it did yours. In the television series *Sex and the City*, Carrie, the main character, meets an ex-boyfriend at a funeral she is attending with her girlfriend, Miranda. Her friend is attracted to the ex and asks for an introduction. Carrie is reluctant. She warns Miranda that this guy is a jerk. Miranda starts dating Carrie's ex, only to eventually discover (you guessed it) that he is indeed the big jerk that Carrie warned her about. Only after Miranda and the jerk break up does she realize that Carrie was reluctant to introduce her to this man not because she was jealous, but because she knew he had a fatal flaw, and she didn't want her friend to get hurt!

Some ex-partners can come back as long-lasting friends, but it rarely happens. However, no matter how pure your intention to keep a once-romantic relationship platonic, it's tricky. You new partner cannot help but sense the history and ease you have with an old love. Even if your new partner is superconfident and trusting, there may be a worry that if you were close with this ex before, you might rekindle the flames. You do *not* want to put an ex between you and your new partner.

FACT

When you break up with someone and become a couple with someone else, the best thing to do is put your friendship with your ex on the back burner—at least for a while. Focus solely on your new partner until you are absolutely solid as a couple. Then, if you wish, slowly reintroduce your ex back into your life. One way to do this is to introduce your ex to your new partner and let *them* develop a friendship.

Sometimes it's not the ex-partners that come back as long-lasting friends, but the ex's family members. Usually, when a relationship ends the couple's parents don't see the ex-partner, but in some cases there may be lasting friendships that evolve:

> "Mom and Dad love my new man, but even after twenty years they are still close to my ex, Stephen. He and his wife are often at my family's dinners. As the father of my child, I realized Stephen would always be a part of my life, but I never expected him to be part of my parents' lives, too. I guess it is a bit strange, but it seems to work out okay for all of us. (Ernestine, 56, High School Teacher)"

Cheating

Even if you are part of a happy couple, there may be times when you think about what "might have been" with a former love, or with someone new. Truthfully, everyone has such thoughts. The question is whether or not you act on them. There is no rule about infidelity other than that it isn't something you should do if you're in a committed relationship. Whether an opportunity is unanticipated and falls in your lap, or you go looking for it, if you act on your impulses you are bound for trouble.

In some cases a couple can survive a cheating incident but it will change the relationship forever. Some say that these types of situations make them stronger as a couple, but in general, the longer a person has been deceived or cheated on, the harder it will be to bounce back. Even if you cheat because you think your partner will forgive you, you may be surprised to find that your partner is too wounded to continue the relationship.

If you are willing to cheat it is a signal that you are also ready to leave your primary relationship. The only exception to this is if both you and your partner have established an open relationship where you are both free to seek other partners for emotional and/or physical intimacy. If you don't have this kind of arrangement, don't confuse being friendly with crossing the line. You know what the difference is. You are an adult, and adults are responsible for the choices they make—along with the resulting consequences.

Wisdom to Take with You

This book and your dating journey are at an end. Hopefully, you have met your relationship goals and your dreams have come true. Love is an amazing gift that should be cherished. Now that you have it, your goal is to make every day of your life with your partner a *great* one filled with success, happiness, and love.

There are countless pieces of advice out there telling you how to make your relationship work. However, a good relationship has to have a firm foundation to begin with. Couples in happy relationships are there because they want to be with each other, and they are committed to their relationship with each other as the most important thing in their lives. They are individuals, but they work as a team. They are willing to do whatever it takes to keep their relationship strong. They understand that being part of a couple means that they won't always be right or get their way, but whatever they sacrifice is worth the payoff of being together. They acknowledge, respect, and appreciate their partner every day.

As a new couple, how you interact will be based on the mixing of your personalities and your goals. However, in general, successful partners:

- Show their affection for one another in little ways, every day
- Use terms of endearment and never say disrespectful things to one another
- Learn and do new things together
- Say "I love you" every day
- Fight constructively
- Support one another
- Choose their battles carefully
- Feel sure that they have found the right one, not just any one
- Notice, appreciate, and compliment each other, often
- Are not afraid to express their feelings
- Trust and believe in each other
- Feel comfortable being alone as well as with each other

If you recognize these characteristics as being present in your relationship, then you can consider yourself one half of a successful couple! Congratulations on completing your dating journey. If you haven't yet found the right one, don't give up. Reread this book as many times as you like and keep your dating journal going as long as you need to. Your special someone is out there—perhaps right around the corner!

Appendix A

Additional Resources

The following are suggested resources to use in addition to this book to help you in your dating journey. However, keep in mind that Web site addresses and content change frequently. The best way to get information is still through personal recommendations from people you know and trust. The resources listed here are for reference, but should not be considered the only options.

Books

Baldrige, Letitia. *Letitia Baldrige's New Manners for New Times: A Complete Guide to Etiquette* (New York, NY: Simon & Schuster Adult Publishing Group, 2003).

Dunham, Alison B. *YOU ARE THE PRODUCT: How to Effectively Sell Yourself to Anyone!* (New York, NY: Piggle Press, 2001). Available through the author. E-mail: *askalisonb@nyc.rr.com*.

Dunham, Alison B. and Freedman, Jessica B. *Recruiting Love: Using the Business Skills You Have to Find the Love You Want* (Nipomo, CA: Cyclone Books, 1998). Available through the author. E-mail: *advicesisters@advicesisters.net*.

Post, Peggy. *Emily Post's Etiquette, 17th Ed.* (New York, NY: Harper Collins, 2004).

Tuckerman, Nancy and Dunnan, Nancy. *Amy Vanderbilt's Complete Book of Etiquette, 50th Anniversary Ed.* (New York, NY: Doubleday, 1995).

Warner, Ralph, Ihara, Toni, and Hertz, Frederick. *Living Together: A Legal Guide for Unmarried Couples, 12th Ed.* (Berkeley, CA: Nolo, 2004).

Advice and Counseling

The Advice Sisters
www.advicesisters.net

This is a large site, created by the author of this book, with a wide variety of general, relationship-oriented content appealing to adults of all ages and lifestyles. Virtually everything on the site is free and easy to access. The private advice services are well defined and reasonably priced. For adults who want to create an easier, happier, more satisfying life.

The American Psychiatric Association
1000 Wilson Boulevard
Suite 1825
Arlington, VA 22209-3901
703-907-7300
✐ *www.psych.org*

This is the nation's oldest medical specialty society with more than 35,000 members. The Web site has general information about psychiatry and tips for choosing a psychiatrist.

Engaged Encounter
✐ *www.engagedencounter.org*

This site has information about the Catholic premarital education program, primarily for couples who are planning to marry in the Catholic Church in the United States. However, couples who are not Catholic are also welcome to attend meetings.

Relationships911.com
✐ *www.relationships911.org/index.html*

This Web site offers 1,000 articles on relationships, marriage, anger, conflict, and interpersonal communication, including a section with advice about online relationships.

Self-Growth.com
✐ *www.selfgrowth.com*

Large directory of self-help resources with thousands of free articles written by self-help experts and links to more than 4,000 success-related Web sites.

National Toll-Free Help Line Numbers

Centers for Disease Control National AIDS Hotline: 800-342-2437

Centers for Disease Control National Sexually Transmitted Diseases Hotline: 800-227-8922

Impotence Information Center: 800-328-3881

National AIDS Hotline: 800-342-AIDS (800-342-2437) (24 hours a day)

National Domestic Violence Hotline: 800-799-SAFE (800-799-7233) or 800-787-3224

National Drug and Alcohol Treatment Hotline: 800-662-HELP (800-662-4357)

National Mental Health Association: 800-969-6642 (9 a.m.–5 p.m. Mon–Fri)

National Organization for Victim Assistance: 800-879-6682

National Suicide Hotline: 800-SUICIDE (800-784-2433)

Planned Parenthood Hotline: 877-4ME-2ASK (877-463-2275)

Rape, Abuse, and Incest National Network: 800-656-4673

Sexual Assault Hotline: 800-656-4673

Volunteer Organizations

Habitat for Humanity International
✍ *www.habitat.org*
121 Habitat Street
Americus, GA 31709-3498
229-924-6935, ext. 2551 or 2552

Politicians, celebrities, and even a few U.S. presidents have participated in this organization's hands-on efforts to build affordable houses in partnership with those who lack adequate shelter.

USA Freedom Corps

✍ *www.usafreedomcorps.gov/index.asp*
1600 Pennsylvania Avenue NW
Washington, DC 20500
877-USA-CORPS (877-872-2677)

Housed at the White House and chaired by President George W. Bush, this volunteer initiative strives to help Americans begin to volunteer. The Web site helps people find volunteer opportunities that match their interests and talents in their hometowns, across the country, or around the world. The site also has tips for volunteers.

Volunteer Match

✍ *www.volunteermatch.org*

This online site allows you to choose a volunteer activity in the United States based on your geographic location by zip code, the amount of time you wish to spend, and your interests.

Online Dating Sites

American Singles

✍ *www.americansingles.com*

Connect with single men and women for dating, romance, and friendship.

E-Harmony.com

✍ *www.eharmony.com*

Online matching uses an extensive personality profile to help you find a match.

Glimpse.com

⌨ *www.glimpse.com*

Connect with gay and lesbian singles for dating and friendship.

JDate

⌨ *www.jdate.com*

Very large online dating service matches Jewish men and women.

Match.com

⌨ *www.match.com*

This dating service has more than 8 million members.

For Adults Starting Over

Divorce Online

⌨ *www.divorceonline.com*

An electronic resource for people involved in, or facing the prospect of, divorce. Free articles and information on the financial, legal, psychological, real estate, and other aspects of divorce.

Parents Without Partners

⌨ *www.parentswithoutpartners.org*

Parents Without Partners is the largest international, nonprofit membership organization in the United States and Canada devoted to the welfare and interests of single parents and their children. Meetings and activities provide single parents with support and opportunities for social interaction and friendship. Single parents may join one of approximately 200 chapters; they may be male or female, custodial or noncustodial, separated, divorced, widowed, or never-married.

WidowNet

✑ *www.widownet.org*

This Web site has information and self-help resources for, and by, widows and widowers.

For Singles Over Forty

50 Years Plus.com

✑ *www.50yearsplus.com*

Here you can connect with men and women over age fifty. However, be aware that there is no quality control.

More Magazine

✑ *www.more.com*

A magazine by the Meredith Corporation celebrating women over age forty. Also has an online Web site with additional resources.

Silver Singles

✑ *www.silversingles.com*

This online dating site is powered by American Singles and focuses on mature adults who are looking for romance, friendships, and more. However, the site does not limit younger people born as late as 1988 from becoming members.

Suddenly Senior

✑ *www.suddenlysenior.com/links.shtml*

Not just for dating and singles, this Web site has links to more than 200 sites for the over-forty crowd including magazines, organizations, and Web sites.

Index

THE EVERYTHING SERIES!

BUSINESS & PERSONAL FINANCE

Everything® Budgeting Book
Everything® Business Planning Book
Everything® Coaching and Mentoring Book
Everything® Fundraising Book
Everything® Get Out of Debt Book
Everything® Grant Writing Book
Everything® Home-Based Business Book, 2nd Ed.
Everything® Homebuying Book, 2nd Ed.
Everything® Homeselling Book, 2nd Ed.
Everything® Investing Book, 2nd Ed.
Everything® Landlording Book
Everything® Leadership Book
Everything® Managing People Book
Everything® Negotiating Book
Everything® Online Business Book
Everything® Personal Finance Book
Everything® Personal Finance in Your 20s and 30s Book
Everything® Project Management Book
Everything® Real Estate Investing Book
Everything® Robert's Rules Book, $7.95
Everything® Selling Book
Everything® Start Your Own Business Book
Everything® Wills & Estate Planning Book

COMPUTERS

Everything® Online Auctions Book
Everything® Blogging Book

COOKING

Everything® Barbecue Cookbook
Everything® Bartender's Book, $9.95
Everything® Chinese Cookbook
Everything® Cocktail Parties and Drinks Book
Everything® College Cookbook
Everything® Cookbook
Everything® Cooking for Two Cookbook
Everything® Diabetes Cookbook
Everything® Easy Gourmet Cookbook
Everything® Fondue Cookbook
Everything® Gluten-Free Cookbook
Everything® Glycemic Index Cookbook
Everything® Grilling Cookbook

Everything® Healthy Meals in Minutes Cookbook
Everything® Holiday Cookbook
Everything® Indian Cookbook
Everything® Italian Cookbook
Everything® Low-Carb Cookbook
Everything® Low-Fat High-Flavor Cookbook
Everything® Low-Salt Cookbook
Everything® Meals for a Month Cookbook
Everything® Mediterranean Cookbook
Everything® Mexican Cookbook
Everything® One-Pot Cookbook
Everything® Pasta Cookbook
Everything® Quick Meals Cookbook
Everything® Slow Cooker Cookbook
Everything® Slow Cooking for a Crowd Cookbook
Everything® Soup Cookbook
Everything® Tex-Mex Cookbook
Everything® Thai Cookbook
Everything® Vegetarian Cookbook
Everything® Wild Game Cookbook
Everything® Wine Book, 2nd Ed.

CRAFT SERIES

Everything® Crafts—Baby Scrapbooking
Everything® Crafts—Bead Your Own Jewelry
Everything® Crafts—Create Your Own Greeting Cards
Everything® Crafts—Easy Projects
Everything® Crafts—Polymer Clay for Beginners
Everything® Crafts—Rubber Stamping Made Easy
Everything® Crafts—Wedding Decorations and Keepsakes

HEALTH

Everything® Alzheimer's Book
Everything® Diabetes Book
Everything® Health Guide to Adult Bipolar Disorder
Everything® Health Guide to Controlling Anxiety
Everything® Health Guide to Fibromyalgia
Everything® Hypnosis Book

Everything® Low Cholesterol Book
Everything® Massage Book
Everything® Menopause Book
Everything® Nutrition Book
Everything® Reflexology Book
Everything® Stress Management Book

HISTORY

Everything® American Government Book
Everything® American History Book
Everything® Civil War Book
Everything® Irish History & Heritage Book
Everything® Middle East Book

GAMES

Everything® 15-Minute Sudoku Book, $9.95
Everything® 30-Minute Sudoku Book, $9.95
Everything® Blackjack Strategy Book
Everything® Brain Strain Book, $9.95
Everything® Bridge Book
Everything® Card Games Book
Everything® Card Tricks Book, $9.95
Everything® Casino Gambling Book, 2nd Ed.
Everything® Chess Basics Book
Everything® Craps Strategy Book
Everything® Crossword and Puzzle Book
Everything® Crossword Challenge Book
Everything® Cryptograms Book, $9.95
Everything® Easy Crosswords Book
Everything® Easy Kakuro Book, $9.95
Everything® Games Book, 2nd Ed.
Everything® Giant Sudoku Book, $9.95
Everything® Kakuro Challenge Book, $9.95
Everything® Large-Print Crosswords Book
Everything® Lateral Thinking Puzzles Book, $9.95
Everything® Pencil Puzzles Book, $9.95
Everything® Poker Strategy Book
Everything® Pool & Billiards Book
Everything® Test Your IQ Book, $9.95
Everything® Texas Hold 'Em Book, $9.95
Everything® Travel Crosswords Book, $9.95
Everything® Word Games Challenge Book
Everything® Word Search Book

Bolded titles are new additions to the series.
All Everything® books are priced at $12.95 or $14.95, unless otherwise stated. Prices subject to change without notice.

HOBBIES

Everything® Candlemaking Book
Everything® Cartooning Book
Everything® Drawing Book
Everything® Family Tree Book, 2nd Ed.
Everything® Knitting Book
Everything® Knots Book
Everything® Photography Book
Everything® Quilting Book
Everything® Scrapbooking Book
Everything® Sewing Book
Everything® Woodworking Book

HOME IMPROVEMENT

Everything® Feng Shui Book
Everything® Feng Shui Decluttering Book, $9.95
Everything® Fix-It Book
Everything® Home Decorating Book
Everything® Homebuilding Book
Everything® Lawn Care Book
Everything® Organize Your Home Book

KIDS' BOOKS

All titles are $7.95
Everything® Kids' Animal Puzzle &
  Activity Book
Everything® Kids' Baseball Book, 4th Ed.
Everything® Kids' Bible Trivia Book
Everything® Kids' Bugs Book
Everything® Kids' Christmas Puzzle
  & Activity Book
Everything® Kids' Cookbook
Everything® Kids' Crazy Puzzles Book
Everything® Kids' Dinosaurs Book
**Everything® Kids' Gross Hidden Pictures
  Book**
Everything® Kids' Gross Jokes Book
Everything® Kids' Gross Mazes Book
Everything® Kids' Gross Puzzle and
  Activity Book
Everything® Kids' Halloween Puzzle
  & Activity Book
Everything® Kids' Hidden Pictures Book
Everything® Kids' Horses Book
Everything® Kids' Joke Book
Everything® Kids' Knock Knock Book
Everything® Kids' Math Puzzles Book
Everything® Kids' Mazes Book
Everything® Kids' Money Book
Everything® Kids' Nature Book

**Everything® Kids' Pirates Puzzle and
  Activity Book**
Everything® Kids' Puzzle Book
Everything® Kids' Riddles & Brain Teasers Book
Everything® Kids' Science Experiments Book
Everything® Kids' Sharks Book
Everything® Kids' Soccer Book
Everything® Kids' Travel Activity Book

KIDS' STORY BOOKS

Everything® Fairy Tales Book

LANGUAGE

Everything® Conversational Japanese Book
  (with CD), $19.95
Everything® French Grammar Book
Everything® French Phrase Book, $9.95
Everything® French Verb Book, $9.95
**Everything® German Practice Book with
  CD, $19.95**
Everything® Inglés Book
Everything® Learning French Book
Everything® Learning German Book
Everything® Learning Italian Book
Everything® Learning Latin Book
Everything® Learning Spanish Book
Everything® Sign Language Book
Everything® Spanish Grammar Book
Everything® Spanish Phrase Book, $9.95
Everything® Spanish Practice Book
  (with CD), $19.95
Everything® Spanish Verb Book, $9.95

MUSIC

Everything® Drums Book (with CD), $19.95
Everything® Guitar Book
**Everything® Guitar Chords Book with CD,
  $19.95**
Everything® Home Recording Book
Everything® Playing Piano and Keyboards
  Book
Everything® Reading Music Book (with CD),
  $19.95
Everything® Rock & Blues Guitar Book
  (with CD), $19.95
Everything® Songwriting Book

NEW AGE

Everything® Astrology Book, 2nd Ed.
Everything® Dreams Book, 2nd Ed.
Everything® Love Signs Book, $9.95

Everything® Numerology Book
Everything® Paganism Book
Everything® Palmistry Book
Everything® Psychic Book
Everything® Reiki Book
Everything® Tarot Book
Everything® Wicca and Witchcraft Book

PARENTING

Everything® Baby Names Book, 2nd Ed.
Everything® Baby Shower Book
Everything® Baby's First Food Book
Everything® Baby's First Year Book
Everything® Birthing Book
Everything® Breastfeeding Book
Everything® Father-to-Be Book
Everything® Father's First Year Book
Everything® Get Ready for Baby Book
Everything® Get Your Baby to Sleep Book,
  $9.95
Everything® Getting Pregnant Book
Everything® Homeschooling Book
Everything® Mother's First Year Book
Everything® Parent's Guide to Children
  and Divorce
Everything® Parent's Guide to Children
  with ADD/ADHD
Everything® Parent's Guide to Children
  with Asperger's Syndrome
Everything® Parent's Guide to Children
  with Autism
Everything® Parent's Guide to Children with
  Bipolar Disorder
Everything® Parent's Guide to Children
  with Dyslexia
Everything® Parent's Guide to Positive
  Discipline
Everything® Parent's Guide to Raising a
  Successful Child
**Everything® Parent's Guide to Raising
  Boys**
**Everything® Parent's Guide to Raising
  Siblings**
Everything® Parent's Guide to Tantrums
Everything® Parent's Guide to the Overweight
  Child
Everything® Parent's Guide to the Strong-
  Willed Child
Everything® Parenting a Teenager Book
Everything® Potty Training Book, $9.95
Everything® Pregnancy Book, 2nd Ed.

Bolded titles are new additions to the series.
All Everything® books are priced at $12.95 or $14.95, unless otherwise stated. Prices subject to change without notice.

Everything® Pregnancy Fitness Book
Everything® Pregnancy Nutrition Book
Everything® Pregnancy Organizer, $15.00
Everything® Toddler Book
Everything® Toddler Activities Book
Everything® Tween Book
Everything® Twins, Triplets, and More Book

PETS

Everything® Boxer Book
Everything® Cat Book, 2nd Ed.
Everything® Chihuahua Book
Everything® Dachshund Book
Everything® Dog Book
Everything® Dog Health Book
Everything® Dog Training and Tricks Book
Everything® German Shepherd Book
Everything® Golden Retriever Book
Everything® Horse Book
Everything® Horse Care Book
Everything® Horseback Riding Book
Everything® Labrador Retriever Book
Everything® Poodle Book
Everything® Pug Book
Everything® Puppy Book
Everything® Rottweiler Book
Everything® Small Dogs Book
Everything® Tropical Fish Book
Everything® Yorkshire Terrier Book

REFERENCE

Everything® Car Care Book
Everything® Classical Mythology Book
Everything® Computer Book
Everything® Divorce Book
Everything® Einstein Book
Everything® Etiquette Book, 2nd Ed.
Everything® Inventions and Patents Book
Everything® Mafia Book
Everything® Mary Magdalene Book
Everything® Philosophy Book
Everything® Psychology Book
Everything® Shakespeare Book

RELIGION

Everything® Angels Book
Everything® Bible Book
Everything® Buddhism Book
Everything® Catholicism Book

Everything® Christianity Book
Everything® Freemasons Book
Everything® History of the Bible Book
Everything® Jewish History & Heritage Book
Everything® Judaism Book
Everything® Kabbalah Book
Everything® Koran Book
Everything® Prayer Book
Everything® Saints Book
Everything® Torah Book
Everything® Understanding Islam Book
Everything® World's Religions Book
Everything® Zen Book

SCHOOL & CAREERS

Everything® Alternative Careers Book
Everything® College Major Test Book
Everything® College Survival Book, 2nd Ed.
Everything® Cover Letter Book, 2nd Ed.
Everything® Get-a-Job Book
Everything® Guide to Being a Paralegal
Everything® Guide to Being a Real Estate Agent
Everything® Guide to Starting and Running a Restaurant
Everything® Job Interview Book
Everything® New Nurse Book
Everything® New Teacher Book
Everything® Paying for College Book
Everything® Practice Interview Book
Everything® Resume Book, 2nd Ed.
Everything® Study Book
Everything® Teacher's Organizer, $16.95

SELF-HELP

Everything® Dating Book, 2nd Ed.
Everything® Great Sex Book
Everything® Kama Sutra Book
Everything® Self-Esteem Book

SPORTS & FITNESS

Everything® Fishing Book
Everything® Golf Instruction Book
Everything® Pilates Book
Everything® Running Book
Everything® Total Fitness Book
Everything® Weight Training Book
Everything® Yoga Book

TRAVEL

Everything® Family Guide to Hawaii
Everything® Family Guide to Las Vegas, 2nd Ed.
Everything® Family Guide to New York City, 2nd Ed.
Everything® Family Guide to RV Travel & Campgrounds
Everything® Family Guide to the Walt Disney World Resort®, Universal Studios®, and Greater Orlando, 4th Ed.
Everything® Family Guide to Cruise Vacations
Everything® Family Guide to the Caribbean
Everything® Family Guide to Washington D.C., 2nd Ed.
Everything® Guide to New England
Everything® Travel Guide to the Disneyland Resort®, California Adventure®, Universal Studios®, and the Anaheim Area

WEDDINGS

Everything® Bachelorette Party Book, $9.95
Everything® Bridesmaid Book, $9.95
Everything® Elopement Book, $9.95
Everything® Father of the Bride Book, $9.95
Everything® Groom Book, $9.95
Everything® Mother of the Bride Book, $9.95
Everything® Outdoor Wedding Book
Everything® Wedding Book, 3rd Ed.
Everything® Wedding Checklist, $9.95
Everything® Wedding Etiquette Book, $9.95
Everything® Wedding Organizer, $15.00
Everything® Wedding Shower Book, $9.95
Everything® Wedding Vows Book, $9.95
Everything® Weddings on a Budget Book, $9.95

WRITING

Everything® Creative Writing Book
Everything® Get Published Book, 2nd Ed.
Everything® Grammar and Style Book
Everything® Guide to Writing a Book Proposal
Everything® Guide to Writing a Novel
Everything® Guide to Writing Children's Books
Everything® Guide to Writing Research Papers
Everything® Screenwriting Book
Everything® Writing Poetry Book
Everything® Writing Well Book